The
MESSAGE *of* ACTS
in the
HISTORY *of* REDEMPTION

The
MESSAGE *of* ACTS
in the
HISTORY *of* REDEMPTION

Dennis E. Johnson

P U B L I S H I N G

P.O. BOX 817 • PHILLIPSBURG • NEW JERSEY 08865-0817

Composition by Colophon Typesetting

Printed in the United States of America

Library of Congress Cataloging-in-Publication Data

Johnson, Dennis E. (Dennis Edward)
    The message of Acts in the history of redemption / Dennis E. Johnson.
        p.   cm.
    Includes bibliographical references and index.
    ISBN-10: 0-87552-235-1 (pbk.)
    ISBN-13: 978-0-87552-235-7 (pbk.)
    1. Bible. N.T. Acts—Criticism, interpretation, etc. I. Title.
BS2625.2.J6   1997
226.6'06—dc21   96-48100

CONTENTS

ABBREVIATIONS

A	Codex Alexandrinus
א	Codex Sinaiticus
B	Codex Vaticanus
BAG	W. Bauer, W. F. Arndt, and F. W. Gingrich, eds., *A Greek-English Lexicon of the New Testament and Other Early Christian Literature*. Chicago: University of Chicago Press, 1957
BC	*The Beginnings of Christianity, Part I: The Acts of the Apostles.* Edited by F. J. Foakes-Jackson and K. Lake. London: Macmillan, 1920
BJRL	*Bulletin of the John Rylands Library*
C	Codex Ephraemi Rescriptus
ExpTim	*Expository Times*
JBL	*Journal of Biblical Literature*
JETS	*Journal of the Evangelical Theological Society*
JSNT	*Journal for the Study of the New Testament*
KJV	King James Version
LN	J. P. Louw and E. A. Nida, eds., *Greek-English Lexicon of the New Testament Based on Semantic Domains*. 2d ed., 2 vols. New York: United Bible Societies, 1989
LS	H. G. Liddell and R. Scott, *A Greek-English Lexicon*. 8th ed. New York: American Book Co., 1882
LXX	Septuagint
NAC	New American Commentary
NCB	New Century Bible
NICNT	New International Commentary on the New Testament

NIDNTT   *New International Dictionary of New Testament Theology*, ed.
            C. Brown. 3 vols. Grand Rapids: Zondervan, 1975–78
NIGTC   New International Greek Testament Commentary
NIV   New International Version
NovT   *Novum Testamentum*
NTG   Eb. Nestle, Er. Nestle, K. Aland, and B. Aland, eds., *Novum
            Testamentum Graece*. 26th ed. Stuttgart: Deutsche Bibel-
            stiftung, 1979
NTS   *New Testament Studies*
SNTS   Studiorum Novi Testamenti Societas
TDNT   *Theological Dictionary of the New Testament*, ed. G. Kittel and
            G. Friedrich, tr. G. Bromiley. 10 vols. Grand Rapids: Eerd-
            mans, 1964–76
UBS   K. Aland, M. Black, C. M. Martini, B. M. Metzger, and
            A. Wikgren, eds., *The Greek New Testament*. 3d ed. (cor-
            rected). Stuttgart: United Bible Societies, 1983
WBC   Word Biblical Commentary
WTJ   *Westminster Theological Journal*
WUNT   Wissenschaftliche Untersuchungen zum Neuen Testament

PREFACE

Bridges are simple but wonderful devices. Imagine a river flowing through an unexplored meadow or forest. One day a few rugged explorers, weary from fighting the current, find a resting place on the riverbank. Time passes. Settlers follow: some build simple shelters on the east bank, while others put down roots on the west bank. As the community grows, its needs for connection between east and west outgrow the capacities of the shallow ford or the makeshift ferry. What the town needs is a bridge, a link between pieces of land that would otherwise remain unconnected, a span that brings people together.

At its most basic, a bridge is a connection that overcomes distance and separation, a span that links diverse or divided regions, creating new possibilities for human contact, commerce, and culture. The building of a bridge does not evaporate the bay or river, nor fill in the canyon that makes the two pieces of land distinct. But the bridge makes it possible to travel back and forth across that otherwise uncrossable divide. Bridges are the arteries, the essential connections in the circulatory systems that unify and vivify many of the world's great cities—London, New York, Paris— whose various neighborhoods grew up on opposite banks of well-traveled waterways.

God is a bridge builder. This metaphor could well sum up a diverse but consistent set of themes that run through the book of Acts. This study arises out of a conviction that attention to bridges of various kinds will enrich our reception of the powerful message of Acts.

Consider, in the first place, the bridge between God's *word of promise* to Israel, which Christians call the Old Testament, and his *word of fulfillment* to Israel and the nations in Jesus Christ, who is proclaimed by the apostles at the dawn of the New Covenant (which we also refer to as the New Testament). Although he was a Gentile concerned with the Gentiles' inclusion among the people of God, the author of Luke-Acts nevertheless manifests marvelous understanding of the Scriptures given to Israel. He shows us the bridges by which we can walk across from the monumental redemptive events, actors, and anticipations of ancient times into the fulfilled reality of the Redeemer himself, Jesus Christ. At the start of his two-volume work, Luke states that he is transmitting the good news that was announced by eyewitnesses of Jesus' ministry (Luke 1:1-4). At the end of that volume, he describes the way in which Jesus opened up for those eyewitnesses the true meaning of the Old Testament Scriptures: the Law of Moses, the Prophets, and the Psalms (and by implication the other Writings) (Luke 24:44). Then, as he writes the second volume (Acts), he shows us the unfolding of that Old Covenant word of promise, not only through the preaching of the eyewitnesses, but also in the way in which he himself (under the Spirit's control) frames his narrative of the church's early years. Luke invites us again and again to walk back and forth across the bridge linking Old Covenant promise with New Covenant fulfillment in Christ —to see, compare, and discover afresh the manifold wisdom of God in his plan of redemption, glimpsed in many parts and ways in the words of the prophets, but now blazing from the glorious face of the Son.

Second, Luke invites us to reflect on the bridge between *Jew* and *Gentile* in the saving plan of God. Like the other New Testament writers, Luke takes pains to emphasize that the word of salvation that has now come in Jesus and is being spread through his messengers among the Gentiles, is not a repudiation of the faithful words that God spoke to Israel of old. Although Luke's words differ from Paul's, he nevertheless joins the Apostle to the Gentiles in giving a resounding *no!* to the question "Has God rejected his people?" (Rom. 11:1). A central theme to be explored, then, in the apostolic history recorded in Acts, is the unity of the church as the one people of God, a unity that bridges the division that once excluded Gentiles from the community of God's covenant and brings them into the salvation achieved by the Messiah.

Finally, there is a bridge that lies just outside the purview of Luke's narrative, but is implied in the theology of the New Testament. It is the bridge between the *apostolic events* narrated by Luke and *our own day*, as we continue to see how the risen Jesus builds his church on the foundation of the apostolic word proclaimed by his eyewitnesses in Acts. This bridge is foreshadowed in Jesus' parable of the wheat and the tares (Matt. 13:24-30), which suggests a period of delay before the final judgment and separation of the redeemed from the rebellious. Jesus' commission to his servants to proclaim his salvation "to the ends of the earth" (Acts 1:8; 13:47) likewise implies a worldwide mission for the church that reaches beyond the geographical and temporal boundaries of the apostles' personal ministry, down through the centuries and around the world—a mission that includes the challenges facing Jesus' people today. Likewise, the promises in Acts that Jesus will return at the end of the age, bringing times of refreshing and restoration, unite Christians today with the apostles and other believers of long ago as together we eagerly await that blessed hope (Acts 1:11; 3:19–21).

As the following chapters will show, there are some important differences between our day and that foundational period, in which eyewitnesses, who had lived with Jesus and had heard his teaching and seen his miracles, bore their testimony to the fact that he was alive forevermore. Today we hear their testimony not through their physical presence, but rather through the words of Scripture. Nevertheless, a bridge connects these two phases in the life of the New Covenant church. The same Spirit who pierced hardened hearts as Peter and others preached long ago is still present in the church to drive home his convicting and life-giving message today. The purpose for the church, as revealed by her Savior and Lord in Acts, must continue to be her goal today. The shape of the church in those early days continues to set the contours for the church's growth and service to her Lord until that day when Jesus returns in the clouds of divine glory. With this third bridge in mind, I have tried to show the connection between the identity of the church as defined in the pages of Acts, on the one hand, and the issues confronting the church in our own day, on the other.

This book is itself a kind of bridge, spanning the gap between the disciplined study of Acts and its application to the church today. It is neither a full commentary nor a specialist's work of technical exegesis. No attempt is made to expound every passage or to resolve every exegetical difficulty in Acts. Much that would be of interest to professional scholars is bypassed without comment. Then again, this book is not intended to be "popular," if that implies a sacrifice of thought to entertaining imagination, so that readers relax, expecting to be carried along on a feather bed of pleasant impressions, their minds in neutral. I am convinced that Christians who have not had the opportunity for formal theological study nevertheless are keenly interested in understanding the Bible and are willing to reflect seriously on the intricate connections by which God's word manifests its splendid unity and variety, always pointing us to the Lord Jesus.

In addition to enriching the appreciation of thoughtful Christians in general as they read Acts, I hope that this book will also help pastors, Bible study teachers, and others directly involved in teaching and preaching the Bible to the church, by pointing out the *major thematic threads* woven through Acts, the patterns that tie passages and events together, the landmarks that signal major intersections in the route taken by Christ's Spirit and his servants to bring salvation to the ends of the earth. Our focus will be on seeing individual passages in *context:* the context of the whole of Acts, of Luke-Acts, and of other pertinent Scriptures. As a preacher and a trainer of preachers, I pray that we will see afresh in Acts the mighty work of our risen Lord through the Spirit; that seeing it, we will preach it; and that as his saving lordship is preached, Jesus will demonstrate his holy and gracious presence in his church, reaching out to the nations with his sovereign summons: "Turn to me and be saved, all you ends of the earth; for I am God, and there is no other" (Isa. 45:22 NIV).

ACKNOWLEDGMENTS

I am thankful:

(1) to Professor Richard B. Gaffin, Jr., of Westminster Theological Seminary (Philadelphia), whose introductory lectures on the theology of the Spirit in Acts during my Master of Divinity program sparked my interest in the Acts of the Apostles, and who wisely supervised my thesis, *Conversion and the Gift of the Spirit in Acts 2:38*, which was accepted by Westminster Seminary for the Master of Theology degree in 1977;

(2) to Westminster Theological Seminary in California for a study leave in 1988, during which this manuscript was begun, and for the privilege of teaching the New Testament to Christians preparing to serve and lead the church;

(3) to New Life Presbyterian Church in Escondido and my fellow elders for the opportunity to live in the midst of an attempt (imperfect but joyfully serious) to implement the New Testament portrait of the church;

(4) to my colleagues in the teaching of the New Testament at Westminster, especially Allen Mawhinney (now of Reformed Theological Seminary, Orlando campus), who read some early chapters and offered helpful exegetical comments, and Steven Baugh, who read chapters 10 and 11, and whose expertise in Hellenistic culture rescued me from repeating some oft-cited "truisms" that are unsupported by evidence;

(5) for my mother, who entered the presence of Christ as I was completing this manuscript, and to my father, whose example of Christian faith, hope, and love, even in sorrow, continues to encourage me;

(6) to Eric, Christina, Peter, and Laurie, young men and women whose growing maturity in Christ gives their mother and me great joy;

(7) to my wife, Jane—friend, encourager, soul mate—who not only

ACKNOWLEDGMENTS

kept me believing that this book could be finished, but also proofread drafts of each chapter, and whose editorial expertise has made the book more user-friendly; and, preeminently,

(8) to the One who is the Light to the Gentiles, who even today is bringing salvation to us and through us at the ends of the earth.

ONE

LISTENING TO LUKE

WHO NEEDS ACTS?

Scenario One: Churches drift off to sleep. Small groups turn in on themselves. Bible studies and Sunday school classes tread predictable, timeworn paths. Worship becomes routine. Witnessing becomes the work of specialists. And compassion? "Let's see . . . I have an hour open next Thursday."

When familiarity breeds contentment and complacency, when good order calcifies into rigid regularity, then people who love Jesus sense that something is amiss. They know that it was not always this way, and they turn to the Book to see again what is truly normal for Christ's church. In particular, when our zeal flags and our focus blurs, we need to listen to Luke, apostolic associate and documenter of the deeds of the Lord, as he recounts the Spirit's acts in the Spirit's words. We need the Acts of the Apostles.

Scenario Two: Emotions run at a feverish pitch, expressing the joy of restoration to God's friendship. The birthrate of God's daughters and sons soars, and the infants cry out for food and care. Churches spring up faster than gardeners can fertilize, train, and trim them. False shepherds slip in among the newborn lambs to cut them off from the flock. "Living stones," newly hewn from pagan quarries, with all sharp edges, rub on each other in Christ's new spiritual house, and the friction generates heat. The Spirit's life-breath blows with such force that everyone is thrown off balance.

When the fires of revival set the church alight, when the earth quakes at the holy and gracious presence of God, when the glad message of Christ's merciful power embraces people who have abandoned hope, then too we need to turn to Acts. Sadly, the joy of salvation can be faked—there can be an empty "high" without lowliness of heart; passion can be fixated on

I

itself, rather than focused on the One worthy of all adoration. Spirit-filled authority can be counterfeited for personal profit, harming Jesus' little ones and his name. Seedlings of faith must be fed from the Word, nurtured in the truth, if they are to bear lasting fruit. God's toddlers need to hear from him what family life in Christ is all about. When the Spirit shakes us up, no less than when we need shaking, we must go to the touchstone of the Spirit's word. We need the Acts of the Apostles.

Whatever our condition as the church of Jesus Christ may be, and wherever we may be scattered among the nations, Luke's second volume, which we call "Acts" or "The Acts of the Apostles," is God's call to remember and reflect on his design for his church, and reconsider how our fellowship fits—or fails to fit—the blueprint.[1] As we return to those thrilling days of yesteryear, we see the New Testament epistles' instructions for living fleshed out in real history. The history in Acts is, after all, real. It is full of people who don't get along, who don't catch on, and who don't always rise eagerly to the challenge of discipleship. On the other hand, this history is also real in demonstrating the powerful impact of Jesus, risen and enthroned, at work among these flawed people by his Spirit's quiet but invincible strength.[2]

HOW SHOULD WE READ ACTS?

Two Crucial Questions

It is obvious that we need light from the church's early days to shine on our churches today. To learn from Acts what God wants us to learn, however, is not an obvious and easy matter. God's Spirit speaks in Acts not in the form of explicit instructions or answers tailored to twentieth-century questions, but in the form of historical narrative. Whenever in God's word we find accounts of events that transpired in the past, we face two crucial questions: (1) What is *God's verdict* on those events? (2) What does God intend us to learn *here and now* from what happened *there and then?*

(1) What is God's moral verdict on the events narrated? It is clear that God does not approve of every action and event that he caused to be recorded in his word. Biblical narratives teem with accounts of the sordid, sensual, foolish, and violent acts of human beings—all of which God severely condemns (as the biblical narrators signal the reader in various ways). Old Testament history is intimately bound up with the Torah, the law for the covenant people of Israel. As the structure of the Hebrew Scriptures shows, the faithfulness of God and the faithfulness or unfaithfulness of his servants are set down in *prophetic* history as a solemn testimony and warning to com-

ing generations.³ So it is in Acts. Actions are recorded, of which the Lord of the church clearly disapproves. For example, we read about the hypocrisy of Ananias and Sapphira, the Samaritan Simon's quest for power, the greed of Ephesian silversmiths, and jealousy of Jewish leaders. In such cases, we have little difficulty seeing that God does not want the church today to duplicate everything we read in the pages of Acts.

(2) *What is normative for the whole church in all ages?* This second question raises a more difficult issue: When we read about an event or a practice in biblical history of which God does approve, should we assume that he wants that feature reproduced by us today? Abraham, for example, is commended by God for his willingness to sacrifice his son Isaac. Should we, then, imitate Abraham? Or, more precisely, if we should imitate Abraham, how should we do so? Should we imitate his *action* by offering our child in sacrifice, or should we imitate his *attitude* of unwavering faith and absolute loyalty to the Lord? Likewise, when we read in Acts that in the early church "no one claimed that any of his possessions was his own, but they shared everything they had" (4:32 NIV), what lesson should we learn for our life together today? Should we take this commendation of the early church's readiness to share as God's hint that he desires radical economic communalism in today's church? Or does the culture-transcending lesson of this text demand a deeper response than simple imitation, namely, a heartfelt and radical commitment to costly fellowship—whatever it may cost to express our unity in Jesus?

Two Extreme Answers

Our dilemma has been called "the problem of historical precedent."⁴ How is the historical portrait of the early church in Acts a normative precedent for the church today? Two extreme answers might be given to this question:

(1) *Everything* in Acts that the Lord approves should be reproduced in the church today. Some Pentecostal and charismatic portions of the church have talked as if everything that is good in Acts would be seen in today's church, if only we would take the Bible seriously. Some conclude from Acts 2 that "the baptism of the Spirit" comes to believers long after we come to trust in Jesus. Others believe that church leaders must be chosen by lot (chap. 1), or that those who are "in the Spirit" can handle snakes safely (chap. 28). However, I know of no one who applies this answer consistently. If we did, we would have to conclude that all of the following should be found in every church: (a) apostles who had walked Galilean trails with Jesus, bearing eyewitness testimony to his resurrection; (b) the Spirit coming in an earthquake and the roar of wind; (c) angels leading preachers out

of prison; and (d) church discipline by instantaneous, divinely administered capital punishment.

But the real problem with this extreme answer is not our pragmatic inconsistency. The real difficulty is that the "everything" answer is itself inconsistent with the theology of the New Testament. Acts, along with the rest of the New Testament, indicates that there is something *special* about the apostles who were chosen by Jesus to give evidence that he had been raised (Acts 1:2–3, 22; 2:32; etc.). Together with the prophets, the apostles formed the church's foundation (Eph. 2:20). Therefore, their testimony was confirmed by God himself through signs and wonders (Heb. 2:3–4; 2 Cor. 12:12). We should expect, then, to find some of the marvelous events associated with the apostles to be unique. They are visible "signs," which, like the miracles of Jesus' earthly ministry, unveil a salvation that goes deeper and farther than the eye can see. These acts of power in the visible world illustrate the hidden healing of the heart and provide a preview of the cosmic renewal that will accompany Jesus' return. Therefore, a church today that does not exhibit these foundational power-signs that we see in Acts is not defective or unspiritual. Rather, it may be a church that focuses on the uniqueness of Jesus' death and resurrection, and respects the special role of the apostles as witnesses to that redemptive turning point.

On the other hand, the uniqueness of the apostolic period should not be stressed to the point that Acts is denied any role at all in forming our life today as Jesus' disciples, as in the error at the opposite extreme:

(2) *Nothing* in Acts is normative for the church today. Again, it is doubtful that anyone holds this extreme view consistently. But when the vitality of the early church's life challenges our own status quo, we may be tempted to argue that, although Acts accurately describes the church's infancy, this description is not supposed to guide our lives today. Some, for example, would attribute the early Christians' pooling of resources exclusively to the unusual circumstances of the days just following Pentecost, when pilgrims who had believed Peter's sermon stayed on after the feast for instruction—thus, no challenge here to Americans' infatuation with their private property! Others have critiqued Paul's apologetic strategy at Athens as a misguided use of intellectual argument, even though Luke and God's Spirit include Paul's speech on Mars Hill as a positive example of gospel proclamation.

This extreme answer, invoked to let us off the hook when something in Acts makes us uncomfortable, violates the purpose that emerges from Luke's writings. Luke is concerned to write history, to be sure, but he is not writing to satisfy dispassionate historical curiosity. He writes to Theophilus and those like him, who have been catechized in the message of Jesus, but who need a thorough and orderly written account to confirm the life-changing message they have heard. Among the New Testament Evangelists, Luke alone has written a sequel to the earthly career of Jesus. This may be because he is writing for people who lacked person-to-person contact with the apostolic eyewitnesses themselves.

At any rate, Luke takes his stand in the tradition of biblical narrative —that is, prophetically interpreted history. He writes history that *must make a difference to our faith and life*, just as his mentor, Paul, described the purpose of Old Testament history as ethical instruction (1 Cor. 10:11) and teaching (Rom. 15:4; see also 2 Tim. 3:16). Certainly the foundational, apostolic period may have some unique features about it, just because it is foundational, but the foundation also determines the contours of the building to be constructed on it.

GUIDELINES FOR DISCOVERING AND APPLYING THE MESSAGE OF ACTS

If neither the "all" nor the "nothing" answer is a reliable guide to the normative impact of Acts on the church today, how can we understand and apply the Spirit's message correctly?

1. Read Acts in the Light of Luke's Purpose
Luke is writing about the climax of God's redemptive acts in history. As in Old Testament history and the Gospels, *what God has done* occupies center stage in Acts. God's saving acts always have implications for our response, of course. But in Scripture the starting point of instruction on right behavior is not a list of our duties, but a declaration of God's saving achievement, bringing us into a relationship of favor with him. Although Acts contains information on the early church's life and outreach, the book may frustrate us if we try to turn it into a manual of church polity or mission policies. Its purpose is more profoundly practical (and cross-cultural) than so many of our questions about procedures and strategy. Here God's Spirit unveils the identity of the church between Jesus' two comings, the divine power at work in this church, the results of that powerful Presence, and the environment in which we are to pursue our mission until "this same Jesus, who has been taken from you into heaven, will come back in the same way you have seen him go into heaven" (1:11 NIV).

2. Read Acts in the Light of the New Testament Epistles

Luke is both a historian and a theologian. As he records "the things that have been fulfilled among us" (Luke 1:1 NIV), he also makes sense of these events, indicating their significance as an interpreter guided by the Spirit of Christ. Nevertheless, the very fact that he communicates this significance through the genre of historical narrative (rather than in a theological essay, for example) has both advantages and limitations.

One advantage is that as Luke demonstrates the interface between God's salvation and the details of Hellenistic history (Luke 1:5; 2:1; 3:1–2), he shows how different the Christian faith is from religions rooted in mysticism, mythology, or speculation. The gospel of Christ is not abstract theory or poetic symbol. It is the account, attested by witnesses, of the personal God's intervention in history to rescue human beings.

One limitation, on the other hand, is that the genre of historical narrative itself permits theological explanation only indirectly, through the placement of material, the recounting of sermons, and verbal allusions to Old Testament texts and themes. To stay true to his historical aim, Luke the narrator cannot jump into the story with extensive commentary or theological essays to clear up all possible misunderstandings.

The epistle is the ideal genre for direct address and straightforward exposition of the gospel's meaning and its behavioral implications for those who believe it. Therefore, the New Testament epistles, written expressly to direct and correct the church's faith and life, provide a necessary check on the applications that we may draw from Acts for the church today. Without minimizing the special contribution of Acts to the teaching of the New Testament as a whole, once we recognize the purpose of Acts, we will be cautious about accepting as normative today any element of its narrative that is not confirmed in the exhortation of the epistles.

3. Read Acts in the Light of the Old Testament[5]

The prominence of the Old Testament in the speeches and sermons of Acts is obvious to any reader of the Bible. Especially where their hearers acknowledged the Scriptures' divine authority, the witnesses of Jesus quoted and interpreted the Scriptures in the light of the Messiah's coming, demonstrating how his ministry, death, resurrection, and pouring out of the Spirit fulfilled these prophetic writings.

Luke's debt to the Old Testament goes deeper than the citation of passages in sermons. He has embedded in his own narrative style echoes of Hebrew ways of speaking, quietly but pervasively reinforcing the message that he is writing in the tradition of Hebrew prophetic history, bearing witness to the climax of that tradition in the work of the Messiah.[6] Moreover, the connection between Acts and the Old Testament is more than a matter of words and grammar. Repeatedly we will see Old Testament themes (the Spirit, the servant, holy judgment, dispersion, persecution of the prophets) brought to new realization through the presence of the risen Lord in his church.

4. Read Acts in the Light of Luke's First Volume

The brief prologue of Acts (1:1–3) draws together Luke's two volumes, summing up the content of the Third Gospel even as it turns our vision toward what is to come.[7] Likewise, the Gospel closes with Jesus' prophetic interpretation of the Scriptures, a statement that anticipates the drama that unfolds in Acts:

> Thus it stands written: The Christ will suffer and rise from the dead on the third day, and repentance leading to forgiveness of sins will be preached in his name to all nations/Gentiles,[8] beginning at Jerusalem. You are witnesses of these things. And note this: I myself am sending upon you what my Father promised, but you must stay in the city until you have been clothed from on high with power. (Luke 24:46–49)

Parallels between Luke's gospel and Acts abound. In the Gospel, Jesus receives the Spirit when anointed in his baptism to proclaim good news; in Acts, the church receives the Spirit from the glorified Jesus and declares the wonders of God. In the Gospel, Jesus is the servant of Isaiah's Servant Songs; in Acts, the church is the servant-witness foreseen by Isaiah (but so also is Jesus, Acts 3:13!). In the Gospel, Jesus is repeatedly referred to as "the Lord"; in Acts, his glory and authority as Lord are displayed by his resurrection from the dead. The centrality of the word, the welcoming of the Gentiles, the arrival of salvation (a central theme in Luke-Acts), and many other themes bind Acts closely to Luke's gospel, demanding that we explore both volumes together in order to understand either.

5. Read Acts in the Light of Its Structure

Luke writes Greek well. He is at home with the written word, and his skill in the use of language is evident. In order to get his message—God's message through him—we must pay attention to the way in which this craftsman has put his books together. Are there overarching themes to guide us through the flow of incidents that we find in Acts? Is there a framework, a structure, to help us see how one section leads to the next? We do well to note four structural signals by which Luke points our way through his account.

STRUCTURAL SIGNPOSTS IN THE NARRATIVE OF ACTS

1. Acts 1:8 and 9:15

It is often observed that Acts 1:8, containing Jesus' promise of the Spirit and of the apostles' role as his witnesses, provides a preview of the phases of the gospel's spread: in Jerusalem (chaps. 1–7), through Judea and Samaria (chaps. 8–12), to the last part of the earth (chaps. 13–28). This of course involves geographical expansion, but there is more afoot here than miles. Things begin in Jerusalem, "the city of the great King" (Ps. 48:2), the site of the sanctuary, the center of Israel's worship of the living God. By the close of Acts, Paul, bearer of the Lord's word, has reached Rome, the city of the Caesars, the center of Gentile world power.[9] The word has crossed not only spatial distance, but also religious, ethnic, and cultural distance. The "word of this salvation" (Acts 13:26) has come not only to Jewish people within the Holy Land, but also to those dispersed throughout the Roman Empire— moreover, not only to Jews descended from "the fathers," but also to Samaritans (whose religious and ethnic heritage, though related to the Jews, was tainted by intermarriage and pagan syncretism), to Gentile proselytes,[10] to Gentile God-fearers,[11] and even to Gentiles enmeshed in idolatry.

In taking Jesus' word of promise for his outline, then, Luke highlights the powerful force of God's Spirit, propelling divine vitality, purity, and grace out from the ancient holy place to bring the nations under the redemptive rule of the Lord and his Christ.

In Acts 9:15, another statement of Jesus' complements the promise of Acts 1:8, suggesting in more detail the contents of the third major section of the book, the apostolic witness "to the ends of the earth." That statement describes Saul of Tarsus, the witness whose mission dominates chapters 13–28: "But the Lord said to [Ananias], 'Go! This man is a select vessel belonging to me, to carry my name in the presence both of Gentiles and of kings and of Israel's sons' " (Acts 9:15). As in Acts 1:8, we see here three spheres of witness: (1) Gentiles, (2) kings, and (3) sons of Israel.[12] This threefold description nicely sums up the targets of Paul's preaching as Luke has recorded it: his primary focus on the Gentiles (chaps. 13–20), his speeches before kings/rulers (chaps. 24–26), and also his testimony to his own people, the sons of Israel (chaps. 22, 28). Thus, Paul's final words of witness in Acts contain a rebuke to Israel, reminiscent of Stephen's prophetic testimony against stiffness of neck and hardness of heart and hearing (see 7:51–53), and an expression of hopeful expectation that the gospel will be welcomed by the Gentiles (28:25–29).

These two promises of Jesus trace out for us the overarching framework for the twenty-eight chapters of Acts, in which Luke chronicles the spread of the word of salvation:

1–7	Jerusalem (Peter/Stephen/[Saul approves Stephen's death])
8–12	Judea and Samaria ([Saul initiates dispersion]/Philip to Samaria, Ethiopian/[Saul converted]/Peter initiates Gentile mission)
13–28	The last part of the earth (Paul/[Peter confirms Gentile mission])

13–20	Before Gentiles
24–26	Before kings
22, 28	Before Israel's sons

2. Summary Statements

Within the larger sections, Luke's method is to give us snapshots or vignettes of the development of the church's life and witness, samples of the Spirit's work, which are then joined to one another by summary statements.[13] These statements, though perhaps lacking the dramatic appeal of the action narratives, are vital to the purpose of Acts.[14] They show us the ongoing results of each incident, and they set the scene for the next event that Luke intends to recount. As they perform these tasks, the summaries quietly but constantly set the tone for our perception of the Spirit's presence and activity in the church: *the word of the Lord grew powerfully.*[15] Early in Acts, several extended summaries place Pentecost, the healing of the lame man in the temple, and the judgment on Ananias and Sapphira in the context of the continuing manifestations of the Spirit's power in the church: bold and effective evangelism, mutual compassion expressed in practical help, joy mingled with a healthy fear (2:42–47; 4:32–35; 5:12–16; see also 9:31; 16:5). Then, after the appointment of the Seven Servers, Luke introduces a theme on which he will present variations in the rest of his narrative: "So the word of God was growing and the number of the disciples in Jerusalem was multiplying exceedingly, and a large crowd of priests were obeying the faith" (Acts 6:7). As Luke's narrative expands to embrace Judea and Samaria, "the word of God was growing and being multiplied" (12:24). In Pisidia "the word of the Lord was permeating through the whole region" (13:49). Likewise, at Ephesus "the word of the Lord was growing powerfully and exerting strength" (19:20).[16]

Luke introduced his two-volume narrative by referring to "those who from the first were eyewitnesses and servants of the word" (Luke 1:2 NIV), signaling from the outset the importance that he attached to the powerful word about Jesus. Now in Acts his repeated reference to the dynamic growth of the word underscores the theme that the Holy Spirit's power is focused in the glad announcement of salvation in Jesus the Christ.

3. Repeated Accounts

A third feature of Luke's structure is a device borrowed from those who told the story of Israel in the Old Testament Scriptures. Although modern readers have little patience for what seems to us to be needless duplication, biblical narrators preferred to underscore an event's importance by repeating the story with slight variations, like the repetition and development of a musical motif in a symphony.[17] If we compare, for example, Genesis 24:1–27 with Genesis 24:34–49 (as we should, since they belong to the same story), we find that the narrator leads us, step by step, through Abraham's servant's successful search for Isaac's bride not once, but twice. Why the "wasted" words? Because Isaac is the son of promise, through whose descendants God will keep his promises to Abraham, and therefore because Isaac's marriage is crucial to the fulfillment of the divine promises. We are invited to marvel —yes, and marvel again!—at the astounding guidance and provision of God in giving the bride of his own choosing to the covenant heir.

Similarly, Luke uses repetition to underscore the importance of three pivotal events: (1) the outpouring of the Spirit at Pentecost, (2) the conversion of Cornelius and his associates, and (3) the conversion of Saul of Tarsus.

(1) The Spirit's coming at Pentecost is described in chapter 2, but it is also recalled by Peter in his report to the Jerusalem church regarding Cornelius, together with a specific reminder of the words of Jesus quoted by Luke prior to Pentecost: "Then I remembered what the Lord had said: 'John baptized with water, but you will be baptized with the Holy Spirit' " (Acts 11:16 NIV; see 1:5). Again, at the Jerusalem council, Peter recalls the gift of the Spirit at Pentecost (15:8). By these references, Luke reminds us that reception of the Spirit is the touchstone of Christian experience.

(2) The conversion of the Gentiles at Cornelius's house is described not only by Luke as the narrator in chapter 10, but also by Peter upon his return to the church in Jerusalem (including the details of Peter's preparatory vision—again!) (11:4–17). Peter refers again to the turning point in Cornelius's home when he speaks at the council of apostles and

elders in Jerusalem: "Brothers, you know that some time ago God made a choice among you that the Gentiles might hear from my lips the message of the gospel and believe" (15:7 NIV). Why belabor the point? Because the pouring out of the Spirit, God's gift of welcome, on the Gentiles in Peter's presence makes him the witness who can testify that God's salvation has burst the boundaries of Israel's cultic and cultural distinctiveness. The risen Lord summons the ends of the earth to turn to him for salvation, and as they come, he sweeps from their path the ruins of the walls that had kept un-Law-ful aliens out of Israel's covenant privilege. Circumcision, sanctuary, calendar, diet—all are bypassed as the God of glory lavishes *himself* on outsiders.

(3) Finally, we read three times of the conversion of Saul of Tarsus: first from the narrator (9:1–30), then twice in Paul's own speeches (22:1–16; 26:2–18). Although intriguing differences in detail puzzle us, the account of the awesome Christophany on the road to Damascus is essentially the same in all three accounts. We may find it odd that Luke did not economize papyrus by inserting a terse summary in chapters 22 and 26, such as: "Then Paul told them about his conversion." But Luke's extravagant repetition is the better way: he will not let us forget the world-changing significance of the call of the Apostle to the Gentiles. He will have us listen to that call again and again, and with each repetition he adds details that increase the luster of this conquest of grace: persecutor turned into propagator, paragon of self-righteousness reduced to penitent dependence on Another's righteousness, aloof zealot for Israel's purity sent to mingle with polluted pagans as the preeminent exhibit of God's cleansing mercy (see 1 Tim. 1:12–16).

4. The Prominence of Preaching

Luke illustrates his persistent reminders that "the word was growing" by preserving a substantial sample of Christian preaching. At least thirty percent of the text of Acts consists of apostolic preaching, either in fairly full form or in summary.[18] Many miracles recorded in Acts are pretexts for preaching, introducing sermons that interpret the miracles' true significance. The preaching, in fact, receives more extended treatment than the related signs of power. For example, although the events associated with the Spirit's coming at Pentecost are recorded in thirteen verses, Peter's sermon explaining the events takes up twenty-three (chap. 2). Similarly, the healing of a lame man in the temple is described in ten verses; it is followed by two speeches of Peter's, totaling twenty-two verses, to explain its implications (chaps. 3, 4).

Luke has selected speeches strategically, including samples of how the gospel was addressed to various audiences in its expansion from Jerusalem, through Judea and Samaria, to the ends of the earth.

In *Jerusalem*, Peter's speech at Pentecost shows the connection between the Spirit's coming and Jesus' exaltation (chap. 2). Peter's speech in Solomon's Colonnade (chap. 3) and its follow-up before the Sanhedrin (4:8–12) focus on the power of Jesus' name to bring the blessings of the last days. Stephen's speech is a prophetic indictment of Israel's rebellion against the deliverers sent by God (chap. 7), leading to the spread of the gospel beyond Jerusalem.

The next phase in the expansion of the gospel—in *Judea and Samaria* —is transitional. We have brief summaries of Philip's preaching to Samaritans and an Ethiopian (8:12, 32–35), but the major speeches center on the conversion of Cornelius and his friends through the proclamation of Peter (chaps. 10, 11).

As the word moves to *the ends of the earth*, we hear it preached in a synagogue of the Dispersion (13:16–41, 46–48), among superstitious pagans (17:22–31; see 14:14–18), to elders of the church in deliberation (15:13–21) and in farewell (20:17–35), and in circumstances of legal defense (chaps. 22, 26). At the close of Acts, Luke leaves us, in a sense, with Paul's preaching ringing in our ears: "He was explaining, solemnly testifying concerning the kingdom of God and persuading them about Jesus from the Law of Moses and the Prophets, from morning until evening" (28:23). "He was preaching the kingdom of God and teaching about the Lord Jesus Christ with all boldness and without hindrance" (28:31).

If we are to understand Acts and its message for the church today, we must certainly pay careful attention to the sermons of Acts, those divinely given, apostolic commentaries on the stirring events that marked the church's entrance into the age of the Spirit's power.

CONCLUSION

Our study of Acts will be enriched as we pay attention to the bridges that link God's mighty work through the apostles with other dimensions of his redeeming work and revealing word: the bridge to Old Testament words of promise and deeds of anticipated deliverance; the bridge to the ministry of Jesus, recounted in Luke's gospel; the bridge to the epistles of Paul and other apostles, through whom the Spirit set his works in theological context and clear focus; and the bridges within the narrative of Acts itself, which signal turning points and interwoven strands of continuity as the message of salvation in Jesus Christ bridges chasms and breaks down barriers to extend God's grace to Jew and Gentile alike.

Notes

¹ The author of the Third Gospel is also the author of Acts, as the introductions to the two documents (Luke 1:1–4; Acts 1:1–2), as well as their style, make clear. The author never identifies himself by name. The most natural understanding of certain sections of Acts (16:10–17; 20:5–21:18; 27:1–28:16), in which the narrator uses the first person pronoun "we," is that the author accompanied Paul during those portions of his travels. From the second century onward, the Third Gospel and Acts were associated with Luke, a physician whom Paul praised highly in Col. 4:14 and mentioned in Philem. 24 and 2 Tim. 4:11. No evidence from the books themselves refutes this ancient tradition, although influential modern scholars have argued that Acts could not have come from an associate of Paul's, either because the portrait of Paul in Acts seems to them to contradict the impression gained from his epistles, or because Acts seems to reflect a church situation that did not arise until after the apostolic period. See, e.g., Ernst Haenchen, *The Acts of the Apostles: A Commentary* (Philadelphia: Westminster Press, 1971). Persuasive answers to Haenchen's argument that the Paul of Acts is irreconcilable with the Paul of the epistles are found in Jacob Jervell, *The Unknown Paul: Essays on Luke-Acts and Early Christian History* (Minneapolis: Augsburg, 1984), and W. Ward Gasque, *A History of the Interpretation of the Acts of the Apostles* (Peabody, Mass.: Hendrickson, 1989), 235–47.

² Some scholars in the historical-critical tradition, such as Martin Dibelius (*Studies in the Acts of the Apostles* [London: SCM, 1956]), Ernst Haenchen (*Acts*), and Hans Conzelmann (*The Theology of St. Luke* [New York: Harper and Row, 1961], and *Acts of the Apostles*, ed. E. J. Epp, trans. J. Limburg, A. T. Kraabel, and D. H. Juel [Hermeneia; Philadelphia: Fortress, 1987]) have argued that the author of Acts was not concerned to recount history as it actually occurred, but rather was propounding his own theology through the form of historical narrative. Their extreme separation of theology from history has been answered by I. Howard Marshall, *Luke: Historian and Theologian*, enlarged ed. (Grand Rapids: Zondervan, 1989), 21–76; Martin Hengel, *Acts and the History of Earliest Christianity* (Philadelphia: Fortress, 1980), 35–49; and others. See also F. F. Bruce, *New Testament History* (Garden City, N.J.: Doubleday, 1972); D. Guthrie, *New Testament Introduction*, 4th rev. ed. (Downers Grove, Ill.: InterVarsity, 1990), 365–82. More recently, the posthumously published study by Colin J. Hemer, *The Book of Acts in the Setting of Hellenistic Historiography*, ed. Conrad J. Gempf (WUNT, 49; Tübingen: J. C. B. Mohr, 1989), develops a nuanced defense, meticulously documented in light of current archaeological knowledge, not only of Luke's intention to report historical events reliably, but also of his effectiveness in achieving this purpose.

³ In the Hebrew Scriptures, unlike our English versions, the books of Joshua, Judges, Samuel, and Kings are regarded as the Former *Prophets*, and therefore grouped with the Latter Prophets such as Isaiah, Jeremiah, etc. The history in the Pentateuch is all prologue or epilogue to the covenant made with Israel at Sinai, and the Former Prophets and Latter Prophets then go on to bear witness concerning Israel's response to the covenant and the consequences that would follow. Biblical history is narrated not to satisfy readers' curiosity

about the past, but to summon us to covenant faithfulness. For a sensitive discussion of the blending of historical, theological, and literary-artistic purposes in biblical history, see V. Philips Long, *The Art of Biblical History* (Foundations of Contemporary Interpretation; Grand Rapids: Zondervan, 1994).

⁴ For a good discussion, see the chapter bearing this title (chap. 6) in Gordon D. Fee and Douglas Stuart, *How to Read the Bible for All It's Worth* (Grand Rapids: Zondervan, 1981), 87–102.

⁵ On this point and the next, see Carey C. Newman, "Acts," in *A Complete Literary Guide to the Bible*, ed. Leland Ryken and Tremper Longman III (Grand Rapids: Zondervan, 1993), 438–39: "Generic riddles can be solved, in part, by reading Acts within its two primary literary contexts—the Jewish Scriptures and the gospel of Luke" (p. 438).

⁶ A few examples here will illustrate the point: (1) "and he lifted up his voice" (Acts 2:14; 14:11; 22:22; see Judg. 9:7); (2) "pierced to the heart" (Acts 2:37; see Ps. 109:16); (3) the report "was heard into the ears" of the church (Acts 11:22; see Isa. 5:9). See Max Wilcox, *The Semitisms of Acts* (Oxford: Clarendon, 1965).

⁷ The first-century Jewish historian Josephus's two-part defense *Against Apion* is unified by a similar introduction to the second book: "In the former book, most excellent Epaphroditus, I have demonstrated our antiquity and confirmed the truth of what I have said."

⁸ The Greek word εθνη (a plural form) refers to "nations" in the sense of "ethnic groups," but often specifically those ethnic groups that are not the "people" (λαος) of Israel —namely, the Gentiles.

⁹ Reading Luke's gospel and Acts together, we observe that the Gospel traces Jesus' movement toward Jerusalem (Luke 9:51; 13:22; 17:11; 19:11), while Acts traces the gospel's spread away from Jerusalem (Acts 8:1, 26, 40; 9:19, 32; 10:1; 11:19; 13:4).

¹⁰ Proselytes were full converts to Judaism, who submitted to circumcision and "shouldered the yoke of the Torah," obligating themselves to keep the ceremonial as well as the moral instructions of the Mosaic law.

¹¹ God-fearers (οι σεβομενοι τον θεον or οι φοβουμενοι τον θεον) were attracted to Judaism's monotheism and high ethical ideals, but balked at submitting to the cultural distinctives of Judaism: circumcision, kosher diet, and observance of the Levitical calendar.

¹² H. N. Ridderbos, *The Speeches of Peter in the Acts of the Apostles* (London: Tyndale Press, 1962), 6.

¹³ Since the summaries describe circumstances and activities that took place consistently over a period of time, they stand out clearly in the Greek text as Luke shifts between verbs in the aorist tense, describing specific acts in the "vignette" sections, to verbs in the imperfect tense, describing continuing conditions or customary behaviors in the summaries. For example, every verb in the summary of Acts 4:32–35 is in the imperfect tense, but in 4:36 Luke shifts back to the aorist tense—a signal that Barnabas's gift is both a specific example of the general trend sketched in the summary and the immediate introduction (instigation) to the hypocritical generosity of Ananias and Sapphira (5:1–11). In 5:12–16— another summary—the characteristic verb tense is the imperfect.

¹⁴ Luke used this method at several points in his Gospel as well: 1:80 (John grew); 2:40, 52 (Jesus grew). Luke's gospel, like the other Synoptic Gospels, Matthew and Mark, also comments on the spread of the news about Jesus after some of his miracles: Luke 4:14–15, 37; 5:15; 7:17; Mark 1:28; 7:36–37; Matt. 4:24; 9:26, 31.

¹⁵ H. Alan Brehm, "The Significance of the Summaries for Interpreting Acts," *Southwestern Journal of Theology* 33 (1990): 29–40.

[16] Luke uses metaphors of organic growth to express both the expansion of the word's sphere of influence and the vitality of the message itself: αυξανω ("grow") in 6:7; 12:24 (with πληθυνω, "multiply"); 19:20 (with ισχυω, "be strong"). In 13:49 the verb is διαφερω (in the passive voice: "be carried through" a region).

[17] Robert Alter, *The Art of Biblical Narrative* (New York: Basic Books, 1981), 88–113. This is a stimulating study of narrative conventions in the Hebrew Scriptures, but it also (despite Alter's judgment on p. ix) is relevant to the study of the Gospels and Acts, inasmuch as they were significantly influenced by the style of earlier historical writing in the Bible.

[18] This figure excludes normal conversation and the narrative introductions to sermons.

T W O

THE ACTS OF THE LORD

PRACTICAL DEISM IN THE CONTEMPORARY CHURCH

One of my professors posed the question, "How could New England slip so quickly from the vibrant evangelical Christianity of the Pilgrims, the Puritans, and Jonathan Edwards—strongly affirming God's personal control of every detail of their lives—first into deism and, finally, into the pantheism of the Transcendentalists?" What influences could have infected the spiritual tone of a region so radically within a few generations? What went wrong?

His hypothesis was that long before the church folk of New England accepted deism in *theory*, they were already operating as deists *in practice*. What is deism? It is the belief that, although the universe reflects the intelligent design and power of a Creator, God's direct and personal involvement with his creatures ceased after that moment of creation, when he established a network of orderly and regular processes, with which not even he himself will interfere. Deism thus enjoyed the perks of a doctrine of creation—meaning, intelligent design, and order in the universe, and even a theoretical basis for morality—without the uncomfortable meddling of a God who intervenes in history through miracle, judgment, or salvation.[1]

Deism as an ideology passed from the scene long ago. It was only an unstable halfway house on the way to the naturalistic determinism that seized the intellectual centers of the West by the middle of the nineteenth century, only lately to be challenged by waves of neopagan spirituality. More persistent and more troubling was the practical deism that had wormed its

16

way into the churches of colonial New England, paving the way for theoretical deism and Transcendentalism to follow. Such practical deism is alive and well today, even in churches that take their stand on the Bible. However correct their statements in Bible studies or Sunday school classes may be, in practice many Christians really assume that God's "interference" in people's lives pretty much came to a halt sometime in the past—perhaps in the apostles' time, perhaps at the Reformation or some revival of bygone days, but surely before our time.

Would we say this out loud? Never! But our meager prayer lives, our anxiety, our dependence on novel techniques in evangelism, our hope in technology to solve spiritual problems, our doubt that loving discipline can restore wandering brothers or sisters to repentance and reconciliation—all these testify to our unspoken assumption that God's *real* action is in the past and in the future, but not in the present. We act as though Jesus wound up the church and then *flung us out on our own* when we say, "Our church can't grow in this neighborhood," or "I won't apologize until she does—and she won't!" or "He says he's sorry, but he'll do it again," or "What will become of us?"

Could any of these attitudes survive if we were convinced that God is present and at work among us? The presence of his power would dispel our discouragement. His authority would melt our stubbornness. His terrible purity would banish our temptation to compromise. Surrounded by his peace, we would laugh at our fears.

There are, of course, differences between the way that God worked in the days of the apostles and the way he is working today. As God has led his people along the path of his saving plan, there have been some towering milestones. By far the greatest of these (qualitatively superior to all the rest!) was the redemptive mission of God's Son: Jesus' birth, ministry, death, resurrection, heavenly enthronement, and bestowal of the Spirit on the church in celebration of his victory. To underscore the once-for-all importance of Jesus Christ's redemptive achievement, God gave his own testimony on behalf of this Messiah-Savior in direct and amazing ways: "Jesus the Nazarene, a man *attested from God* to you by acts of power and wonders and signs, which God did through him among you" (Acts 2:22). This testimony through miracle came not only while Jesus was on earth, but also after his enthronement in heaven, through his witnesses, the apostles (Heb. 2:3–4). The miraculous signs through which the Father bore witness to his Son (and the Son's apostles) mark those days and those ways of divine working as extraordinary, since they are especially linked to that once-for-all turning point in God's plan of salvation.[2]

Having recognized the extraordinary actions of God when Jesus and his apostles walked the earth, however, we may fail to see how the God of saving surprises is still present and active in the church today. It is not that we don't "know" that Christ is with his people, but too often we hold such "knowledge" as a piece of data on an almost unreadable sector of some mislaid floppy disk of the mind. We need to "boot up" this astounding reality, giving it ready access to our thoughts and attitudes, so that it impacts everything we do and think in connection with the church's life and mission.

Here is where we need to listen to Luke, to contemplate his portrait of the church as God sees her. Jesus said not only to those first disciples but to us as well, "I will not leave you as orphans; I will come to you" (John 14:18 NIV). Luke says to us, in effect, "Let me show you *how* Jesus has come to us."

THE FIRST THING TO KNOW ABOUT THE CHURCH

Luke sets the scene for his narrative in Acts by summing up the contents of his gospel: "I produced the first discourse concerning all things, O Theophilus, which Jesus *began* both to do and to teach, until the day when, having commanded through the Holy Spirit the apostles he had chosen, he was taken up" (Acts 1:1–2). This summarizing device was used by other ancient historians to signal to readers that they are entering the narrative "midstream,"[3] but in Luke's hands it does more than this.

Luke's gospel is aptly described as an account of Jesus' actions and teachings. What may surprise us is that his first book dealt with "what Jesus *began* to do and teach,"[4] for with this turn of phrase Luke not only sums up his first volume, but also indicates the contents of this second installment: "Now I will narrate all the things which Jesus *continued* to do and to teach, *after* he was taken up to heaven."[5] Luke's story, from beginning to end, is the story of the acts and teachings of Jesus. This is the first thing Luke wants us to know about the church: *Jesus is still at work, here and now.*

Of course, very few people in the apostolic church actually *saw* Jesus at work with their physical eyes or *heard* his voice with their ears after his resurrection. With respect to his resurrected body—the body that his friends touched and with which he ate among them (Luke 24:39–43)—Jesus is now in heaven. God's messengers promise that he will return physically, visibly, as he departed (Acts 1:11), but not until the divinely scheduled sea-son of total restoration (3:21). How, then, can Jesus "do and teach" on earth in the interim between his departure and his return, when he is at the right hand of God in heaven (2:34; 7:55)? Reading Acts with an eye for the activity of Jesus will sensitize us to the supernatural character of the church.

JESUS CONTINUES TO CHOOSE LEADERS FOR HIS CHURCH

"Who's in charge here?" is a vital question for any group of people. There are only so many possible answers, whether we are thinking of political structure, business, the local softball league, or a religious gathering. A group's leadership may be exercised by one person, a few, or a majority of all its members. If it is governed by one or a few, those leaders may be chosen by the whole membership (democracy), or they may hold the reins of power without the consent of those whom they govern. So then, who's in charge of the church?

Democracy (or a democratic republic) has much to commend it. Decentralization of power, accountability to the people, and a system of checks and balances can limit totalitarian abuses of power by one or a few leaders. Nevertheless, the church is not a democracy. The New Testament proclaims Jesus not as president, prime minister, coordinator, or facilitator, but as Messiah—the anointed King. He is the head of the church, the Lord of the church, the lawgiver of the church. His wish is our command.

But it has looked to many people over the centuries as though Jesus is now a king in absentia. Some, in fact, wonder whether his royal rule has even begun. Is Jesus an absent monarch or a ruler in waiting? Was Peter jumping the gun to announce at Pentecost, "God has made this Jesus, whom you crucified, both Lord and Christ" (Acts 2:36 NIV)?

Completing the Number of the Apostles (Acts 1:2, 12–26)
Luke's answer to these questions begins with the central role of the apostles appointed by Jesus. In the prologue to Luke's gospel, they are called "those who from the beginning became eyewitnesses and servants of the word" (Luke 1:2); in Acts they are "the apostles whom he had chosen" (Acts 1:2). Very possibly, Theophilus (like us) had not met an apostle in person and so had never heard directly the testimony of one who could say, "I saw him eat fish, I touched his wounds—he was alive after his death on the cross!" But Theophilus needed access to the apostles' testimony that Jesus had been raised from the dead (as we do), and so Luke emphasizes

that it is precisely this eyewitness testimony that Theophilus now holds in his hands, in written form.

The fact that Luke opens his second volume with the reminder that Jesus himself chose the apostles suggests that this selection is of no small significance. Between his resurrection and his ascension, Jesus gave instructions and "presented himself alive by means of many convincing proofs" to "the apostles whom he had *chosen*" (Acts 1:2–3). These words echo Luke's account of the appointment of the Twelve when, after a night of prayer, "he summoned his disciples and *chose* from them twelve, whom he also named apostles" (Luke 6:13). Of the four Evangelists, only Luke speaks of Jesus "choosing" (εκλεγομαι) the apostles,[6] and his repetition of the verb in Acts 1:2 reminds us that Jesus sovereignly selected the witnesses who would testify to his resurrection and lordship.

Unlike the situation in Luke 6, however, at the beginning of Acts the number of the apostles is not twelve, but eleven. One has defected, betraying the Lord with a kiss. The number is significant: Judas had been "numbered" among the apostles (Acts 1:17).[7] Since the apostles were to be the chiefs of the twelve tribes of the new Israel (Luke 22:30; Matt. 19:28), the gap left by Judas had to be filled. The apostolic number had to be restored to fullness before the promised arrival of God's Spirit. The filling of this gap is the one event that Luke records in the ten-day period between Jesus' ascent to heaven and the Spirit's descent from heaven (Acts 1:15–26).

When Peter explains why another must take Judas's place, we sense that he has taken to heart Jesus' post-resurrection lessons in biblical interpretation (Luke 24:44–49, 25–27). Now Peter recognizes that "it was necessary" (εδει) that the psalmists' laments over treachery by intimates would reach their climax in the betrayal of the Messiah himself by one from his own inner circle (Pss. 41; 69; 109).[8] God had planned and announced in the Scriptures that the righteous Sufferer would be betrayed by a companion, and that this false friend would thereby forfeit his leadership privilege.

How, then, was Judas's replacement to be identified? The apostles' distinctive task was to bear witness to Jesus' resurrection (Acts 1:22). Therefore, Judas's replacement was required to have traveled with Jesus before his death and seen him alive from the dead (Acts 1:21–22). The new apostle had to be able to attest that Jesus was the same person before and after his death and resurrection. When this criterion was applied, the field was narrowed to two candidates: Joseph (Barsabbas Justus) and Matthias. But from this point on, the believers did not presume to make the final decision. Instead, they prayed for direct revelation from the Lord and used lots, an ancient method of seeking to discern God's will without the interference of human reasoning (Lev. 16:8–10; Num. 26:55–56; Prov. 16:33; Jonah 1:7).

Luke implies that this prayer of the early church was addressed to Jesus, whose death they had witnessed only weeks before. Although the title "Lord" (κυριος) is sometimes applied to God the Father (Acts 4:29), it is characteristically applied to Jesus in Luke-Acts (including the language of prayer, as in 7:59–60). The Lord who is addressed by the church's prayer in Acts 1:24 is clearly the Lord Jesus, for their request, "Show us which one of these two you have *chosen* [εκλεγομαι]," echoes the language of Acts 1:2: It was *Jesus* who *chose* (εκλεγομαι) his apostles.[9] Moreover, the Lord addressed here knows the secrets of the human heart (καρδιογνωστης), just as the Lord Jesus does in Luke's gospel.[10] So Jesus the Lord chooses apostles to proclaim his resurrection, both before his suffering and after his triumph over death. Although he is in heaven, Jesus is at work here on earth.

Saul, Servant-Witness to the Gentiles
The call of Saul of Tarsus reveals the same presence and activity of Jesus the Lord. Although Saul unwittingly called "Lord" (κυριε) the glorious figure who confronted him on the road (Acts 9:5), Ananias of Damascus knew precisely who it was. Jesus the Lord, who appeared to Saul on the road, sent Ananias to Saul (v. 17).[11] This Lord declared to Ananias that Saul was "my chosen instrument" (σκευος εκλογης) to carry the Lord's name before Gentiles, kings, and the sons of Israel (v. 15). Thus, Jesus chose one who had *not* traveled with him before his crucifixion. From his heavenly throne, Jesus reached down and seized that violent persecutor and pressed him into service as a proclaimer of the faith he had been trying to destroy (Gal. 1:23).

Seven Servants Appointed by Jesus Through the Church's Discernment
It is not surprising that Luke portrays Jesus as directly involved—even from heaven—in the appointment of apostles through direct revelation. But does Jesus still appoint leaders for his church today, or was this activity of Jesus limited to the time of the apostles? Must we receive special revelation (by casting lots or seeing a vision of Christ's glory) in order to have confidence that King Jesus is governing us through church officials?

The Seven Servants in Acts 6 were chosen by a different means than were Matthias and Paul. However, Luke implies that their selection by the decision of the church, no less than a revelatory casting of lots or prophetic vision, was the action of Jesus the Lord. The Seven were appointed not by divine revelation or by the apostles' decision. Because their task arose from a growing discontent with perceived inequities in the church's care for its needy members, it was essential that these leaders be men who had already earned the confidence of the whole Christian community. They were to be "seven men from among you *on whose behalf testimony is given* that they are full of the Spirit and wisdom" (6:3).[12] The believers themselves were instructed and invited to select men to carry out this important ministry.

Is this, then, a transition from Jesus' "hands-on" monarchy to a democratic model? No, for Luke gives two indications that, although the discernment and decision of the whole congregation were the means of their appointment, the Lord himself was appointing them to this position of service.

First, as with the appointment of Judas's replacement in Acts 1, the field of candidates was narrowed from the outset by certain essential criteria. In the case of the Seven, the crucial criterion was not an external circumstance (having followed Jesus from his baptism to his ascension), but an internal, prior work of God in their lives: they were to be "full of the Spirit and wisdom" (6:3). Stephen, the most prominent of the Seven, was indeed "full of faith and of the Holy Spirit" (v. 5), and "full of God's grace and power" (v. 8). These qualities set these men apart from others in the church. Although the Holy Spirit is present in all who trust Jesus (Rom. 8:9; 1 Cor. 12:13), the description "full of the Spirit" marks out these men as having had an unusual degree of maturity, of sensitivity to the Spirit's divine presence, of bold and joyful faith, and of godly wisdom and compassion.[13] In other words, the church's choice of these men was a response to, and a recognition of, the extraordinary work of the Spirit of God within them. Since Jesus was the one who poured out the Spirit (Acts 2:33), these believers were following his lead in presenting the Seven to the apostles for official recognition through prayer and the laying on of hands. Similarly, although elders were appointed through decisions made by human beings (Acts 14:23; Titus 1:5), it was preeminently the Holy Spirit who appointed elders to oversee God's flock (Acts 20:28). To Luke, the risen Lord's initiative, imparting Spirit-given abilities and maturity to lead, on the one hand, and the church's responsive recognition of Spirit-filled leaders, on the other, do not stand in tension with one another. Rather, the Lord Jesus, who sends the Spirit, makes his choice of leaders clear through the dependent discernment of believers.

Second, the Old Testament background to the appointment of the Seven also sends the signal that the Lord himself is involved in their selection. Several elements of this account are parallel to the Lord's selection of Joshua as Moses' successor (Num. 27:15–23), and some of these will be discussed in a later chapter. Relevant here is the unusual word in Acts

6:3, which the NIV translates "choose" (NASB: "select"). Luke's verb here is not the one we noted earlier in Acts 1:2, 25,[14] but another one that typically means "oversee, visit, give special attention to, intervene to judge or save."[15] This is the word used in the Septuagint, the Greek translation of the Old Testament, at Numbers 27:16, where Moses asks God to designate a leader to succeed him. But here is the point to notice: in Numbers 27, Moses asks *the Lord* to "oversee" a man to lead Israel, and the Lord points him to Joshua, "in whom is the Spirit." But in Acts it is *the fellowship of disciples* that is to "oversee" men full of the Holy Spirit, who will meet the widows' needs. The change from the Lord's choice of Joshua to the church's choice of the Seven does not mean that the King has abdicated his throne or ceded his power to the people. Rather, it shows that the Lord uses his Spirit-baptized people as he appoints leaders who are full of the Spirit. Through these leaders, as through Joshua, the Lord will extend the reach of his rule into new territory, as we shall see.[16]

Whether through direct revelation or through the spiritual discernment of his followers, Jesus appoints leaders for his church. Although the process by which pastors, elders, and deacons are selected today may involve ballots and tallies, God is telling us through Luke that we should not understand church elections as expressing the "will of the people," but rather as discerning the will of the Lord.[17] Clearly, then, such processes of seeking and discerning leaders gifted and called by God must be immersed in fervent, humble, confident, dependent prayer to the Lord (Acts 1:24; 6:6; 14:23), for he gives such gifts to his people as the "spoils of war" won in the victory of his crucifixion and resurrection (Eph. 4:7–13).

JESUS CONTINUES TO TEACH AND TO DO

Luke's summary of Jesus' earthly ministry in Acts 1:1 focuses attention on what Jesus began "both to *do* and to *teach*," that is, on his miracles and his teachings, both of which disclosed the arrival of the era of salvation (Luke 4:18–21; 7:18–23). In Acts, Luke portrays Jesus' continuing activity in bringing salvation in *word* and in *deed*.

Jesus the Teacher
In the apostolic church, Jesus taught the word both by empowering his messengers to preach and by working in those who heard their proclamation.

Extraordinary phenomena (wind, flames, and tongues) attended the

Spirit's coming at Pentecost, but the spotlight in Acts is on the *declaration* of the wonders of God (2:11), exemplified by Peter's sermon (2:14–40). In that sermon, Peter explains the origin of this bold proclamation of the wonderful acts[18] of God: "God has raised this Jesus, of whom we are all witnesses. Therefore, having been exalted to God's right hand and having received the promised gift—the Holy Spirit—from the Father, he has poured out what you see and hear" (vv. 32–33). Thus, as John the Baptist had prophesied, Jesus was indeed the one who would baptize with the Holy Spirit (Luke 3:16). As Joel had predicted, this outpouring of the Spirit produced prophetic proclamation (Joel 2:28, cited in Acts 2:17). Because Jesus is the one who pours out the Spirit, references to the Spirit's actions should be seen as references to the activity of Jesus, proclaiming his salvation to the ends of the earth.

Empowering His Messengers. The Spirit who guides and empowers the bearers of the word is "the Spirit of Jesus" (Acts 16:7). At times, the form that the Lord's guidance takes is related to the unique role of the apostles as recipients of revelation from the risen Lord. When Paul encountered Jewish opposition at Corinth, for example, the Lord encouraged him in a vision: "Do not be afraid, but go on speaking and do not be silent. For I myself am with you, and no one will attack you to harm you, because many people in this city belong to me" (18:9–11).[19] Although the revelatory *form* of this direction from Jesus may have been extraordinary, the encouraging truth that it communicated—that Jesus was with him and that many people were his—was not unique to the apostles' experience. These words recall the risen Jesus' promise at the close of Matthew's gospel, a promise made not only to his apostles, but also to his whole church until he returns: "Surely *I am with you* always, to the very end of the age" (Matt. 28:20 NIV). In the transition from Moses, mediator of the exodus from slavery, to Joshua, captain of the conquest of the Gentiles, the Lord assured Joshua: "As I was with Moses, so *I will be with you*; I will never leave you nor forsake you" (Josh. 1:5 NIV). So now Jesus, whose earthly ministry, death, and resurrection have accomplished the supreme exodus from slavery for his people,[20] assures the messengers through whom he carries out his conquest of the Gentiles, "I am with you."

Illumining Their Listeners. Jesus is also active in those who listen to the apostles' proclamation. Although the message of Christ is good news,[21] human hearts that are blind to the wonders of God will not perceive the message of life for what it is, unless the Lord intervenes to give spiritual insight as his servants are preaching (Acts 28:26–27, quoting Isa. 6:9–10). Those leaders and residents of Jerusalem who concurred in bringing Jesus to the cross needed a profound change of conviction and attitude—that is, repentance—in order to escape the wrathful judgment to come on those who have taken their stand against the Lord and against his Anointed One (Ps. 2:1–2, quoted in Acts 4:25–26). Therefore, Peter's preaching summoned them to repent (Acts 2:38; 3:19). But how can callous hearts be brought to repentance? "This man [Jesus] God exalted as Captain and Savior at his own right hand, in order to give repentance and forgiveness of sins to Israel" (Acts 5:31). The exalted Jesus celebrates his enthronement by bestowing on enemies the change of heart that leads to forgiveness.

This gift is not only for hardened Israelites. The gift of the Spirit to Gentiles assembled at Cornelius's house to hear Peter's message is described in terms that echo Pentecost: "The Holy Spirit had been poured out[22] even on the Gentiles" (Acts 10:45; see v. 47; 11:15–17). In response to Peter's report on these amazing events, the church in Jerusalem "praised God, saying, 'Consequently, even to the Gentiles has God given repentance leading to life' " (11:18). The wording here attributes the gift of repentance specifically to God (the Father).[23] Luke's versatility in ascribing saving initiative either to God the Father or to the risen Christ attests to the complete harmony in the saving purposes and actions of the Father, the Son, and the Spirit. The Father exalted Jesus as Savior and Lord, and from the Father the exalted Lord Jesus received the Spirit, whom he now bestows in saving power.

From the Jerusalem church's confession that God gives repentance even to Gentiles (11:18), Luke immediately turns to the spread of the Word among Gentiles in Antioch (11:19–26). As Jewish Christians from Cyprus and Cyrene told the good news about the Lord Jesus to Greeks, "*the hand of the Lord* was with them, and a great number who believed turned to the Lord" (11:21). "The Lord's hand" is an Old Testament symbol for mighty divine intervention (e.g., Isa. 41:20; see Luke 1:66), but in view of the context in Acts 11, it is clear that the Lord whose mighty hand empowered his evangelists' message is the Lord Jesus, about whom they preached.[24] So also, when Paul preached to the businesswoman Lydia at Philippi, "*The Lord opened her heart* to respond to Paul's message" (Acts 16:14 NIV), with the result that she became "a believer in the Lord" (v. 15). The Lord Jesus became the object of her faith because he had opened her heart to the message that called her to faith.

Jesus the Doer: The Power of a Name

Jesus also continues his saving *deeds* after his ascension, particularly by producing physical healing, which is a sign pointing toward the final "time for God to restore everything" (Acts 3:21). This point is demonstrated especially in the frequent references to the "name of Jesus" in the healing of the lame man in the temple (3:1–4:31). Peter commanded the man to walk in the *name* of Jesus (3:6). When the crowd gathered around the apostles, Peter made it clear that he and John had no intrinsic power or superior piety to bring about the healing; rather, faith in Jesus' *name* had enabled the lame man to leap (3:12, 16). Questioned before the Sanhedrin regarding the power or *name* by which the lame man had been healed (4:7), Peter not only announced that the *name* of Jesus Christ of Nazareth had been responsible for this healing, but also went on to declare that "there is no other *name* under heaven given among human beings by which it is necessary[25] that we be saved" (4:10, 12). Salvation in Luke-Acts can include physical healing (as in Acts 4:9, containing the same word [σωζω] as that translated "saved" in 4:12); but Jesus' name—and this name alone—brings a deeper, more comprehensive restoration than merely a restoration to physical wholeness. Elsewhere in Acts we learn more fully what it means to be saved, particularly in Peter's statements that sins are forgiven through Jesus' *name* (2:38; 10:43). Thus, the Lucan formula "call upon the *name*" of the Lord (Jesus), epitomizes the prayer of dependence that God answers with salvation: "And everyone who calls on the *name* of the Lord will be saved" (2:21 NIV, citing Joel 2:32). "Get up, be baptized and wash your sins away, calling on his *name*" (22:16 NIV). Christians are those who "call on the *name*" of the Lord Jesus (9:14, 21). In response to the church's prayer, God performs signs and wonders "through the *name* of your holy servant Jesus" (4:30).

There is great power in Jesus' name, but Luke later emphasizes an implication of Acts 3:16—that the name of Jesus brings salvation only when it is invoked in *faith*. At Ephesus, Jewish exorcists tried to use his name to expel demons: "In the name of Jesus, whom Paul preaches, I command you to come out" (19:13–14 NIV). Their attempt to use his name as a magic "power word" to invoke and manipulate Paul's god—perhaps one of a number of divine names accumulated in the hope of overpowering the demonic[26]—not only failed to achieve their ends, but also brought them deserved pain and shame: "Then the man in whom the evil spirit was overpowered them so that, naked and traumatized, they fled out of the house" (19:16).

Why is faith so crucial in using Jesus' name? Because this name, like the name of Yahweh in the Old Testament, represents the person himself, demonstrating his presence in power and glory through his name. When they moved into Yahweh's promised land, Israel was to worship him together at one place, "the place the LORD your God will choose from among all your tribes to put his *Name* there for his dwelling" (Deut. 12:5 NIV; see 1 Kings 9:3). The Lord had promised, "Wherever I cause my *name* to be honored, I will come to you and bless you" (Ex. 20:24 NIV). David joined battle with the Philistine champion Goliath not with sword, spear, or javelin, but " in the *name* of the Lord Sabaoth, the God of the battalions of Israel" (1 Sam. 17:45). The psalmists extolled the protective force of God's name (Pss. 20:1; 54:1; 118:10–12, 26; see also Prov. 18:10). Thus, often in the Old Testament the name of the Lord is nothing less than his powerful presence with his people, openly proclaimed, so that they might place their hope and trust in the God who is with us. So also in Acts, Jesus' name wields power to save, for it speaks of the presence of Jesus among people in need, calling the desperate and the weak to rest their faith in his strength and grace.

TOWARD A CURE FOR OUR PRACTICAL DEISM

What would change if churches took more seriously Luke's message—the Holy Spirit's message—that the life of the church is the continuing "teaching and doing" ministry of Jesus Christ, the risen and exalted Lord? Let us begin to reflect on this question by considering two areas of church life.

First, how would an awareness of Christ's presence affect all the issues surrounding the *control and direction* of the church: planning, strategizing, budgeting, chain-of-command, church councils, etc.? It is clear from Acts that it would not mean dismantling all structures of human leadership, leaving the church as an amorphous, emotion-driven mass of spontaneity, flowing in whatever direction the Spirit seems to "lead." Christ gives leaders to the church, men full of wisdom and the Spirit. And those leaders, in that Spirit-given wisdom, gauge their actions and choose their words in ways calculated to bring the greatest harvest for Christ's kingdom. The presence of Jesus among us by his Spirit does not exempt us from careful planning and courageous leadership. But it does demand that we not take *our* plans too seriously. We dare not *trust* in our plans for success, nor can we "bend" God's word or our consciences to fit what seems expedient. Do church leaders so idolize their own control of the church that the Spirit's gifts to all its members are shackled? Do we resent the delays and detours that the Lord of the church may decide to inject into our itineraries for church growth? The presence of Jesus demands that we formulate and re-formulate our fallible plans in order to keep in step with his invincible plan. We must stay alert to unplanned, unexpected opportunities for witness and service, remaining patient and full of hope when encountering setbacks, and being sensitive to the surprising resources he gives to all his people.

Second, how would a vivid consciousness of the presence of Jesus affect the *prayer life* of the church? Prayer is often portrayed as a Christian duty; it is often enjoined upon us in exhortations heavily laced with guilt in-ducers. Like the holiday phone commercial that scolds wayward adults—"Call your mother"—the definition of prayer as duty (though not wrong) often leaves the impression that we have an uncomfortable obligation to a distant "loved one" who is out of touch with our daily lives. At the op-posite extreme are pastors and teachers who try to move us to prayer by portraying Jesus as our buddy, our pal, eager to hear our monologues of self-pity and to come to our assistance. Here too there is a grain of truth (Jesus is compassionate, and he does bring help to those who turn to him in faith), but the casual and self-centered embellishment added to that grain puts the truth out of focus.

Acts shows us what prayer is like when praying people recognize the presence of Jesus the Lord. It is joyful and confident, for the one who is Lord and Christ is among us to hear our needs. There is awe-filled fear when we recognize his terrifying holiness. There is a preoccupation not with ourselves—our ailments, comforts, conveniences, hurt feelings—but with the great cause of the King who walks in our midst. We ask to receive from his hand whatever will make us serviceable to him, useful for his saving purposes. We pray not because we must, but because we may; not out of lust for his gifts, but out of love for the Giver; not to bend his will to ours, but to bend our wills to his.

Jesus is here, teaching and doing, preaching and performing the saving work of God through his Spirit and the Spirit-gifted people he gives to his church. How will this truth affect what we expect preaching to accomplish, what we expect Sunday school classes, Bible studies, small groups, and va-cation Bible schools to accomplish? How will it affect our hopes for the resolution of conflict in the church, our hopes for the fruit of sharing our faith with others, our hope for the discipling of the world's peoples through missions? Because our King is not an aloof designer or absentee landlord, but a living Shepherd walking among his sheep, there is hope for change in the church beyond anything human ingenuity can invent. Our King is intimately present and powerfully active as the champion and the chastener of his church.

Notes

1 Consistent with his deistic convictions, Thomas Jefferson could write in the Declaration of Independence of the "Creator" who endowed all men "with certain inalienable rights," and could also excise from his own "edition" of the New Testament all reference to the miracles. For a brief description of deism, see "Deism," by Vergilius Ferm, in *Dictionary of Philosophy*, ed. Dagobert D. Runes (Totowa, N.J.: Littlefield, Adams, 1967), 75.

2 Richard B. Gaffin, *Perspectives on Pentecost: Studies in New Testament Teaching on the Gifts of the Holy Spirit* (Phillipsburg, N.J.: Presbyterian and Reformed, 1979), 89–116.

3 See the opening to the second volume of Josephus, *Against Apion*, cited in chap. 1, n. 7.

4 Greek: ηρξατο ο Ιησους ποιειν τε και διδασκειν. Ernst Haenchen views "began . . . to do and to teach" as a roundabout (periphrastic) way of saying simply "did and taught," adopted by the author of Acts for stylistic reasons (*The Acts of the Apostles: A Commentary* [Philadelphia: Westminster Press, 1971], 137, n. 4). In his view, then, "began" (αρχομαι) is a meaningless helping verb that implies nothing about the relationship between Luke's gospel and Acts. It is more likely, however, especially in view of the activity ascribed to the ascended Jesus in Acts, which we will survey in this chapter, that Luke intends us to see "that the works and words of Jesus, recounted in the Gospel, were the real *beginning* of the story of the Church, and that Jesus *is still acting* through his Spirit in the missionary campaigns of the Apostles" (William Neil, *The Acts of the Apostles* [London: Oliphants, 1973], 63 [emphasis added]).

5 "Luke's thesis is this: Jesus remains active, though the manner of his working has changed. Now, no longer in the flesh, he continues to 'do and teach' through his 'body,' the church" (David J. Williams, *Acts* [Good News Commentary; San Francisco: Harper and Row, 1985], 2). See also Everett F. Harrison, *Interpreting Acts: The Expanding Church* (Grand Rapids: Zondervan, 1986), 42; I. Howard Marshall, *The Acts of the Apostles* (Grand Rapids: Eerdmans, 1980), 56; F. F. Bruce, *Commentary on the Book of the Acts* (NICNT; Grand Rapids: Eerdmans, 1954), 32.

6 Mark 3:14: "And he made [ποιεω] twelve, whom he also named [ονομαζω] apostles." Matt. 10:2: "And the names of the twelve apostles are these."

7 Καταριθμεω here echoes Luke's comment in the betrayal account that Judas was "of the number [αριθμος] of the Twelve" (Luke 22:3).

8 The Greek verb δει, "it is necessary" (or, in the imperfect, εδει, "it was necessary"), in Luke-Acts often marks events that are necessary because they have been planned and purposed by God—and in many cases already announced by him through his prophets in the Old Testament. See Luke 2:49; 4:43; 9:22; 13:16, 33; 17:25; 19:5; 24:7, 26, 44; Acts 1:21; 3:21; 9:16; 14:22; 17:3; 19:21; 23:11; 27:24.

9 Marshall, *Acts*, 66. See also R. T. France, "The Worship of Jesus: A Neglected Factor in Christological Debate?" in *Christ the Lord: Studies in Christology Presented to Donald Guthrie*, ed. H. H. Rowden (Leicester: InterVarsity Press, 1982), 17–36.

10 Luke 5:22; 6:8; 9:46–47; 22:21–22.

¹¹ "The Lord has sent me—Jesus, who appeared to you . . ." (ο κυριος απεσταλκεν με, Ιησους ο οφθεις σοι . . .).

¹² The cumbersome italicized phrase translates a single Greek word: the present passive participle of μαρτυρεω, "I bear witness, give testimony" (ανδρας . . . μαρτυρουμενους). Since the theme of testimony and witness (μαρτυς, μαρτυρεω, μαρτυρια) is so prominent in Acts (the apostles as Jesus' witnesses, testifying to his resurrection), Luke has chosen his word here advisedly.

¹³ Although Luke speaks of large groups of believers being "filled" (πιμπλημι) with the Holy Spirit (Acts 2:4; 4:31), he reserves the description "full [πληρης] of the Spirit" for individuals (Jesus in Luke 4:1; Stephen here and in Acts 7:55; Barnabas in Acts 11:24). Those "filled with the Spirit" are empowered with spiritual gifts to proclaim the Word (in addition to Acts 2:4; 4:31, see Luke 1:15, 41, 67; Acts 4:8; 9:17, 29; 13:9). The expression "full of the Spirit," on the other hand, calls attention to the demonstration of the Spirit's holiness in these individuals—obedience in temptation, wisdom, faith, goodness—rather than to displays of spiritual gifts.

¹⁴ Greek: εκλεγομαι.

¹⁵ Greek: επισκεπτομαι. This word is often used in the LXX to translate the Hebrew verb פקד, "visit, intervene, care for." Elsewhere in Luke-Acts, it typically refers to a saving intervention by God to rescue his people and judge his enemies: see Luke 1:68, 78; 7:16; Acts 7:23 (of Joseph visiting the Israelites in their affliction); 15:14, 36 (of missionaries "visiting" churches previously planted).

¹⁶ See chapter 6, "Diversity in Unity."

¹⁷ A further example of the early church's confidence in the Lord's intimate leadership and guidance is found in the letter framed by the Jerusalem council (Acts 15). The decision regarding the Gentiles' status in the church was reached through the give-and-take of discussion, in which the apostles and elders came to discern the implications of God's present actions in the light of Scripture. Luke gives us no hint of special revelation from God at this point (through vision or prophetic word), as he does in some other situations. Nevertheless, the council was confident that the outcome of its deliberations was the Lord's decision: "It seemed good to the Holy Spirit and to us . . ." (Acts 15:28).

¹⁸ In Acts 2:11, the expression rendered "wonders of God" in the NIV is μεγαλεια του θεου. Although the English word wonder might be taken to refer to God's eternally supreme attributes, the use of μεγαλεια in the Greek version of the Old Testament (it does not appear elsewhere in the New Testament) makes it clear that this expression refers to the wonderful acts of God—particularly in redeeming his people. See, for example, Pss. 71:19 ("O God, unto the highest [heavens] you who have done magnificent things"); 105:1 ("Announce among the nations his magnificent acts" [Codex Sinaiticus]; 106:21 ("They forgot the God who saved them, who had done magnificent things in Egypt" [Codex Alexandrinus]); Deut. 11:2–3 ("Know today that your children are not those who know and who saw the discipline of the Lord your God and his magnificent acts and his mighty hand and his uplifted arm and his signs and his wonders which he did in the midst of Egypt to Pharaoh king of Egypt and all his land").

In citing the Old Testament, I will normally offer my English translation of the Septuagint (abbreviated LXX), the Greek version of the Old Testament that was widely used in Dispersion synagogues and among the Gentile Christians to whom Luke addressed his gospel and Acts. Thus, some Old Testament citations may vary slightly from the standard English versions, which are based (as was the LXX) on the original Hebrew and Aramaic

Scriptures. It appears that the LXX translators worked from a Hebrew text that differed in wording at points from the Masoretic text of later Jewish tradition, and that in some of these instances the text underlying the LXX is reflected in the Hebrew Old Testament manuscripts found at Qumran (the Dead Sea Scrolls), which are centuries older than the oldest Masoretic text manuscripts. The Septuagint also differs from the Hebrew Old Testament in the chapter numbering and versification of the Psalms and some other books; in giving references I use the chapter and verse divisions of the English versions, which follow the Hebrew Scriptures. Those wishing to consult the LXX directly will find that the standard editions contain information on locating corresponding passages in the Hebrew Scriptures and the LXX.

[19] Similar visions of encouragement are described in 23:11; 27:23–24.

[20] In the Greek text of Luke 9:31, Jesus' "departure," which he discusses with Moses and Elijah on the Mount of Transfiguration, is called his εξοδος (the LXX title for Moses' second book, descriptive of Israel's departure from Egyptian slavery).

[21] Although the noun "gospel, good news" (ευαγγελιον) does not appear in the Third Gospel (in contrast to Matthew and Mark) and is used only twice in Acts, Luke uses the verb "evangelize, announce good news" (ευαγγελιζομαι) more than any other New Testament author: 25 times in Luke–Acts, 20 in Paul, 8 in other books.

[22] Greek: εκχεω, as in Acts 2:33.

[23] Likewise, in 14:27 we read: "God . . . opened for the Gentiles a door of faith."

[24] In Acts 2:47 (*"The Lord added to their number* daily those who were being saved"), "the Lord" probably refers to Jesus, whom God "has made . . . both *Lord* and Christ" (v. 36).

[25] Greek: δει, a reference to God's plan and purpose.

[26] An Egyptian magical papyrus, dating from about A.D. 300, illustrates an exorcist's heaping up of divine names from Jewish, Christian, and pagan sources to overpower demons. For the wording, see chap. 10, n. 43 below. Paris Magical Papyrus, lines 3019–27, from Adolf Deissmann, *Light from the Ancient East* (London: Hodder and Stoughton, 1910), 252 (Greek text), 256 (Eng. trans.).

THREE

THE SPIRIT AND THE SERVANT

RECOGNIZING THE SPIRIT

Would you recognize a Spirit-filled church if you met one? How could you tell? By measuring the decibels of the singing in worship? By checking the clapping, raising, or waving of hands in praise? Or are you suspicious of such rowdy joy? Do you sense the Spirit's presence more in the silence of meditation, in a stilled sanctuary and a liturgy rich in reverence and reflection?

The presence of God's Holy Spirit in the church—in all sorts of churches that acclaim Jesus as Lord—makes the church different from every merely human organization. On this point, at least, Christians agree, although our views about the marks of the Spirit's presence may differ.

The mighty activity of the Holy Spirit in the church is a major theme in Acts. Luke reinforces the importance of the coming of the Spirit by recording repeated references to Pentecost. The risen Lord Jesus instructed his disciples "through the Holy Spirit" (Acts 1:2), promising them that the Spirit would soon be poured out on them in power (Luke 24:49; Acts 1:5, 8). Later in Acts, key transitions in the gospel's spreading to the ends of the earth are explained in the light of Pentecost, as the outpouring of the Spirit is extended to the Samaritans (Acts 8:17) and especially to the Gentiles (10:44–47; 11:15–17; 15:8).

What is the significance of this new bestowal of God's Spirit? What does the Spirit intend to do among us? What does his presence say about the church's calling and our resources for accomplishing that calling? We need to know not only *that* the Spirit came at Pentecost, but also *why* he came.

The New Testament shows how easy it is to misunderstand the Spirit's work. We read of people who attributed the Spirit's holy activity to unholy influences such as liquor or demons (Acts 2:13; Mark 3:20–30). Others, fooled by satanic counterfeits, attributed unholy activity—cursing Jesus—to the Spirit (1 Cor. 12:3; 1 John 4:1–3). To recognize what is genuinely the Spirit's work, we need discernment that is informed by divine wisdom. Whether our part of the church associates the Spirit with buoyant celebration or with hushed awe, the externals can be faked and empty. Enthusiasm can be manipulated, liturgy can be mechanical, and meditation can be self-absorbed rather than Christ-centered. How, then, can we filter out the static of the counterfeit, in order to recognize the real signs of the Spirit's presence?

The Holy Spirit himself must be our guide, through the words he has spoken through Luke and the other Spirit-borne authors of Scripture (2 Peter 1:21). Luke was both a historian and a theologian, both *recording* and *interpreting* the Spirit's world-changing arrival.

Through Peter's sermon at Pentecost (Acts 2:14–39), Luke imparts an apostolic commentary on Jesus' sending of the Spirit on the church. But even before Peter's sermon, in Luke's record of Jesus' own promise of the Spirit's coming (Acts 1:5, 8), readers are prepared to grasp the significance of Pentecost. The outpouring of the Spirit means that the Father is keeping his promise, announced long ago through his servants the prophets.

THE PROMISE OF THE FATHER
(LUKE 24:49; ACTS 1:4)

At the end of Luke's gospel and at the opening of Acts, we find two versions of the same command and assurance of Jesus:

> I am sending *the promise of my Father* upon you; but you must stay in the city until you are clothed from on high with power. (Luke 24:49)

> Do not separate yourselves from Jerusalem, but wait for *the promise of the Father,* about which you heard from me. For John baptized with water, but you will be baptized with the Holy Spirit after not many days. (Acts 1:4–5)[1]

Both in the conclusion of Luke's first volume and in the opening of the second, Jesus designates the Spirit as the gift promised by God the Father. At the end of Luke's gospel, the Father's promised gift is simply described as a new power coming from heaven to clothe Jesus' disciples; the Spirit is

not mentioned by name. In Acts, on the other hand, Jesus immediately interprets "the promise of the Father" as the soon-coming baptism in the
Spirit. But in both texts the Spirit's coming will fulfill the Father's promise.

When, then, did the Father first promise that the Spirit would come? Ob-
viously, the Father's promise was announced in Jesus' own teaching—"about
which you heard from me" (Acts 1:4). It was spoken through John the Baptist as well, since the contrast that Jesus draws between John's water baptism and the coming Spirit baptism (v. 5) echoes John's announcement of
the Messiah (Luke 3:16). Did the Father speak this promise even earlier?

John's announcement of a coming Spirit baptizer was not spoken in a
vacuum. Through the ancient prophets long before, God had promised a
rescue and restoration at last, and the eschatological outpouring of the
Spirit was to be central to this new creation. Thus, Luke reports the risen
Jesus' teaching that "it is written" that the Christ would suffer and be
raised, and that repentance leading to forgiveness would be proclaimed to
all the nations by witnesses clothed with heavenly power—power promised
by the Father and sent by Jesus himself (Luke 24:46–49). The expression
"it is written" points to the prophetic Scriptures of the Old Testament. The
promise spoken through the prophets, that the Lord's salvation would
reach Gentiles at the ends of the earth, included the Spirit's coming to empower the bearers of this saving message.

Peter's sermon at Pentecost points to the fulfillment of the promise announced through the prophet Joel, that the outpouring of the Spirit would
give all of God's people the power to speak God's words:[2] "And it shall be
in the last days, God says, that I will pour out my Spirit on all people" (Acts
2:17). The prophetic promise of the Spirit is not limited to Joel's prediction, however. It is also found in Isaiah, Jeremiah, Ezekiel, and other
prophets. In fact, the promises of the Spirit in Isaiah are particularly influential on Luke's theology of the Holy Spirit, and Luke introduces them
even before he narrates the events of Pentecost.[3] The Spirit's work in the
church is a climax of God's plan, announced through Isaiah, to heal and
empower his people to be his servant-witnesses among the nations.

WITNESSES TO THE ENDS OF THE
EARTH (ACTS 1:8)

We have noticed that Acts 1:8 provides the narrative skeleton for the
whole book of Acts. This saying of Jesus' also has much to teach about
the purpose of the Spirit's coming. Jesus had been teaching his apostles

about his resurrection and its implications for the coming kingdom of God. When they asked him whether his resurrection marked the dawn of restored dominion for the people of Israel, Jesus responded (as he so often did) not with a direct answer, but with a redirection of his questioners' attention.

He did not deny outright that a restoration of Israel was coming.[4] Indeed, Israel's true restoration had begun in John's call to repent in view of the nearness of God's kingdom (Matt. 17:11–13), and Peter would later announce the hope of future "times of the restoration[5] of all things," when Jesus the Messiah would return to earth (Acts 3:19–21). Nevertheless, his answer (if we can call it that) implied a twofold correction of their expectations. In the first place, they needed to understand that God's timing was none of their business (Acts 1:7). Second, and more importantly, their concept of restoration needed to be expanded to worldwide, even cosmic, dimensions. The disciples' ethnocentric focus on Israel's military-political ascendancy was far too small. In order to coincide with the Father's plan, their mental picture of the Messiah's kingdom would have to be magnified far beyond the boundaries of their imagination. They needed to see the expanding horizons of the Lord's work of rescue, repair, and restoration, embracing not only Israelites, but all peoples, in a triumphant conquest of grace. "But you will receive power when the Holy Spirit comes on you; and you will be my witnesses in *Jerusalem*, and in *all Judea and Samaria*, and to *the ends of the earth*" (1:8 NIV).

This statement is a composite of words and ideas from prophecies in Isaiah, a carefully designed concentration of rich imagery to alert us to the epochal importance of the outpouring that was soon to come. Consider the following parallels:

Acts 1:8	Isaiah (LXX)
"when the Holy *Spirit comes upon you*"[6]	"until the *Spirit comes upon you* from on high" (32:15)[7]
"*you shall be my witnesses*"[8]	"*Become witnesses for me*,[9] and I myself am witness, says the Lord God, and my servant whom I have chosen" (43:10).
	"*You are witnesses for me*,[10] and I myself am witness, says the Lord God" (43:12).
	"*You are witnesses*,[11] whether there is any god besides me" (44:8).

Acts 1:8	Isaiah (LXX)
"to the ends of the earth"[12]	"Is it a great thing for you to be called my servant to cause Jacob's tribes to stand and Israel's dispersion to return? I will appoint you for a covenant of the people, for a light to the Gentiles, that you may be for salvation *to the ends of the earth*" (49:6).[13]
	"Turn to me and be saved, you who are from *the ends of the earth*;[14] for I myself am God, and there is no other" (45:22).

Thus, this statement of Jesus, which is programmatic for Luke's entire narrative of the gospel's progress to the "ends of the earth," brings together three themes from Isaiah's prophecies concerning the Servant of the Lord:

1. The *Spirit of God* is poured out upon God's people.
2. God's people are *his witnesses*, testifying on the basis of the saving acts that they have seen that he alone is God and Savior.
3. Their witness extends *to the ends of the earth*, calling pagan nations to abandon their idols and turn to the Lord for salvation.

These three themes are woven into the heart of Isaiah's announcement concerning the Servant of the Lord (Isa. 42–53, 61). Often, when the New Testament writers quote the Old Testament, they refer not only to the words they actually quote, but also to the surrounding context of those words.[15] Therefore, we will find it enlightening to look at the contexts of these statements from Isaiah, from which the wording and content of Jesus' words in Acts 1:8 have been drawn.

WITNESSES IN THE LORD'S LAWSUIT: THE SPIRIT AND THE SERVANT IN ISAIAH[16]

Throughout the later chapters of Isaiah, the Lord announces his lawsuit against the idols. At the start of Isaiah's prophecy, the Lord "sues" his people, charging them with spiritual adultery and infidelity and calling heaven and earth to testify to Israel's guilt (Isa. 1; see Deut. 4:26; 30:10; 32:1). But in Isaiah 41 the Lord lodges a different lawsuit, a challenge to the idols served by the pagan Gentiles (and too often by Israel as well), accusing these false gods of *false advertising*. Their worshipers have claimed that these dead, deaf, impotent images could hear prayer and respond, rescuing their devotees from danger and death. But it is all a lie. Those other gods are dead stone and wood, products of the craft of those who blindly trust in them. They cannot foretell the future because they cannot control or influence it.

The Lord taunts the pagan peoples, challenging them to present evidence that their gods can do what they claim:

> Let them come near and speak together; then let them announce judgment. Who raised up vindication from the east, calling it to his feet, and it will come? . . . Who has accomplished and done these things? I am the one who called it from ancient generations. I, God, am first, and into the coming [ages] I AM! (41:1-2, 4)

> "Your judicial case is drawing near," says the Lord God. "Your purposes have drawn near," says Jacob's king. "Let them draw near and report to you what is going to happen. Or the first things—tell what they were, and we will understand their insight and know what the last things will be, and you must tell us things to come. Declare to us the things to come at the last, and we will know that you are gods. Do good or cause harm, and we will marvel and see it together." (41:21-23)

Israel, Witnesses of the Lord

So the Lord lodges his lawsuit, charging the gods of the nations with false advertising, breach of promise, and blatant perjury. When the case of *The Lord v. the Idols* is tried, both sides have the opportunity to present witnesses to substantiate their claims:

> All the nations have been gathered together and their rulers will be gathered. Who will announce these things, or who will report to you the things from the beginning? Let them present their witnesses and let them be proved right and let them say, "It is true." "You must become my witnesses, and I myself am witness," declares the Lord God, "and [you are] my servant whom I have chosen, so that you may know and believe and understand that I AM. Before me no other god came into existence, and after me none shall be." (43:9-10)

> Gather together and come; take counsel together, you who are being saved from the nations. Those who carry about an engraved

figure of wood, who pray to gods who do not save.[17] If they are going to make an announcement, let them draw near—so that they may know who made these things heard from the beginning. Then I, God, was announced to you, and there is no other besides me. . . . Turn to me and be saved, all you from the last part of the earth; for I am God, and there is no other. (45:20–22)

The idols have no witnesses who can testify to their power or activity. Israel's God, on the other hand, is Lord of creation and history and can call his people, his chosen servant, to the witness stand. They have seen and heard the saving acts that he has performed, fulfilling his promises. Therefore they can support his claim to be the only living God, the only Savior.

Israel, Blind Eyewitnesses

But there is a problem: Has Israel indeed seen the mighty deeds of her God, which he has performed in her presence down through her history? His saving achievements have been there to see: the Exodus, the conquest of Canaan, the kingdom, and even the return from exile by Cyrus's decree, which, though still future, is certain to come by the Lord's sure word (Isa. 45:1–6). But the Israelites' history of infidelity puts in question whether they have actually perceived the significance of these events. In the language of Isaiah's original call, "Go and tell this people: 'Be ever hearing, but never understanding; be ever seeing, but never perceiving' " (6:9 NIV). The Lord's eyewitnesses are blind!

> You deaf, hear; and you blind, receive sight to see! Who is blind except my servants, and deaf except those who rule them? And *the servants of God have been blinded.* (42:18–19)

The Lord's servants are blind and deaf, but the problem is not that their physical sense organs are defective, for Isaiah continues: "You have seen many things, but have not kept them; your ears are opened, but you have not heard" (42:20). Israel's problem is *spiritual inattention*, a deliberate "ignorance" of God's faithful, saving deeds.

The Healing of Israel's Blindness and Deafness

Can such inattentive witnesses be of any use in the Lord's lawsuit against the idols? Why call to the stand witnesses who have refused to admit what they have seen and heard—who are, in the deepest sense, blind and deaf? The only hope is a healing of blind eyes and deaf ears. In Isaiah 42:6–7 the Lord promises such a cure:

> I, the Lord God, called you in righteousness, and I will empower your hand and strengthen you. And I have given you to be a covenant for the people, to be a light for the Gentiles, to *open the eyes of the blind*, to lead captives out of their chains from prison and those who sit in darkness out of the prison-house.[18]

A few lines later, just before the Lord speaks of his servants' willful blindness (42:18–20, quoted above) he repeats the promise of healing: "I will *lead the blind* in the way they have not known, and on paths that they have not perceived I will make them walk; for them *I will make the darkness into light* and make the crooked places straight" (42:16). In this future exodus, with the daylight of God's glory blazing on the trail ahead, Israel will indeed "see the light" at last.

The court scene in Isaiah 43 begins with the entrance of the blind and deaf (v. 8). These are apparently the Gentiles, assembled in the courtroom to testify blindly and deafly on behalf of their blind and deaf idols (v. 9). Over against these false and futile witnesses for empty gods who cannot speak or save, the Lord subpoenas his own people as his witnesses, whose eyes and ears he has healed and whose darkness he has turned to light. When the healing of Israel's blindness takes place, says Isaiah, Israel will be the Lord's witnesses at last (v. 10, where they are first called witnesses). Healed of their own blindness, they in turn will guide the idol-blinded Gentiles out of darkness and into light.

The Life-Giving Spirit Makes Israel Fruitful in Witness
How will the Lord heal the blind and deaf? This question is answered by an agricultural metaphor in Isaiah 44:1–11. Life-giving rain, the Israelite farmer's hope and delight, becomes an image of the Spirit's outpouring, a great hope of the people of God (vv. 3–5):

- *Heavenly irrigation—the metaphor:* "I will give water on the thirsty land, streams on the waterless ground."
- *Heavenly irrigation—the reality:* "I will bestow my Spirit on your seed, and my blessing on your children."
- *Resulting growth—the metaphor:* "They will spring up like grass in the midst of water, like poplar trees by flowing streams."
- *Resulting growth—the reality:* "This one will say, 'I belong to God'; and this one will be called by the name of Jacob; and still another will write, 'I belong to God,' taking the name of Israel."

The life-creating arrival of the Spirit will open the mouths of Israel's children to confess the Lord's name. When the Spirit comes, Israel's fearful trembling will be over and they will take the stand with confidence: "You are my witnesses, whether there is any god besides me" (44:8). Their testimony will expose the blindness of those who try to testify on the idols' behalf (v. 9). Like the promise of the spread of Spirit-given prophecy in Joel 2, Israel's healing by the Spirit in Isaiah focuses on the *proclamation of the Lord's self-revelation* as the fruit of the Spirit's coming. The Spirit comes to turn the Lord's blind servants into bold, clear-sighted witnesses.

The Other Servant, the Faithful Witness

Isaiah prophesies not only that Israel's healing will come through the Spirit, but also that this healing will come through *another servant*, one who (unlike Israel) will be faithful to his mission from God. In the Servant Songs of Isaiah, there is an intriguing and puzzling vacillation in the referents to whom the title "servant" is applied. In some passages, the people of Israel are the Lord's servant (e.g., 42:19–22; 44:1–8), while in others the servant is an *individual* who is contrasted to the people, is faithful where they have failed, and is instrumental in their atonement and restoration (e.g., 42:1–7; 49:1–6; 53:1–12). Even in the "individual" passages, the Servant is addressed as Israel because in this "other servant" the true mission of Israel (to declare God's glory among the nations, 42:12) is to be accomplished. But the obedient, individual Servant is not only a righteous *replacement* for the wayward people, but also the redemptive *restorer* of this people. Through the one faithful Servant, the failing servant Israel will be restored to sight and hearing, to health and usefulness.

The faithful Servant's healing, saving mission, however, reaches far beyond the bounds of Israel. This is the truth that the disciples, with their narrow focus on restored political autonomy for Israel, failed to grasp. It is the point that Jesus is making in his allusion to Isaiah 49:6, "to the ends of the earth." According to Isaiah 42 and 49, the individual servant would have a two-pronged ministry, both to Israel and to the Gentiles. Because the Spirit of God would be upon him (42:1), he would bring righteousness on earth, even to the distant islands of the Gentiles (v. 4). God has assured him:

> I, the Lord, have called you in righteousness; I will take hold of your hand. I will keep you and will make you to be a covenant for the people *and a light for the Gentiles*, to open eyes that are blind,

to free captives from prison and to release from the dungeon those who sit in darkness. (42:6–7 NIV)

In his own person, this Servant would reunite the Lord and his people in covenant, but he would do even more that this. He would bear the light of God's glory to the Gentiles. Both Israel and the nations needed sight and release from dark dungeons, and this Servant would heal and liberate them both.

In chapter 49, the Lord comforts the Servant, whose labor seems to have come to nothing, with the assurance that a regathering of Israel to favor and faithfulness, though a part of his mission, is too small to encompass God's purpose for this true Servant: "I have appointed you to be a covenant for the people, *a light for the Gentiles*, that you may become salvation *to the ends of the earth*" (49:5–6). Although this great task would bring the Servant suffering and repudiation at the hands of his own people, he would in the end receive incomparable honor from the Lord (49:7; 52:13–15; 53:2–3, 10–12). Condemned, although innocent, he would suffer for those who scorn him, and his suffering would bring mercy and healing to his despisers (53:4–6, 11–12). Who could this Servant be?

THE "OTHER SERVANT" IN LUKE'S GOSPEL

While various New Testament writers portray Jesus as the suffering Servant,[19] this theme is particularly prominent in the writings of Luke, the only author to refer to Jesus as God's "servant" (Greek: παις) (see Acts 3:13, 26; 4:27, 30).

At Jesus' birth, echoes of Isaiah hinted that he was the Servant who would restore Israel and bring light to the nations. John the Baptist was to prepare the way for the daybreak that would "shine on those who sit in darkness and the shadow of death" (Luke 1:79; see Isa. 42:7).[20] The aged Simeon greeted the infant Jesus with praise to God, who had prepared his salvation in the sight of all peoples (see Isa. 52:10), "a light for revelation to the Gentiles and for glory to your people Israel" (Luke 2:32 NIV; see Isa. 49:6).

In his baptism, when Jesus was first "numbered with transgressors" (receiving a "baptism of repentance for the forgiveness of sins," Luke 3:3; see Isa. 53:12), the Spirit of God came upon him as the Servant and the royal Son. Therefore, the Father's words from heaven acknowledged him as messianic king, "You are my Son" (cf. Ps. 2:7), and as faithful Servant, "with you I am well pleased" (cf. Isa. 42:1—"my chosen one, whom my soul welcomes") (Luke 3:22 NIV). When Jesus was later transfigured on the mountain, the Father again spoke from heaven, acclaiming Jesus as the Son and chosen Servant, who speaks with God's authority and must be heeded (Luke 9:35).[21]

Full of the Spirit, Jesus was led by the Spirit into the desert (as Israel had been) for the initial trial of his faith and faithfulness (Luke 4:1). Upon his triumphant return from the desert in the Spirit's power, he entered the synagogue at Nazareth and read publicly these words of the Spirit-anointed Servant in Isaiah:

> The Spirit of the Lord is on me, because he has anointed me to announce good news to poor people. He has sent me to proclaim to captives, freedom; and to blind people, restoration of sight; to send out the oppressed in release; to proclaim the year acceptable to the Lord. (Luke 4:18–19; Isa. 61:1–2)[22]

This was the service for which Jesus had received anointing with the Spirit's power in his baptism. He was the herald of liberty for the poor and the prisoners, of clear sight for those in darkness. In reading this Scripture, he was carrying out his mission (Luke 4:21). Therefore, he began to experience the rejection that Isaiah foresaw as the Servant's lot (Luke 4:29).

John the Baptist—a prisoner needing release—sent his disciples to ask Jesus, "Are you the coming one or should we expect someone else?" (Luke 7:20). Jesus pointed them to the signs of the Servant's mission that he was accomplishing: blind people receive sight, lame people walk, lepers are cleansed, deaf people hear, dead people are raised, poor people are told good news (v. 22, alluding to Isa. 61:1; 35:5–6). However, it was possible for one to misunderstand the method and the timing of Jesus' liberating work as Servant, thus becoming confused and disillusioned when he did not move immediately to overthrow the existing military-political establishment and set the prisoners (such as John) free. Therefore, Jesus pronounced a special blessing on those who do not "stumble" over him and the way he comes to bring rescue and freedom (Luke 7:23; compare Isa. 53:1–3).

While Jesus' way of salvation involved a delay of deliverance for the faithful such as John, it was far more costly for Jesus himself. Knowing the rejection and anguish that awaited him there, Jesus "set his face to go to Jerusalem,"[23] as the Servant who, in the confidence of final vindication, "set [his] face like flint" to face beating, mocking, and spitting (Isa. 50:7;

Luke 9:51–53). On the eve of his suffering, when establishing the memorial meal of the New Covenant (Jer. 31:31–34), Jesus implied that he would become the "covenant for the people" (Isa. 42:6) through his death. The accounts of the Last Supper contain two allusions to the Servant's suffering (Isa. 53:12). First, Jesus spoke of his death as the "pouring out" of his blood—an even closer echo of "he poured out his life to death" than is found in the Septuagint (Luke 22:20; Mark 14:24; Matt. 26:28).[24] Second, Jesus' death was to be "for many," as Isaiah announced that the Servant would justify many by bearing their sins (Mark 14:24; Matt. 26:28—Luke 22:20 has "for you").[25] The bond between the Lord and his faulty servants would be reestablished in the suffering of Jesus, the righteous Servant. It was necessary that the Scripture, "And he was numbered with the transgressors" (Isa. 53:12), be fulfilled in Jesus (Luke 22:37).

The individual Servant's story does not end with his suffering. Though once "despised and abhorred by the nation," he will be honored by kings (Isa. 49:7); though once "despised and rejected by men" (Isa. 53:3), the Lord's servant "will be raised and lifted up and highly exalted" (Isa. 52:13 NIV—in the LXX, "lifted up and glorified" [δοξαζω]). So Luke shows us the glory of Jesus the Servant, declared in the preaching of his apostles and the prayer of his church. Only in the early chapters of Acts do we find the title "servant," as it is found in Isaiah, applied to Jesus.[26] As Peter spoke in the temple courts at the dawn of the day of salvation, he focused attention on Jesus, the exalted Servant. Although the people of Jerusalem had disowned the Righteous One (a title applied to the Servant in Isaiah 53:11), God had glorified (δοξαζω) his servant Jesus (Acts 3:13–14), raising him up and sending him "first" to Israel, blessing his rejecters with the gift of repentance from their evil practices (Acts 3:26). The fact that Israel received the blessing first implies that others would receive blessing afterwards through Jesus the glorified Servant, as Peter made plain by citing God's promise to Abraham, "Through your offspring all peoples on earth will be blessed" (Acts 3:25 NIV, citing Gen. 22:18). As Isaiah foretold, the restoration of Israel would be too small a task for this Servant; he would bring the Lord's salvation to the ends of the earth.

The suffering and glory of the individual Servant, Jesus, brings comfort and courage to those who have been transformed into the Lord's servant-witnesses through him. Thus, when Jesus' messengers were threatened by the religious-political establishment in Jerusalem, they appealed to a higher court in prayer, rehearsing before their Sovereign the way he accomplished his announced plan through the suffering of Jesus, his anointed Servant (Acts 4:24–30). As servants also (although they call themselves δουλοι, "slaves," reserving the Isaianic title παις for Jesus[27]), their only request in the face of threats is for courage to carry out their mission—"to speak your word with great boldness" (Acts 4:29 NIV).

CHRISTIANS AS THE LORD'S SERVANT IN ACTS

How does this connection between Servant and Spirit, drawn from Isaiah and woven through Luke-Acts, help us to understand the Spirit's work among us?

The Servant Is Lord

Although Jesus is proclaimed by the apostles to be God's Servant, in Acts *he acts as Lord*. Jesus, the despised Servant, who walked and wept among his disciples, who hungered and thirsted, who served beggars, widows, and children, whose face endured spitting and whose back was torn by flogging, now takes on his own lips the words of the Lord, the God of Israel: *"You will be my witnesses"* (Acts 1:8). The contexts in Isaiah from which these words come underscore the uniqueness of the Lord, the only God and Savior, in contrast to all his "rivals," the false gods in whom the Gentiles hoped. Jesus is claiming to be this unique Lord, the God and Savior of the new Israel, whom he empowers with the Spirit and commissions as his witnesses. Those who worship Jesus as Lord, who pray to him and serve him, bear witness that he, not the idols, is the only God and Savior. The Spirit is sent to empower us to testify to the divine glory that the Son deserves.

Witnesses Attest God's Saving Actions in History

We learn from Luke what it means to be a witness. "Witnessing" and "giving testimonies" in evangelical circles have been thought of as telling your personal life pilgrimage out of a life of sin (the more flagrant the better!) into a life of faith. This way of speaking reflects a sound instinct, since an indispensable qualification for witness is to have experienced the subjective transformation that the Spirit brings, making blind eyes to see and deaf ears to hear. But evangelical testimonies too often get twisted in on themselves, wrapped up with the subjectivity of our own experience. Then, in our "live and let live" culture, it becomes easy for the people to whom we bear witness to shrug off what we say: "It's great that Jesus is true for you. As for me, I'm into Zen. We all have our own concept of God and reality."

But in Isaiah and Acts, the *subjective* healing of the Lord's witnesses enables them to declare the *objective* events of God's redemptive plan. Through Isaiah, God calls upon his people to give evidence of the ways in which he has shown his lordship over history by predicting deliverance or catastrophe and fulfilling his prediction. In Acts, Jesus' witnesses testify to his deeds of kindness and healing (10:38–39) and especially to his resurrection from the dead (1:22; 2:32; 3:15; 4:33; 10:41; 13:30–31; 22:15–16; 26:16). This means that the concept of witness is closely tied to the apostles who can give *eyewitness* testimony concerning Jesus' resurrection (1:22).

On the other hand, this does not mean that those who are not apostolic eyewitnesses must be silent concerning these great events. As the Lord in Isaiah summoned his people to be his witnesses, so now all believers, empowered by the Spirit, can speak the word of God boldly (Acts 4:31). In fact, the first steps in the gospel's spread to the earth's ends are taken not by apostles, but by other Christians, who are scattered by persecution as the apostles remain in Jerusalem (8:1). These scattered believers "announce the word as good news" as they travel through Judea and Samaria (8:4). Their announcement of good news is centered on Jesus Christ (8:5, 12), and is therefore firmly rooted in the apostles' testimony that Jesus is alive from the dead.

The apostle Peter says to the Sanhedrin, "We are witnesses of these things, and so is the Holy Spirit, whom God has given to those who obey him" (Acts 5:32 NIV). The witness of the apostles, who traveled with Jesus before his death and saw him after his resurrection, is central and foundational. But Peter also affirms that the divine witness, the Spirit, is given not only to apostles, but to all who obey God's call to repentance from sin and faith in Jesus. Those who are God's servants are his witnesses. Who they are and what they do—individually, together, and in relation to those outside the faith—influence the Lord's reputation among the peoples of the world.

The Spirit Must Heal Witnesses' Blind Eyes
Having grasped the *objective* center point of the testimony concerning Jesus, we must also appreciate the *subjective* transformation that is prerequisite to witnessing. We cannot be God's servant unless we have been touched by his Spirit. Sightless eyewitnesses are useless, and only the Spirit of the Servant gives sight.

Why did the radiant glory of the risen Jesus leave Saul in blind darkness at midday on the road to Damascus? The miracles of Jesus are not random blasts of power to impress the crowds and boost publicity. They are *signs* that point to unseen realities in the spiritual realm. Most of Jesus' miracles are signs of mercy, rescue, and repair, but some are tokens of judgment, such as Jesus' cursing of the fig tree and the death of Ananias and Sapphira. In view of this "signing" purpose of miracles, then, why was Saul struck blind? Whatever its humbling effect on Saul's attitude may have been, what does Saul's blindness say to us?

His physical blindness brought to the surface his failure to "see" God's redemption for what it really was. He is a picture in microcosm of Israel's failure to see, to take to heart the saving acts of God. As the Lord promised to lead the blind on a road not known to them (Isa. 42:16), so Saul needed to be led by the hand into Damascus (Acts 9:8). When he received his sight, he heard from Ananias the commission to be the Lord's witness:

> The God of our fathers appointed you to know his will and to see the Righteous One and to hear from his mouth, because *you will be his witness* to all men of the things that you have seen and heard. (Acts 22:14-15)

In Paul's later account before Agrippa, he reported that Jesus had said to him:

> For this purpose I have appeared to you: to appoint you as a *servant* [υπηρετης] and as a *witness* both of the things that you have seen of me and of the things that I will show you, rescuing you from the people and from the Gentiles, to whom I am sending you—to open their eyes and turn them from darkness to light, and from the authority of Satan to God, so that they may receive forgiveness of sins. (Acts 26:16-18)

Saul was appointed as the Lord's servant and witness, restored to sight so that he might "open eyes that are blind" and "release from the dungeon those who sit in darkness" (Isa. 42:7 NIV). He had seen the righteous Servant in his glory (Isa. 52:13; 53:11), and that sight had brought to light Saul's hidden blindness—and cured it. Of his period as a persecutor, Paul writes: "I acted in ignorance and unbelief" (1 Tim. 1:13 NIV). But now he sees himself as an exhibit of the mercy and limitless patience of Christ Jesus, "as an example for those who would believe on him and receive eternal life" (v. 16 NIV).

Service to Christ and witness for Christ must begin with his forgiving and transforming grace. Before we can begin to fulfill his mission in the world, the Lord must heal our blind eyes to take in his glory and open our deaf ears to hear words from his mouth. Apart from the Spirit, all our "right" deeds are infected with self-righteousness. Apart from the Spirit, zeal for God is blind, and blind zeal blunders its way contrary to God's purposes.

Spirit-Healed Servants Carry Their Witness Worldwide

The testimony of God's servants is to reach "the ends of the earth." Jesus picked up this phrase from Isaiah 49:6 to redirect his disciples' attention outward from Israel to the nations of the world. Luke's purpose was to trace the movement of the word of salvation from Jerusalem, the city of David, to Rome, the city of the Caesars. But even when Paul reached Rome, the story was not complete. The book of Acts seems to come to a halt, rather than a conclusion. Its ending is strikingly inconclusive. No outcome of Paul's appeal is recorded. Some scholars believe that no verdict had been rendered when Luke wrote Acts. It is possible, however, that Luke ended the story where he did, not because Paul's appeal was undecided, but to suggest to his readers that "the ends of the earth" lay even beyond Rome.

It is natural for us all to be ethnocentric, comfortable with people like ourselves, and therefore to place the highest importance on our own family, clan, group, race, or nation. We find it easier to love, understand, help, and work with people who are "our kind of people," close to us in space and time and language and culture, than we do people who are different from us. "Citizens of the world" are made, not born.

But Christ the Lord is gathering his church as an *international family* (as paradoxical as this sounds). Jesus' disciples needed to learn this, and so do we. Their ethnocentricity had at least some theological rationale: God had, after all, chosen Israel to be his special people, setting them apart from every other nation for a special purpose. But after Jesus' resurrection, the apostles needed to recognize that Israel's special status had been directed toward the coming of the Messiah, who is not the Savior of Israel only, but (as Samaritans had rightly confessed) "the Savior of the world" (John 4:42). When Jesus spoke of "the kingdom of God," they heard "the kingdom for Israel," so he drew words and themes from Isaiah's Servant Songs to reconfigure his friends' mental picture of his messianic rule. Jesus' suffering and glory as the Servant and their own witnessing mission as servants had vaster dimensions than they had ever imagined (evidenced by the fact that a Gentile of Swedish descent writes this reflection on Jesus' words in the English language on the North American continent—we've come a long way from the Mount of Olives!). If Jewish Christians needed to discover that their special role in God's plan was to lead to God's opening the floodgates of salvation to all peoples, how much more should North

American Christians take to heart God's transcontinental plans for gathering his international family! History and our own nearsightedness have chopped our view of the church into little pieces, randomly sliced apart by mere political boundaries. But that fragmented, myopic view of the church is (as the Lord said through Isaiah) too small. We who trust in Jesus are the truly worldwide church of God, but too often we fail to think and act that way. What would change if, for example, North American Christians were to ask themselves seriously where in the world the Lord could best use the financial resources he has temporarily entrusted to us, or the resources for biblical and theological study at our disposal?

Jesus' Witnesses Challenge People's Hollow Gods, Encountering Suffering

The testimony of the Lord's servants challenges the gods in which people trust. In Isaiah, the gift of the Spirit and the call to be witnesses come to Israel in her confrontation with the idols on which the Gentiles rely—gods whose emptiness and impotence are evident.

Confrontation with futile religious options is equally prominent in Acts. The Lord's word placed the paganism of the Roman world on the defensive. Simon, "the Great Power" of Samaria, recognized in Philip and the apostles a power greater than his own sorcery (8:9–13, 18–19). The sorcerer Elymas Bar-Jesus on Cyprus (a distant island, as in Isa. 41:1) opposed the word of God and was struck blind (Acts 13:6–11)—a judgment befitting one so darkened as to testify against the Lord (Isa. 44:9)! A lame man's healing at Lystra gave the witnesses of Jesus an opportunity to call upon pagans "to turn from these futile things to the living God" (Acts 14:15). Athenian philosophers likewise needed to learn about the true God, the Creator and Lord of heaven and earth, who "does not live in handmade temples" and "is not served by human hands, as if he needed anything, because he himself gives to all life and breath and all things" (17:24–25). Occultists at Ephesus torched their private collections of magical manuscripts, fearing and trusting the name of the Lord Jesus (19:17–20). In Ephesus, Jesus' witness persuaded so many "that gods made by our hands are not gods," that the Artemis shrine industry faltered (Acts 19:23–28).

To bring God's salvation to the ends of the earth, Jesus' witnesses must unmask treasured idols, encountering hostility from those whose security is shaken by God's truth. At Philippi, traffickers in the occult disguised their resentment over lost profits behind a façade of civic pride, coercing local officials into beating and imprisoning the apostles who "advocate customs unlawful for us to accept or practice, since we are Romans" (Acts

16:19–21). Ephesian silver craftsmen likewise hid their true economic motivations behind a veil of loyalty to their city and its divine patroness (19:25–28). The urbane intellectuals of Athens scoffed at Paul's talk of judgment and resurrection (17:32).

Opposition to the Lord's word came not only from Gentile quarters, but also from the entrenched authorities of Judaism. Whether in Jerusalem or among the Dispersion, Jewish leaders, who were "filled with jealousy" as the message of Jesus advanced, opposed the witnesses of the Lord (Acts 5:17; 13:45). Although the Lord had shown mercy to some blind Israelites, such as Saul of Tarsus, many among the ancient people of God were still blind to the Messiah's light. Thus, at the close of Acts, Paul warns the leaders of the Jewish community at Rome in the words of Isaiah's prophecy:

> With your hearing you will hear but never understand; seeing you will see but never perceive. For this people's heart has become calloused; they hear heavily with their ears, and they have closed their eyes, lest they see with their eyes and hear with their ears and understand with their hearts and turn, and I would heal them. (Acts 28:26–27, quoting Isa. 6:9–10)

Although the community of the Lord's servant-witnesses is characterized by a tangible love that is attractive to outsiders (Acts 2:47; 5:13), their testimony makes no peace with any alternative to faith in Jesus. Religious "solutions" apart from Jesus the Savior are dangerous frauds with which there can be no compromise or polite toleration. Jesus' witnesses set out to conquer the world not through military might or political machinations, but through the word of the Lord. As the Lord's servants, they face suffering with courage, even considering it an honor to suffer "for the sake of the Name" (Acts 5:41). Powerless politically and scorned socially, in weakness and hardship they take the stand to testify, and through their testimony Jesus the Lord summons the nations of the world: "Turn to me and be saved, all you ends of the earth; for I am God, and there is no other" (Isa. 45:22 NIV).

CONCLUSION

Jesus' words in Acts 1:8 point us to the Father's promise in Isaiah, that he would send his Spirit to heal the blind eyes and deaf ears of his servant people, so that they could be his witnesses among the nations. Jesus, the faithful Servant, suffered and was glorified, and by his faithfulness he brought healing not only for failing Israel, but also for the Gentiles. He is the Lord, who restores sight to the blind through the gift of the Spirit. Empowered by the Spirit, we at last can see the Lord's mighty acts of redemption and bear witness that he alone is God and Savior. Our testimony confronts and exposes people's pet sources of false security, calling them to live in the light of God's reality. Therefore, to be Jesus' witnesses is to suffer, even as he uses our testimony to extend his redemptive rule to the ends of the earth.

Notes

[1] Την επαγγελιαν του πατρος μου (Luke) and την επαγγελιαν του πατρος (Acts). Often in the New Testament, a "promise" of God is not merely the *words* by which he commits himself to act in the future, but the promised blessing itself, the actual *event* in which God fulfills his earlier word of commitment. Thus, although Abraham received God's promises (i.e., verbal commitments to bring future blessings, Heb. 7:6; 11:33), he and the other patriarchs did not receive God's promises (i.e., the future blessings themselves, Heb. 11:13, 39).

[2] Some English versions (e.g., the NIV) introduce the quotation in v. 16 with "this is what was spoken by the prophet Joel," but Luke's Greek implies that Joel was merely the messenger through whom God himself spoke. The prophecy was spoken not "by" (υπο, as in Luke 2:18, 26; Acts 8:6) Joel, but "through" (δια) Joel. The real subject of the passive participle "what was spoken" (ειρημενον) is God. For similar uses of δια with the genitive, see Luke 18:31; Acts 28:25; note also the construction "through the mouth" (δια του στοματος) in Luke 1:70; Acts 1:16; 3:18, 21; 4:25. See J. W. Scott, "Dynamic Equivalence and Some Theological Problems in the NIV," *WTJ* 48 (1986): 351–61, esp. 358–59.

[3] After writing "Jesus Against the Idols" (see note 16 below) and this chapter, I came across David Seccombe, "Luke and Isaiah," *NTS* 27 (1981): 252–59, now reprinted in *The Right Doctrine from the Wrong Texts? Essays on the Use of the Old Testament in the New*, ed. G. K. Beale (Grand Rapids: Baker, 1994), 248–56. Seccombe's brief survey confirms the connections proposed in this chapter between the Servant and Spirit themes in Isaiah and those themes in Luke-Acts.

[4] The disciples use the verb αποκαθιστανω, which also occurs in Matt. 17:11, where Jesus says, "Elijah . . . *will restore* all things; but I say to you that Elijah already came" (i.e., John).

[5] Greek: αποκαταστασις, the cognate noun of the verb αποκαθιστανω in Acts 1:6.

[6] Greek: επελθοντος του αγιου πνευματος εφ' υμας.

[7] LXX: εως αν επελθη εφ' υμας πνευμα αφ' υψηλου—these last two words probably influenced the promise in Luke 24:49: You will be "clothed with power *from on high.*" Both the Hebrew original (which has slightly different wording) and the Septuagint translation express the promise of the Spirit's coming upon Israel, restoring fruitfulness to the desert and peace to a people desolated by war and injustice.

[8] Greek: εσεσθε μου μαρτυρες.

[9] LXX: γενεσθε μοι μαρτυρες.

[10] LXX: υμεις μοι μαρτυρες.

[11] LXX: μαρτυρες υμεις εστε.

[12] Greek: εως εσχατου της γης.

[13] LXX: εως εσχατου της γης.

[14] LXX: οι απ᾽ εσχατου της γης.

[15] C. H. Dodd, *According to the Scriptures: The Sub-Structure of New Testament Theology* (London: Nisbet, 1957), 126: "The method [of the New Testament writers' use of the Old Testament] included, first, the *selection* of certain large sections of the Old Testament scriptures. . . . These sections were understood as *wholes*, and particular verses or sentences were quoted from them rather as pointers to the whole context than as constituting testimonies in and of themselves" (emphasis Dodd's).

[16] For further development of this theme, see D. E. Johnson, "Jesus Against the Idols: The Use of Isaianic Servant Songs in the Missiology of Acts," *WTJ* 52 (1990) 343–53.

[17] Isaiah's most graphic portrait of the ignorance of idolatry is in 44:9–20, where feverish craftsmen fashion lifeless images, failing to sense the absurdity of deriving firewood and an object of worship from the same tree. "No one stops to think, . . . 'Half of it I used for fuel; I even baked bread over its coals, I roasted meat and I ate. Shall I make a detestable thing from what is left? Shall I bow down to a block of wood?' " (Isa. 44:19 NIV).

[18] Cf. Isa. 35:5; 61:1.

[19] See, for example, the application of Isa. 42:1–4 to Jesus' rejection of celebrity (Matt. 12:18–21); of Isa. 53:4 to his healing ministry (Matt. 8:17); of the title "Lamb of God" in Isa. 53:7 to his atonement for sins (John 1:29); of Isa. 53:4–12 to his role as the innocent substitute who removes the sins of others (1 Peter 2:22–25).

[20] The picture is of prisoners *sitting* in a dark prison both in Luke 1:79 (τοις εν σκοτει . . . καθημενοις) and in Isa. 42:7 (LXX, καθημενους εν σκοτει).

[21] "The chosen one" (ο εκλελεγμενος) is equivalent to ο εκλεκτος μου, in LXX Isa. 42:1.

[22] Although this passage in Isaiah is not explicitly identified with the Servant, the parallels between it and Isa. 42:1–7 (Spirit, release from captivity, and darkness) indicate that it is a statement of the Servant in response to the Lord's commission. The wording quoted in Luke 4:18–19 does not agree exactly with either the Hebrew or the LXX text of Isa. 61:1–2. The most important difference is the following:

Isa. 61:1 (NIV translation of Hebrew text): "He has sent me to bind up the brokenhearted, to proclaim freedom for the captives and *release from darkness for the prisoners*."

Isa. 61:1 (LXX): "He has sent me to heal the brokenhearted, to proclaim freedom for the captives and *recovery of sight for the blind*."

Luke 4:18 (NIV): "He has sent me to proclaim freedom for the prisoners [= captives] and *recovery of sight for the blind, to release the oppressed*."

The unusual Hebrew wording (פקח-קוח), translated "release from darkness" in the NIV, may mean "opening of eyesight" (the verb פקח appears in Isa. 42:7: "to *open* eyes that are blind"). So it would appear that the LXX, which is partially reflected in Luke 4:18, is an appropriate expression of the thought of the Hebrew text.

[23] The expression in Luke is στηριζω το προσωπον, used in the LXX to translate the Hebrew expression שמתי פני, "I have set my face," expressive of firm resolution (e.g., Jer. 21:10). In Isa. 50:7, the LXX translates שמתי פני as *I have set my face as a firm rock* (εθηκα το προσωπον μου ως στερεαν πετραν).

[24] The Hebrew verb in Isa. 53:12 is ערה, "empty out, pour out, expose, abandon." In this

passage, the LXX translates it "was handed over" (παρεδοθη). See Joachim Jeremias, *The Eucharistic Words of Jesus* (London: SCM, 1966), 178, 226–27.

[25] Matthew: "concerning many" (περι πολλων); Mark: "on behalf of many" (υπερ πολλων); Isa. 53:12: "He bore the sins of many" (αυτος αμαρτιας πολλων ανηνεγκεν).

[26] The LXX translated "my servant" (עבדי) as ο παις μου. Although παις can in some contexts mean "child," the background in Isaiah makes it clear that God's παις in Acts 3:13, 26; 4:27, 30 is his "servant."

[27] Jesus is "your holy servant" (ο αγιος παις σου, Acts 4:27, 30), whereas his followers call themselves "your slaves" (οι δουλοι σου, v. 29). Seccombe, in "Luke and Isaiah" (in Beale, *Right Doctrine*, 256), likewise makes the point that, although Paul "continues the Servant mission," Luke never applies to him the Isaianic title παις, expressing Paul's servant role in other terms (δουλος, υπηρετης).

FOUR

DAWN OF THE LAST DAYS

THINGS FALL APART

"Things Fall Apart" is the title given by Nigerian novelist Chinua Achebe to his story of Okonkwo, a strong, clever, ambitious warrior in nineteenth-century Nigeria. The title fits. Okonkwo exerts all of his courage, cunning, self-discipline, and strength to overcome his lowly background and achieve a place of honor in the tribe—only to have his goal snatched away by an accidental death, a seven-year exile, his son's abandonment of tribal ways, and the tribe's capitulation to the new political regime imposed by the British. The expansion of one social order has dissolved the foundations of another. Okonkwo finally hangs himself—a death of untouchable shame. Things have fallen apart.[1]

That sad observation aptly describes not only Africa's experience of European imperialism, but also, in a sense, the history of the whole universe. The second law of thermodynamics, the principle of entropy, observes that the trend is from ordered forms of energy toward disorder. Physicist Stephen Hawking even suggests that our experience of time's passing depends on this tendency of things to "fall apart." For example, if broken dinner plates spontaneously repaired themselves, we would "remember" the future instead of the past! If things didn't run down, break down, and generally fall into disrepair, who would know whether we were living "frontward" or "backward"?[2]

Still, it bothers us that things fall apart. We buy a new house—the drains back up. We buy a new car—it's scratched in the parking lot or the dashboard clock loses time. Clean air and water get polluted. It's easier to foul a coastline with crude oil than it is to clean it up. We ourselves fall apart. Sickness, fatigue, stress, and depression take their toll. Sometimes, with a heavy investment of dollars, expertise, and energy, malignancies and infections can be turned back, and decaying organs can be repaired or replaced. But it's always an uphill battle. AIDS victims don't "catch" good health by sharing a needle with an uninfected person; things go in the other direction. Human relationships are wounded by insensitivity, misunderstanding, anger, unfaithfulness, and deceit; and when things fall apart between us, the brokenness is even harder to repair. Healing can take place, but scars remain.

Mechanics can (generally) repair cars; doctors can (sometimes) help cure our ills; dads can (once in a while) fix broken toys. But who can repair, once and for all, the hurts of the human heart? Who can fix *us*, so that we won't hurt each other anymore? Can the universe itself (or even the soiled globe which is our home) be fixed, or is it destined to run down, as Hawking suggests, from the "big bang" to the "big crunch"?

The Bible tells us realistically that things fall apart now more than they used to—and why. Because Adam was disobedient at the dawn of human history, God said to him,

> Cursed is the ground because of your deeds; in pain you will eat of it all the days of your life. Thorns and thistles it will raise for you, and you will eat the grass of the field. By the sweat of your face you will eat your bread until you return to the ground, for from it you were taken; for earth you are and to earth you will depart. (Gen. 3:17–19)

Into the physical order, which had come "very good" from the Creator's hand (Gen. 1:31), human rebellion introduced the virus of rebellion, decay, and futility. The preacher who counsels us in Ecclesiastes tells us that wherever he looked—at wisdom (Eccl. 1:17–18; 2:15), pleasure (2:10–11), wealth (2:4–8; 5:10; 6:1–6), labor (2:17–23), or justice (5:8–9; 8:14)—he found frustration and futility. Death comes for all alike, and before it does, accident, disease, human fickleness, or injustice may snatch from our fingertips the goals that we pursue.

The Promise of Repair

Through his prophets, however, God promised a coming great day of repair, when the senselessness that now frustrates us will give way to order, inequities will be corrected, wounds healed, and the malignancy that afflicts this world to the bone will be overcome. For centuries God's people waited for the "last days," the "day of the Lord," their hope being sustained by these prophetic promises. In those last days, the Lord himself would step into history in an unprecedented way to set things straight in this out-of-joint world.

Yet, even though the Lord's *eschatological*[3] ("last days") repair would be incomparably greater than anything seen before, his earlier works of power and grace were models, patterns, previews, and prototypes by which the Israelites could see a silhouette of the great restoration to come. The coming day of salvation would bring a new creation (Isa. 65:17–25), a new exodus (Isa. 40:3–5), a new day of judgment on God's enemies (like the Flood and the conquest of Canaan—Isa. 66:14–15, 22–24; Mal. 4:1–3), a new gathering of nations to worship at a new temple in the city of God (Isa. 4:2–6; 25:6–9). In effect, the prophets said, "If you want to get a glimpse of what it will be like when God finally reverses the ravages of our rebellion, look at the patterns[4] of his redemptive interventions in the past: a fresh beginning for the world, a new liberation from enemies, a new sifting to separate God's enemies from his children, a new reconciliation among the world's alienated peoples."

REPAIR IN TWO STEPS

Luke learned from the Spirit that the "last days" of Old Testament eschatology had dawned. The time of repair promised through the prophets had begun with the coming of Jesus the Messiah. We may not have guessed it from the form of the prophetic promises, but the Lord's repair work in the last days comes in *two phases*. The first phase arrived through the Messiah's life, death, resurrection, enthronement, and pouring of God's Spirit on his church.

The initial infection of the created order also came in two phases. First came the "death" that separated Adam and Eve from their God on the day of their disobedience (Gen. 2:17). Then this spiritual and relational death worked itself out in the death of their bodies, which returned to the dust (3:19). Similarly, the cure comes first to deal with the hidden, spiritual source of the decay, our spiritual and relational alienation from our Creator and each other; and then, in the end, it will become visible in the reversal of the body's death through resurrection. The eschatological salvation promised through the prophets has *already* come; but the promised climax of salvation has *not yet* come.

This is an uncomfortable tension in which to live, at the crossroads between cosmic sin-induced entropy, on the one hand, and the inexhaustibly creative energy of God, on the other. Paul writes, "We know that all the creation groans and suffers labor pains together right up to the present. Not only this, but also we ourselves, having the firstfruits—namely, the Spirit —groan in ourselves, eagerly anticipating adoption, the redemption of our body" (Rom. 8:22–23). The presence of the Spirit in our lives is a foretaste, a first installment, of the full restoration that awaits us when Christ returns. And because the Spirit gives us this foretaste of final redemption, he whets our appetite for the full feast.

Despite our frustration that the Lord's work of repair in and around us is not yet *finished*, we can take encouragement from the fact that it has *begun*:

> Therefore, we do not despair, though our outer person is experiencing ongoing decay, yet our inner person is being made newer every day. For the brief, weightless thing, our affliction, is producing for us a superabundantly eternal weight of glory, as we focus our gaze not on things seen, but on things unseen. For the seen things are ephemeral, but the unseen are eternal. (2 Cor. 4:16–18)

The outward fatigue, stress, suffering, and "falling apart" are easy to see. God's inward reassembly, renewal, and refreshment are discernible only to those who (paradoxically) "fix their eyes on what is unseen." It would be easy to conclude from the state of the world, the state of the church, or the state of our own behavior, that nothing significant happened in the months after Jesus of Nazareth was crucified. But in fact that was *the beginning of the end* of the old process of things falling apart, and it was the beginning of a new beginning, *the dawn of the last days*.

This is the perspective on the Spirit's presence in the church that emerges from the account of Pentecost (Acts 2:1–41) and the subsequent healing of a lame man in the temple courts (3:1–4:31). Viewed against the background of prophetic promise, these early signs of Jesus' power to rescue and repair by his Spirit reveal that the church's life is now a first installment and preview of the peace, purity, love, and joy of the world to come, even in the midst of the old creation's present pollution, decay, and death.

PENTECOST: THE SIGNS OF THE SPIRIT'S COMING

As we have seen, Luke shows us not merely the *fact*, but especially the *significance*, of the Spirit's coming to the church at Pentecost. In Acts 2, that significance is revealed through the audible and visible signs that attend the Spirit's arrival (Acts 2:1–11) and through Peter's Spirit-inspired sermon (2:14–36, 38–40). Both the signs and the sermon point back to Old Testament promises as essential background for understanding the Spirit's mission.

Luke even turns our thoughts to the prophetic promises by the wording he chooses to introduce the events of Pentecost: "When the day of Pentecost *was fulfilled*" (συμπληρόω, Acts 2:1). This verb, which appears only rarely in the Greek Bible (LXX and New Testament), designates the prophesied climax of a period of time (e.g., the seventy years of Judah's exile, Jer. 25:12; the ascension of Jesus, Luke 9:51).[5] Haenchen rightly notes "a biblical ring about this beginning,"[6] for the formula alerts us to the arrival of a significant event predicted by God—a promise of the Father's.[7]

Wonder-Signs of a New Creation and Covenant

Three observable signs attest the Spirit's arrival: (1) the roar of a rushing wind from heaven, (2) "tongues" of fire distributed over the heads of the believers, and (3) the spoken tongues through which believers declared "the wonders of God" in the dialects of the Mediterranean world. These signs are echoes of new beginnings in the Old Testament, displaying the new creation, the new exodus, the new revelation, and the new resurrection that the Spirit initiates at his coming.

The Mighty Breath/Wind of God

When we read of the "sound like the blowing of a violent wind," we should remember that in both Hebrew and Greek the words used (רוח in Hebrew, πνευμα in Greek) can refer either to the physical wind or to the Spirit of God.[8] The ambiguity is not accidental, for the movement of physical air aptly portrays important aspects of the Spirit's work.

The Breath of Life. From one perspective, God's πνευμα is like the powerful wind that brings changes of weather. In ancient Israel, breezes from the Mediterranean Sea carried rainstorms eastward across Palestine, making the earth fruitful; so also the Spirit would come like life-giving water on dry ground, restoring Israel's children to fruitful witness (Isa. 44:3).[9]

From another perspective, we are as dependent on the Spirit for life in the presence of God as we are on the breath in our lungs for physical life. Thus, the movement of air into our respiratory systems is another illustration of the Spirit. Adam became a living being only when God "breathed into his nostrils the breath[10] of life" (Gen. 2:7). The prophet Ezekiel, granted a vision of Israel as a valley full of skeletons, was instructed to call the wind (רוח) to breathe into the slain, that they might live (Ezek. 37:9–10). The Lord interpreted the vision: "I will put my Spirit (רוח) in you and you will live" (Ezek. 37:14 NIV). The resurrection that Ezekiel witnessed, after the desolation caused by Israel's unfaithfulness, was nothing less than a *new creation* of the people of God, in which God's Spirit imparted life to the lifeless. Just before this vision, the prophet had recorded God's promise to replace his people's hearts of stone with hearts of flesh and *his own Spirit,* so that they would hear and heed his word (Ezek. 36:26–27).

The sound of wind signaled the arrival of the Spirit, who makes the dead alive. The "wind" was the breath of God, breathed into the new humanity.[11] Pentecost was a new creation. Especially in view of Ezekiel's vision of the dry bones, reordered and returned to life by the word and Spirit of the Lord, we can see that the coming of the Spirit at Pentecost marked a major step in God's restoration of his creation in the last days.

The Windstorm at Sinai. The blast of breath/wind may also have evoked memories of the days following the Passover/Exodus, when Israel gathered at Mount Sinai to enter into covenant with their Redeemer. The Lord's descent to the mountain was accompanied by a terrifying turmoil of thunder, lightning, fire, cloud, and earthquake—and an increasingly loud series of trumpet blasts (Ex. 19:16–19). The first-century Jewish philosopher Philo associated that trumpet sound with the πνευμα of God, the "breath" through which the Lord brought the Torah to his people.[12] The "breathing" out of the law on Sinai now finds its counterpart in the Spirit-empowered announcement of God's marvelous deeds in Jesus by believers given utterance in the languages of the nations, as Peter's quotation from Joel's prophecy will make clear. At Sinai, Israel was formed as a community of faith in response to the Lord's words breathed out in terrifying trumpet blasts. But in Jerusalem, the Lord's word, proclaimed by the church through the breath-Spirit of God, surpassed the revelation given to Moses.

Tongues of Purifying Fire
The second sign was "what seemed to be tongues of fire that separated and came to rest on each of them" (Acts 2:3 NIV). These flames announced

the glorious presence of God, just as the lightning on Sinai (Ex. 19:18) and the fire and cloud over the tent of meeting made the holy glory of God visible in the midst of Israel (Ex. 40:34–38). But when the risen Christ poured out the Spirit, each believer was marked by a miniature "pillar of fire," indicating that each was a temple in which God dwelt by his Spirit (see 1 Cor. 6:19; Eph. 2:22). Peter would later write to suffering believers, perhaps with a memory of this very day in mind: "If you are insulted because of the name of Christ, you are blessed, for the Spirit of glory and of God rests on you" (1 Peter 4:14 NIV). If we face suffering for the Name (see Acts 5:41), it is a sign not of God's absence, but of the presence of his purifying Spirit.[13]

John the Baptist had announced Jesus as the one who would baptize "with the Holy Spirit and with fire," safely gathering the wheat of God's harvest and consuming the chaff with fire (Luke 3:16–17). Fire so often symbolizes and makes visible the presence of God, not only because it radiates light, but also because it destroys through heat. Fire pictures the consuming holiness of the true and living God. His presence "burns away" all that is in conflict with his purity. The Spirit comes with the life-giving power of a new creation, but there is a dangerous side to this *Holy* Spirit. He is so utterly pure that when he is present among human beings, any compromise with spiritual pollution, any toleration of spiritual infection, becomes unthinkable. "Our God is a consuming fire," declares the New Testament (Heb. 12:29), quoting the Old (Deut. 4:24). When God comes to his temple, says Malachi, he shall burn as a refiner's fire, purifying true worshipers and consuming the false (Mal. 3:2–5; 4:1). As we shall see in the judgment of Ananias and Sapphira, the Spirit has come to make Christ's church a community of integrity as well as love.

The tongues of fire also had a second message. Although Luke's vocabulary includes the word *flames* (φλογαι; see Luke 16:24), here he chooses *tongues* (γλωσσαι) to describe the shape of the flames resting on the believers. The third sign consisted of "tongues" that could be heard rather than seen—the languages and dialects of the peoples that made up the Hellenistic world (Acts 2:4, 8, 11). The shape of this visible sign of the Spirit, as he filled the assembled believers, showed his mission to stimulate our speech about the wonders of God. As Philo reflected about Sinai, he discerned in the voice of God that came from the fire a symbol of the twofold effect of God's word, giving light to those who heed the commandments and destruction to those who do not.[14] So, at Pentecost, the sign of fiery tongues alerts our ears to listen to the new words of God, that they might bring us light and not judgment.

The Tongues of the Nations

The third sign was the gift of speaking the "wonders of God" in the "tongues" (languages) of the nations (Acts 2:4). These tongues were not mere ecstatic speech or an angelic language, but rather "dialects" (διαλεκτοι, v. 8) recognized as their mother tongues by members of the crowd who had come from the far-flung reaches of the Jewish Dispersion. They were "other tongues" (v. 4), not learned naturally by the speakers, but imparted supernaturally by the Spirit. The listening crowds were affiliated with Judaism, either by heredity or through conversion (v. 11); but, having come from the Dispersion, they represented the diverse peoples among whom they resided.[15] The meaning of this miraculous speech would be given in Peter's sermon, but two elements of Old Testament background should be noticed here:

Reversing the Confusion of Babel. First, this miracle of languages, which united representatives of the nations in hearing the wonders of God, marked a reversal of the brokenness in human language that began at Babel (Gen. 11:1–9). Part of what "falls apart" in this world is language, which tends to divide the peoples of the earth, breeding suspicion, misunderstanding, and frustration. According to the account of Babel in the book of Genesis, this is a result of human arrogance and resistance to God's command to fill the earth. The coalition of pride at Babel was shattered by the Lord's confusing of the rebels' tongues (LXX: γλωσσα), thereby scattering (διασπειρω[16]) the human race "over the face of the whole earth." Pentecost signaled the reversal of this judgment, a drawing together of people "from every nation that is under heaven" (Acts 2:5), not to erect a monument to their own pride, but to glorify God for his salvation.[17]

God's Law to the Nations at Sinai. This sign, like the wind and the flaming tongues, may allude to the giving of the law at Sinai. Rabbinical tradition held, "Every word which came from the mouth of the Almighty (in the giving of the Law) was divided into seventy tongues,"[18] so that the Gentiles who were traveling with the Israelites might hear and understand the Torah clearly for themselves. Although this thought is not explicit in the Pentateuch, it is likely that the sign of languages at Pentecost is God's eschatological answer to this tradition, which glorified the Torah. Although the law given to Moses was indeed a revelation of God's righteousness to all peoples, the divine word that will bring the Gentiles under his saving rule is not the law, but the good news of Jesus the Messiah.[19]

PETER'S SERMON: THE LAST DAYS HAVE COME

In the structure of Luke's two-volume work, Peter's sermon parallels Jesus' sermon in the synagogue at Nazareth (Luke 4:16–30). Thus, near the beginning of each book we find (1) a reception of the Spirit by the Lord's servant (Jesus, Luke 3:22; his disciples, Acts 2:1–4), (2) a sermon explaining the purpose for the Spirit's coming (Jesus, Luke 4:17–21; Peter, Acts 2:14–39), and then (3) a healing ministry that shows the Spirit's power, but also elicits opposition (Jesus, Luke 4:31–44 and 5:12–26; Peter and John, Acts 3–4).[20]

Peter's sermon reveals three important facts about the Spirit's coming: (1) The outpouring of the Spirit means that the last days have dawned. (2) The gift of tongues signals the arrival of the universal gift of the Spirit of prophecy, desired by Moses and promised through Joel. (3) The Spirit's role is to bear witness to Jesus, drawing people to confess him as Lord and Messiah.

The Last Days Have Dawned

Of the slight verbal variations between Peter's quotation of Joel 2, on the one hand, and the Hebrew and Septuagint texts, on the other, the most important is his replacement of the general expression "after this"[21] with "in the last days," a theologically charged expression derived from other prophetic passages. In the prophets, when the "last days" come, the people of Israel return to the Lord their God and to David their rightful king (Hos. 3:5), and the peoples of the earth stream to the house of God in Jerusalem, to be taught and ruled by him (Isa. 2:2–5 = Mic. 4:1–5). The last days would be days of restoration and reconciliation.[22]

The last days would also be days of crisis, as Joel's prophecy showed. There would be "wonders in the heaven above and signs on the earth below, blood and fire and a vapor of smoke. The sun will be changed into darkness and the moon into blood before the great and glorious day of the Lord comes" (Acts 2:19–20). God's intervention brings trauma as well as relief, judgment as well as blessing. The "wonders and signs" include the miracles of Jesus' earthly ministry (which Peter calls "acts of power and wonders and signs," Acts 2:22), but also the darkening of the sun during Jesus' crucifixion (Luke 23:44–45), his resurrection (Luke 11:29–30), and the heavenly wind, fiery tongues, and spoken tongues of Pentecost.

These tokens of blessing and judgment did not instantaneously bring down the curtain on human history, however. Because God is patient, people have time to repent and "be saved from this twisted generation" (Acts 2:40). Nevertheless, the exaltation of Jesus as Lord and Messiah intensifies the urgency of the summons to faith: It shall be that "whoever calls on the Lord's name will be saved" (Acts 2:21). Jesus is now baptizing in the Spirit and with fire, as John predicted. Although the final separation of wheat from chaff is still to come, his winnowing fork is in his hand, to begin this eschatological sifting by means of the gospel (Luke 3:16–17).

The Spirit of Prophecy Comes to All God's People

When "things fall apart" between humans, the words we speak are often involved. The speech that comes from our mouths, Jesus says, exposes its source in our thoughts and motives (Matt. 12:34–37). That inner source of our speaking can be purified only by the Spirit of God. The Spirit came upon ancient prophets to restore their speech to the original purity of the image of God, so that they could declare God's word (Isa. 6:1–9).[23]

In the Old Testament, the Holy Spirit is mentioned primarily in connection with the abilities he gave to enable certain people to serve the community of Israel: craftsmen to build the tent of meeting, prophets to speak God's word, and judges and kings to defend God's people and administer justice.[24] But the Old Testament also looks forward to the day when the Spirit will equip *every one* of God's people to serve him. The background of Joel's prophecy is a wish expressed by Moses long before. Overburdened with the responsibility of governing the Israelites, Moses had heeded the Lord's command to gather seventy elders to the Tent of Meeting, so that they might receive the Spirit and, through the Spirit, wisdom to share the burden of leadership (Num. 11:16–17). At the appointed time, however, two elders were not with Moses and the others at the Tent of Meeting. Yet they too received the Spirit (with the sign of prophecy) where they were, elsewhere in the camp (vv. 24–26). Joshua, loyally defending Moses' authority as covenant mediator, protested that these two, who were not with Moses, should be forbidden to prophesy. But Moses said, "Are you jealous for my sake? I wish that all the LORD's people were prophets and that the LORD would put his Spirit on them!" (v. 29 NIV). What Moses foresaw and longed for, and what Joel predicted, Peter now declares to have arrived. All the Lord's people have received the Spirit, and to signify this event, they all prophesy, declaring God's great deeds (Acts 2:11) in the dialects of the nations (v. 6), as the Spirit gives them utterance (v. 4).

In Numbers 11:25, it is noted that the Israelite elders prophesied only at their initial reception of the Spirit: "They did not do so again." Similarly in the New Testament, Paul insists that, whereas *all* Christians have received the Spirit (1 Cor. 12:13), *only some* have received the power to prophesy as a constant gift (vv. 29–30). Thus, this initial outpouring of prophecy is a sign that the Spirit, who fills all who trust in Jesus, brings our speech under the control of the God of truth, so that we declare his wonderful, redemptive achievements. This prophecy comes in the diverse languages of the nations to point forward to the spreading witness of the Spirit "to the ends of the earth."

The Spirit Bears Witness to Jesus

Having quoted from Joel to explain the Spirit's signs, Peter seems to drop this topic which gathered his audience. Instead of focusing on the Spirit's wonders, the apostle turns his hearers' attention to Jesus, attested by God through wondrous signs, but then handed over by his people for destruction, and finally raised by the Father to life (Acts 2:22–32). Finally Peter shows how the Spirit and Jesus fit together: "Having been exalted to the right hand of God and having received from the Father the promise, i.e., the Holy Spirit, [Jesus] has poured out what you are seeing and hearing" (v. 33). Because Jesus has sent the Spirit, the Spirit's signs point to Jesus. Because Jesus has sent the Spirit, the Spirit's words (spoken by Peter) center on Jesus, whom God has made Lord and Christ (v. 36). In these last days, the Messiah has taken the throne at the Father's right hand, and he is extending his dominion on earth through the power of his Spirit.

THE LAME MAN LEAPS: SIGN OF FINAL RESTORATION

After a transitional summary portraying the community life of the new believers in Jesus,[25] Luke records a second event that signals the arrival of the last days. In keeping with prophetic promise, the name of Jesus causes the lame to leap for joy, and this physical healing provides a preview of the coming comprehensive restoration.

As we have seen, in this section the name of Jesus is emphasized through repeated references to its saving power. This salvation, or restoration to wholeness through faith in Jesus' name, also confronts us repeatedly in this account, through a striking variety of words that express healing and restoration. No fewer than five different Greek words expressive of healing appear here, and two of these occur nowhere else in Luke-Acts, while another appears only once.[26] "Become strong" (στερεοω) is used by Luke only in this passage (Acts 3:7, 16) and in Acts 16:5 (of the strengthening of churches). To this vocabulary of healing/salvation we could add the general term "good deed" (ευεργεσια, 4:9), which appears only here in Luke-Acts.[27] Peter's sermon contains two terms expressing the promise of a cosmic healing, "times of refreshing" (αναφυξις, v. 20) and "times of the restoration of all things" (αποκαταστασις, 3:21), neither of which appears elsewhere in the New Testament.[28]

Why is there this concentration of "healing" and "restoration" language, some of which is rare elsewhere in Luke's writings? This miracle is a sign, given at the start of Jesus' heavenly ministry, to demonstrate how he has begun the healing of the cosmos by the power of his name in those who have faith. The strengthening of a lame man's ankles prefigures the renewal of the whole creation, as the text signals in several ways:

(1) In an important summary statement, the miracle is called "the sign of healing" (Acts 4:22; see also v. 16). Jesus' healing signs, which could be seen, point to profound dimensions of salvation that cannot be seen because they are spiritual or future.

(2) Peter uses the same verb, "to save" (σωζω), to describe both the healing of lame ankles (4:9) and the comprehensive rescue of which all stand in need: "Salvation [σωτηρια] is found in no one else, for there is no other name under heaven given to men by which we must be saved [σωζω]" (4:12 NIV).

(3) Luke frames his description of the miraculous healing to remind readers of a prophetic promise of the last days: "Then will the eyes of the blind be opened and the ears of the deaf unstopped. Then will the *lame leap* like a deer, and the mute tongue shout for joy. Water will gush forth in the wilderness and streams in the desert" (Isa. 35:5–6 NIV).[29] In view of the symbolic use of blindness and deafness in Isaiah's Servant Songs, we can anticipate that this promise symbolizes a healing that goes deeper than (but does not exclude) physical restoration. Our expectation is confirmed by the summons to courage and hope, portrayed in physical terms, that precedes the promise of sight for the blind, hearing for the deaf, and leaping for the lame: "Strengthen the feeble hands, steady the knees that give way; say to those with fearful hearts, 'Be strong, do not fear; your God will come'" (vv. 3–4). The leaping of the lame is a sign that God will strengthen the step of his pilgrim people as they walk along on his highway, the Way of Holiness (v. 8).[30]

When the imprisoned John had earlier sent his disciples with the question whether Jesus was in fact "the coming one," Jesus alluded to this prophetic promise (Isa. 35:5–6, with 61:1–2) as finding its fulfillment in his healing and preaching: "Go, report to John what you have seen and heard: Blind people receive sight, lame people walk, lepers are made clean, deaf people hear, dead people are raised, and poor people are told good news" (Luke 7:22). At that point, the lame were healed to *walk*. Now the risen Lord gives a greater sign of his power to save: the lame man *leaps* for joy! Faith in Jesus' name has restored him to complete health (Acts 3:16).

This healing may be thought of as both an X-ray and a preview. As an X-ray, it makes visible to outside observers the unseen inner cure that faith in Jesus produces. Astonishing as it is for a man of forty who has never walked to leap in the temple, the cure of hearts paralyzed in sin is even greater. As a preview, it shows the final completion of Jesus' restorative work, when believers' physical bodies will fully experience the salvation which we already taste in the form of firstfruits (see Rom. 8:18–25). Astonishing as it is for a lame man to leap, it is nothing when compared to the *cosmic* restoration to come—"the restoration of all things" (Acts 3:21).

THE NEW CREATION AMID THE DECAY OF THE OLD

This brings us back to the tension that pervades the Christian's life here and now, the tension between salvation "already" and salvation "not yet." Peter's sermon announced that Jesus is the righteous Servant of the Lord (Acts 3:13–14).[31] Although disowned by the people, Jesus was glorified by God (Isa. 52:2–3, 13). In Jesus, salvation had arrived and was then present. "Indeed, all the prophets from Samuel on, as many as have spoken, have foretold *these days,*" said Peter (Acts. 3:24 NIV). The promised blessing of all peoples through Abraham's seed had begun with the sending of the Servant to Israel (vv. 25–26).[32]

Yet the fullness of the messianic restoration has not arrived. The seasons of refreshing and the times of the restoration of all things still await the sending of Jesus, the appointed Messiah, from heaven. That coming of Jesus will indeed complete the fulfillment of the promises spoken by God long ago through his holy prophets (Acts 3:19–21). But the reassembly of the things that fall apart in this creation must await that day. God patiently waits to set right all that's wrong in this creation. This patience prolongs the pain for those who long for his righteous kingdom, but it mercifully holds open a door of repentance for those who have defiled the creation and defied its Creator. In the temple, Peter spoke on behalf of the God of long-suffering mercy: "Repent, therefore, and turn to God, so that your sins may be erased, that seasons of refreshing may come from the presence of the Lord" (v. 19). The gift of repentance is the starting point of the blessing that Jesus, the seed of Abraham, bestows on the Gentiles: "To you first, when God raised up his servant, God sent him, blessing you *by turning each of you away from your wicked ways*" (v. 26). To troubled Christians, Peter later explained the divine patience that dictates the delay of Messiah Jesus' return: "The Lord is not slow about his promise, as some regard slowness. Rather, he is long-suffering toward you, not wanting that any perish, but that all arrive at repentance" (2 Peter 3:9).

At the dawn of the last days, selective and temporary previews of complete, eternal restoration (the leaping of a lame man) provided divine confirmation of the apostles' testimony about Jesus (Acts 4:30; Heb. 2:3–4). He is indeed the righteous Servant by whose "wounds we are healed" (Isa. 53:5, cited in 1 Peter. 2:24). The healing comes not all at once, but in phases. Now "things fall apart," and suffering and death dog our steps, but the reversal of cosmic entropy has begun in the resurrection of Jesus. Faith in the name of Jesus, germinating from the Spirit's witness, is the seed from which will grow the restoration of all things.

Notes

[1] Chinua Achebe, *Things Fall Apart* (New York: Fawcett Crest, 1969).

[2] Stephen M. Hawking, *A Brief History of Time: From the Big Bang to Black Holes* (New York: Bantam, 1988).

[3] The theological term *eschatology* (adjective, *eschatological*) is derived from the Greek word εσχατος ("last"). Thus, it refers to the area of theology that discusses the events that come last in God's plan for the world, events that we normally assume to be still future for us. From the standpoint of the prophets, however, some important "last things" already invaded history when the Son of God became human, died, and was raised from the dead.

[4] The Greek counterpart to "pattern" is τυπος, "type." This noun and other words derived from it are used in the New Testament to identify Old Testament persons and events as patterns that anticipate Christ and his saving work, thus helping God's people to understand the richness of the redemption that Jesus has accomplished (Rom. 5:14; 1 Cor. 10:6, 11). From this Greek word comes our word *typology*, which refers to the recognition and study of these Old Testament "previews" of the Savior.

[5] Συμπληροω is used in the passive voice in these passages, as in Acts 2:1. A predicted time period is "filled up" at its conclusion. The only other use of συμπληροω in the Greek Bible is in Luke 8:23, where it refers to the filling of the disciples' boat with water.

[6] Ernst Haenchen, *The Acts of the Apostles: A Commentary* (Philadelphia: Westminster Press, 1971), 167.

[7] Eduard Lohse translates the opening phrase of Acts 2:1: "When the *promised* day of Pentecost *had come*" ("πεντηκοστη," *TDNT*, 6:50) (emphasis added).

⁸ In discussion with Nicodemus, Jesus exploits this connection by referring to the wind in order to illustrate the Spirit's mysterious movements: "The wind [πνευμα] blows wherever it pleases. You hear its sound, but you cannot tell where it comes from or where it is going. So it is with everyone born of the Spirit [πνευμα]" (John 3:8 NIV).

⁹ On the other hand, hot winds blowing westward from the eastern desert burned and withered crops; so also the Spirit would come as a burning fire of judgment (Isa. 40:7).

¹⁰ Here the Hebrew word is not רוח, but נשמה; and the LXX has πνοη rather than πνευμα. But the movement of air in nostrils (נשמה, πνοη) and the movement of air in the atmosphere (רוח, πνευμα) are sometimes closely related in biblical imagery. See especially Job 32:8 and 33:4 (where the two words appear in synonymous parallelism).

¹¹ "Wind" in Acts 2:2 is not πνευμα but πνοη, the word used in the creation account (Gen. 2:7 LXX: πνοη ζωης, "breath of life"). In biblical Greek (for example, in its only other New Testament usage, Acts 17:25), πνοη normally designates breath which passes through a person's nose and mouth rather than the wind. A parallel between the creation of Adam and Jesus' gift of the Spirit to his followers is suggested also in John 20:22: "And having said this he breathed [εμφυσαω] on them and said, 'Receive the Holy Spirit.' " "Breathe" (εμφυσαω) is the verb used in Genesis 2:7 and Ezekiel 37:9 LXX.

¹² Philo, *The Decalogue* 33–35.

¹³ See D. E. Johnson, "Fire in God's House: Imagery from Malachi 3 in Peter's Theology of Suffering (1 Pet 4:12–19)" *JETS* 29 (1986): 285–94.

¹⁴ Philo, *The Decalogue* 46–49.

¹⁵ These are listed from east to west from Parthia through the provinces of Asia Minor (ending with Pamphylia), then westward along the north African coast (Egypt, Libya/Cyrene), and finally reaching Rome. The two pairs in v. 11 show that the crowd is a comprehensive representation of the Hellenistic world, including both ethnic Jews and Gentile converts to Judaism, both the island peoples (Crete) in the midst of the Mediterranean and the desert peoples (Arabs) on the outskirts of the empire.

¹⁶ Scattering and dispersion, which in the Old Testament connote judgment, fulfill a new purpose in Acts: as suffering scatters (διασπειρω) Christ's servants, they carry the light of salvation to the nations (Acts 8:1, 4; 11:19). See chapter 6, "Diversity in Unity."

¹⁷ On the other hand, as this gift of foreign languages made possible the proclamation of the gospel to the nations, it was also a sign of judgment on Jewish particularism. A hint of this is seen in the way native-born Jerusalemites dismissed the Spirit's sign: "They have had too much wine" (Acts 2:13 NIV). Paul would later warn the Christians at Corinth that tongues function as a sign against unbelievers, hardening them in their resistance to God's message in fulfillment of Isa. 28:11–12: "Through men of strange tongues and through the lips of foreigners I will speak to this people, but even then they will not listen to me" (1 Cor. 14:20–25 NIV). See O. Palmer Robertson, "Tongues: Sign of Covenantal Curse and Blessing," *WTJ* 38 (1975–76): 43–53.

¹⁸ Leonhard Goppelt, *Typos: The Typological Interpretation of the Old Testament in the New* (Grand Rapids: Eerdmans, 1982), 117, quoting Hermann L. Strack and Paul Billerbeck, *Kommentar zum Neuen Testament aus Talmud und Midrash*, 6th ed., 6 vols. (Munich: C. H. Beck, 1974), 2:604–5. The citation is from Rabbi Johachanan (who died in 279), who was explaining Ps. 68:11, "The Lord gave the word of proclamation to a great multitude." A member of the school of Rabbi Ishmael (who died ca. 135) interpreted Jer. 23:29 ("Is not my word . . . like a hammer, which smashes rocks?"): "As a hammer divides itself in many sparks, so also the Word that goes out of the mouth of God divides itself into seventy languages"

(p. 605). Philo also says that from the fire of God's glory came a voice which was understandable in the language familiar to the hearers, although he does not explicitly speak of many languages for the sake of the Gentiles (*The Decalogue* 46).

[19] The allusions to the giving of the law at Sinai that we have seen in this passage are confirmed by the fact that, at least by the second century A.D., Jewish teachers associated the Feast of Pentecost (primarily an agricultural feast in the Old Testament) with the giving of the Torah. Since Pentecost came fifty days after Passover, the timing was fairly close to that indicated in Ex. 19:1, namely, that the Israelites arrived at Mount Sinai at the start of the third month after their exodus from Egypt (fifty-six days or so, using lunar months). Some scholars (e.g., Lohse, "πεντηκοστη," in *TDNT*, 6:48–49) believe that the identification of Pentecost with Sinai was a result of the fall of Jerusalem in A.D. 70—several decades after Jesus' death, resurrection, and bestowal of the Spirit; others (e.g., J. D. G. Dunn, "Pentecost," *NIDNTT*, 2:784) believe that the tradition originated before 70, though earlier written documentation is lacking.

[20] M. D. Goulder, *Type and History in Acts* (London: SPCK, 1964), 54–55.

[21] Hebrew: אחרי־כֵן; והיה; LXX: και εσται μετα ταυτα. The passage quoted by Peter is Joel 2:28–32 in English translations, but is numbered as 3:1–5 in the Hebrew text and the LXX.

[22] Geerhardus Vos, *The Pauline Eschatology* (Grand Rapids: Eerdmans, 1961), 1–7.

[23] On the Spirit, the image of God, and the prophets, see M. G. Kline, *Images of the Spirit* (Grand Rapids: Baker, 1980).

[24] B. B. Warfield, "The Spirit of God in the Old Testament," in Warfield, *Biblical and Theological Studies*, ed. S. G. Craig (Philadelphia: Presbyterian and Reformed, 1952), 127–56.

[25] The healing of the lame man in the temple illustrates several elements in the summary that precedes it: the Christians' devotion to "the prayers" (Acts 2:42), wonders and signs through the apostles (v. 43), daily worship in the temple (v. 46), and the daily addition of those who were being saved (v. 47). For discussion of the portrait of the church's life given in the transitional summaries, see chapter 5, "The Holy Community."

[26] "Complete healing" (ολοκληρια) appears nowhere else in the New Testament (3:16). "Healthy, sound" (υγιης) appears only in 4:10 in all of Luke-Acts. Acts 4:22—"the sign of healing" (το σημειον της ιασεως)—contains another word for healing (ιασις), which appears once more in this section (4:30) and once in Luke 13:32. "Heal" (θεραπευω, Acts 4:14), on the other hand, is used frequently by Luke (13 times in the Gospel, 5 times in Acts). And σωζω, meaning "heal" (Acts 4:9), is a special application of the verb "to save," used frequently by Luke (16 times in the Gospel, 13 times in Acts), sometimes, as in Acts 4:9, with reference to physical healing (indicating "salvation" from weakness, injury, or disease) (Luke 6:9; 8:48, 50; 17:19; 18:42; Acts 14:9).

[27] Its only other New Testament occurrence is in 1 Tim. 6:2.

[28] The verb "restore" (αποκαθιστημι), a cognate of the noun in Acts 3:21, appears in Acts 1:6; Luke 6:10; and a half dozen other times in other New Testament books.

[29] In the LXX, "lame" is χωλος, as in Acts 3:2. Likewise, "leap" is αλλομαι, the word used in Acts 3:8. "He leaped to his feet" at the beginning of this verse represents a compound form of the same basic verb (εξαλλομαι). The verb "leap" (αλλομαι) is used by Luke only here and in his parallel account of the healing of a lame man through Paul in Acts 14:8–10. Of the eight appearances of αλλομαι in the LXX, only Isaiah 35:6 speaks of the *lame* leaping.

³⁰ The epistle to the Hebrews, comparing the Christian life to Israel's desert pilgrimage, uses the imagery of Isa. 35:3 to exhort its readers to a pilgrimage of persistent faith (Heb. 12:12–13).

³¹ "The Righteous One" (ο δικαιος, Acts 3:14; 22:14) is the Servant's title in Isa. 53:11.

³² Peter's statement to his Jewish listeners, that God, having raised up his servant, "sent him *first* to you to bless you" (3:26 NIV), implies that the blessing will eventually include other peoples as well, as promised in Gen. 22:18, just quoted by Peter.

FIVE

THE HOLY COMMUNITY

HEAVEN: CITY OR COUNTRY?

What is your mental picture of Paradise: a still clearing in the Maine woods or a Manhattan city street? Los Angeles freeways, Philadelphia row houses, or Mexico City's *colonias* of cardboard, sheet metal, and mud? Or a footpath through the Rockies, a lakeside log cabin, rolling meadows of wildflowers, or a tropical beach?

For many, "the city" is not exactly synonymous with celestial bliss. Over half of the people on this earth live in cities, by choice or necessity. To be sure, cities have their attractions: impressive architecture, cultural events, and—most importantly—jobs to be done and wages to be earned. But for many, the city's benefits are overshadowed by its threatening ugliness: poverty, crime, pollution, congestion, pressure, and hopelessness. The city often seems to be a dirty, dangerous, drug-ridden, desperate dumping place, littered with leftovers—gutted shells of vehicles, boarded-up husks of buildings, burned-out remnants of humanity. It is hardly surprising that American mythology has romanticized the solitary life in the wild, far from civilization's encroachments. Give us the wide-open spaces any day!

The Bible, on the other hand, states unequivocally that God is a city dweller, and that the goal of his people's pilgrimage is a city resplendent with his own glory—"the heavenly Jerusalem, the city of the living God" (Heb. 12:22). In John's visions, he "saw the Holy City, New Jerusalem, coming down out of heaven from God, prepared as a bride beautified for her husband" (Rev. 21:2). This is a gardenlike city, reminiscent of the unstained garden of God, Eden (Rev. 22:1–2; Gen. 2:8–14). But it is still a place where crowds of people live together—and they do so in peace and joy! The Bible finds in the city a fitting portrait of the Father's home that awaits us, the place of perfect safety, sharing, justice, and joy. The wilderness, on the other hand, symbolizes danger, struggle, testing, and hardship. To be banished, alone and without the protection of kin, neighbor, and social order—worse yet, away from the community in which God dwells—into the uninhabited wasteland: this is a picture of hell itself.[1] The Bible's preference for city over wilderness is not simply a by-product of the hardships of Israel's wilderness wandering, or of the threatening beasts and brigands that lurked outside Israel's walled cities. Scripture's exaltation of the city and suspicion of the wilderness unveil God's purpose for us: We were made to live together, with each other and with our God.

Of course, if you pack sinful, selfish people together in close quarters, the pressure intensifies the destructive tendencies of their fallenness, sometimes to explosive dimensions. But when God packs his city with people who are purified by his Spirit, the crowds will gather in peace and praise. The church is to be a present foretaste of that future heavenly, holy community.

To be honest, however, sometimes the church makes us long for the wide-open spaces. It's one thing to sing "I love thy church, O God" or "I love this family of God," and quite another to bear with an abrasive member of God's family. Didn't the hermits of earlier ages have the right idea in pursuing holiness through solitude? Doesn't godliness grow best "far from the madding crowd," undistracted by the aggravating interference of flawed people?

But God says, in effect, "You grow into the image of my Son only as you grow *together*" (Eph. 4:12–16). The summaries of the church's life and growth in the early chapters of Acts give us a glimpse of how the church behaves when it is a normal, healthy, holy community. Although some scholars have accused the author of Acts of romanticism in portraying the church's infancy as idyllic,[2] in fact Luke honestly shows that the early church, though healthy and growing, was far from flawless. Hypocrisy crept in to mar its purity, and interpersonal friction threatened its unity. Nevertheless, in the aftermath of the Spirit's coming, people who confessed that Jesus is Lord and Christ were molded into a fellowship that was both attractive in its love and terrifying in its holiness.

Luke does not intend his description to be a nostalgic retrospect of "good old days" long gone, but rather a pattern for the present. Although the apostles' days were extraordinary in some respects, when we compare the church soon after Pentecost with the New Testament epistles' instructions for Christians' attitudes and relationships, we find a striking correspondence.[3] In effect, the Spirit is saying to us through Luke's early summaries, "Look here and recognize that my blueprint for the church, commanded in apostolic letters, works!"

We will focus on three early summaries (Acts 2:42–47; 4:32–35; 5:12–16), which are interspersed between accounts of noteworthy events: the coming of the Spirit (2:1–41), the healing of a lame man (3:1–4:31), the judgment of Ananias and Sapphira (5:1–11), and the second arrest of apostles (5:17–40). These are the fullest descriptions of the believers' daily life together.[4] In the Greek text, these summaries are set apart from the narratives of events by a shift in verb tense, from the aorist (simple past) to the imperfect tense, signaling that the action in the summaries occurred repeatedly, as a customary pattern of behavior in the Christian community. At the end of this chapter, in considering the account of the offerings brought by Joseph Barnabas and by Ananias and Sapphira (4:36–5:11), we will note how the narratives of events illustrate themes in the summaries that join them. For example, Barnabas's generosity exemplifies the sharing described in the preceding summary (4:32), while the judgment on Ananias and Sapphira explains the fear of those who "were not daring to associate with" this holy community (5:13).

In Acts 2:42, Luke lists four things to which the believers were "devoting themselves":[5] the apostles' teaching, the fellowship, the breaking of the bread, and the prayers. These items sum up the fuller portrait of the church's life that we find in the passages we are considering. In this chapter, our focus will be on the fellowship, the breaking of bread, and the prayers as strands that bound these earlier believers together into a shared life, a "community."[6] The apostles' teaching, so fully exemplified in the many speeches and sermons of Acts, merits separate attention (see chap. 9).

THE FELLOWSHIP OF THE SPIRIT

Fellowship is at the heart of Luke's portrait of the church. Its importance is shown by the prominence it is given in his summaries. Of the fourteen verses in Acts 2:43–47; 4:32–35; 5:12–16, six deal with fellowship, three with the apostles' ministry of witness and its supportive signs, and five with the impact of the Spirit's work on those outside the church. This is not to say that fellowship is more important than apostolic teaching and witness, but it does show that the church's life is more than preaching, and that the church's internal relationships affect its external testimony.

Although *fellowship* is a familiar piece of Christian jargon, we should not assume that we know what Luke means by the term. As the New Testament speaks of it, fellowship is deep, virile, and costly; too often today it is cheap and superficial. The higher we value our personal privacy and freedom from commitments, the shallower our grasp of fellowship will be— reduced to moments of idle chitchat over steaming coffee before or after a worship service.

Luke corrects our cheapened concept of fellowship. He uses the word κοινωνια only in Acts 2:42, but he offers a clue to its significance by using the related adjective close at hand: "All the believers . . . had everything *in common* [κοινος]" (v. 44 NIV). The focus of fellowship is on what believers have in common with one another, what we share with one another, putting into practice the truth that we are woven together as members of one body. Often in the New Testament, κοινωνια has financial overtones (as it does here), expressing a willingness to share tangible, material resources with other members of God's family.

Partnership in and with God's Spirit

There is, however, a treasure shared by believers in Jesus that is deeper and more valuable than dollars or denarii, a treasure that produces their willingness to part with property for the sake of their partners in God's family. Paul speaks of "the fellowship of the Holy Spirit" (2 Cor. 13:13; cf. Phil. 2:1).[7] Luke does not use these expressions—in fact, in these summaries he does not mention the Spirit by name. Yet he points to the unifying fruit of the Spirit: "All the believers were *in the same place* [επι το αυτο] . . . daily devoting themselves *with one accord* [ομοθυμαδον] in the temple courts. . . . They were *partaking* food *together* [μεταλαμβανω] in celebration and sincerity of heart" (Acts 2:44, 46).[8] "The heart and soul of the crowd of believers were *one*" (4:32). "They were all *with one accord* [ομοθυμαδον] in Solomon's Colonnade" (5:12). The Spirit's coming marked the reversal of the centrifugal momentum of proud humanity's dispersion from Babel. God now regathers scattered exiles from earth's ends and reforges them into his new international family, united not by coercion (as Rome attempted), but by his Spirit of grace, and not for human fame, but for God's glory. People "cut to the heart" over their complicity in the death of Jesus the Lord (2:36–37) call on the name of this Lord (2:21, 38) and are restored to harmony not only with God but also with each other. Luke's repeated references to believers' "togetherness" and unity of heart exemplify what Paul calls "the fellowship of the Spirit."

Hindrances to Spirit-Given Fellowship

Only a powerful magnetic force could draw and hold such a diverse group of people together. Already at this early point, the church mirrored to some extent the diversity of peoples in the Roman world. Although they were Jewish in faith (and most—but not all—were Jewish by descent), cultur-ally they no doubt reflected to some extent the various peoples among whom they had lived (Acts 2:9–11). Tensions between Greek speakers from the Dispersion and Palestinian-born Aramaic speakers would soon arise (6:1).

The early church's setting was no more congenial to a commitment to Christian community than is ours. Are our schedules too full to fit in some fellowship that is more than skin-deep? Jesus had warned his own genera-tion that "the worry of this age and the deceitfulness of wealth" could choke out initial interest in God's kingdom (Matt. 13:22). Even among Paul's col-leagues, some felt the allure of the surrounding culture, pulling them away from Christ's community: "Demas abandoned me, having fallen in love with the present age" (2 Tim. 4:10).

Would "excessive" involvement in the church bring criticism and pres-sure from those who can make us squirm (family, friends, employers)? Jesus warned that a shallow interest in the Word, which wilts under the heat of opposition, is rootless and fruitless (Matt. 13:21). In the early church too, some had formed a habit of neglecting to meet together (Heb. 10:25), pos-sibly under the mounting pressure of persecution (Heb. 12:3–13).

Are the needs of other people so troublesome that we would prefer to keep them at arm's length? This too is no new excuse: "If anyone has earthly goods, sees his brother in need, and closes his heart against him, how can God's love abide in him?" (1 John 3:17). "If a brother or sister has no clothing and lacks daily food and one of you says to them, 'Go in peace; stay warm and eat well,' but does not give them what their bodies need, what good is it?" (James 2:15–16). Some were as reluctant to "get involved" then as we are now.

The Surprising, Deep Fellowship That Grace Creates

The point is this: It was *not* easier in the first century than it is in the twen-tieth to come together and stay together in genuine Christian community. There were no fewer distractions and no fewer temptations toward selfish, aloof individualism, protective of one's privacy. Yet the early church was a gathering of people who rejoiced to be together consistently, to eat, share, and serve together. What force bound them to each other? The grace of God. "And great grace was upon them all" (Acts 4:33).

By the grace of God, they had been born into the family that could call God "Father" (Luke 11:2). How could they not, then, treat each other as brothers and sisters (whatever their previous lineage)? Luke calls the followers of Jesus "the brothers" 25 times in Acts[9]—more often than he calls them "the disciples" (23 times), "the church" (22), "the believers" (5), or "the saints" (4). Luke wants us to understand that the familial bond uniting believers to one another is of utmost importance to the identity of Christ's church and to our identity as individual members. Delight over belonging to the family of God evokes a joyful eagerness to be with and share with new siblings. Luke may not use the verbs (αγαπαω, φιλεω) and nouns (αγαπη, φιλαδελφια) expressing "love" and "brotherly love" as other New Testament writers do,[10] but he shows us Christian brotherly love in action.

The Breaking of the Bread

Because Christian fellowship is fellowship in the Spirit of God, among its activities are "the breaking of the bread and the prayers" (Acts 2:42). Luke's reference to *"the* bread" [του αρτου, with the definite article] suggests that he is referring not to the meals that believers often shared together,[11] but to the Lord's Supper, established by Jesus as a memorial and sign of his redemptive death (Luke 22:14–20; 1 Cor. 11:23–26). It was "in the breaking of the bread" (τη κλασει του αρτου, as in Acts 2:42) that the risen Lord Jesus revealed himself to two downcast disciples at Emmaus (Luke 24:34; cf. vv. 30–31). Luke later records that the church at Troas gathered on the first day of the week for the purpose of breaking bread (Acts 20:7).[12]

No doubt the special ritual of the Lord's Supper was observed in the context of normal meals that Christians enjoyed together (Acts 2:46).[13] But the breaking of the bread and the drinking of the cup had been invested by Jesus with special significance as signs of his sacrificial death as the Servant of the Lord, "poured out for many" (Isa. 53:12). The bread and cup celebrate and commemorate the establishment of the New Covenant (Jer. 31:31–34), and the echo of Exodus 24[14] suggests that the new meal, like the covenant meal at Sinai, is eaten in the presence of the God of Israel himself.

> Moses and Aaron and Nadab and Abihu, and the seventy elders of Israel, went up and saw the place where the God of Israel was standing. Under his feet was like a pavement made of sapphire, its appearance like the firmament of heaven in purity. And not one of these chosen ones of Israel perished. They were seen in the place of God, and they ate and drank. (Ex. 24:9–11)[15]

Paul affirms that the Lord's Supper is "a fellowship [κοινωνια] in the blood of Christ" and the body of Christ (1 Cor. 10:16), but Christ is not merely the slain sacrifice whose blood seals the covenant bond. He is the Lord who offers the cup, the host who welcomes dinner guests into his table fellowship (vv. 21–22). Thus, the breaking of the bread focuses on the center and source of Christian fellowship/partnership/community, the redemptive death of Christ and his presence as the risen Lord among his people through the Holy Spirit.

The Prayers

"The prayers" also exhibited the heart of Christian fellowship in the presence of God's Spirit. Jewish believers continued to gather with the rest of Israel to offer praise and prayer in the temple (Acts 2:46; 3:1). Their devotion to prayer was more than traditional Jewish piety. The distributed flames of God's Spirit of glory marked out the people of Jesus as the new sanctuary, the new house of prayer for all nations (2:3; Isa. 56:7). Because Jesus was present and active among them, they could pray to him to select an apostle to complete the number of the tribal heads of a renewed Israel (Acts 1:24). When confronted by human threats, they could appeal to God, who made human hostility serve his own purposes in the suffering and glory of his Servant, Jesus (4:25–30). The presence of his Holy Spirit emboldened their proclamation of his word (4:31). The church naturally and instinctively reacted to crises and decisions through prayer, showing that the unifying center of their fellowship was communion with God in the Spirit.

The Fellowship in Finances

Pentecost's converts were united by their sharing in the Spirit given by the risen Lord Jesus, but in Acts 2:42, when Luke speaks of "the fellowship" to which they devoted themselves, he is pointing directly to their readiness to treat their possessions as community property, to be used wherever needs arose in the family of God. When the Spirit blows, "you hear its sound" (John 3:8); and in the life of the early church, the observable evidence of the Spirit's presence was a willingness to share financial resources with sisters and brothers in need.

This tangible dimension of fellowship is often prominent when the New Testament uses the noun κοινωνια and the verb κοινωνεω. In Philippians 1:5, for instance, the NIV rightly translates κοινωνια as "partnership," for, like our English word partnership, κοινωνια has financial overtones in Philippians. The Philippians' contribution, for which Paul thanked them plainly in the epistle's closing, was an investment in his gospel proclamation that made them partners in that great project.[16] From the earliest time of their Christian life ("the early days of your acquaintance with the gospel,"

Phil. 4:15; "the first day," 1:5), they "shared with [κοινωνεω]" Paul "in the matter of giving and receiving" (4:15). Christian κοινωνια involves not only investments of time and attention, but also investments of dollars and cents, drachmae and denarii, pounds and shillings, marks, shekels, etc.[17] In Acts 2:42, Luke stresses the financial price tag of Christian partnership, for his commentary on "they devoted themselves to . . . partnership" is found two verses later: the believers "had everything in common [κοινος[18]], and they were selling their properties and possessions and distributing them as anyone had need" (Acts 2:44–45).

Christian Communalism?

These passages in Acts have been taken by some as a pattern for mandatory economic communalism. To join certain Christian communities requires relinquishing one's possessions to the leaders, who administer the group's common budget. This is not, however, what happened in the early church in Jerusalem. Luke makes it plain that wealthier Christians sold lands and houses to care for those in need *as needs arose* (Acts 2:45; 4:34–35). Peter's rebuke to Ananias makes it clear that the liquidation of one's property was not a requirement for church membership: "Could it not have remained in your possession? After it was sold, were not the proceeds still within your authority [to use as you wished]?" (5:4). Unlike the Qumran community, Christians did not withdraw from the cities into monastic enclaves with a common purse; rather, they stayed in the society, where their daily lives were observed by all.[19] First Timothy 6:17–18 shows that later in the first century the church still included "people who are rich in this present age," whom Timothy was to teach to use their wealth generously. Paul's instructions to Timothy presuppose that individual members of the church had the freedom and authority to make decisions regarding the use of their financial resources. Submitting all one's assets to a "common purse" administered by church leaders was not the New Testament norm.

We should not, however, take comfort too quickly in the fact that this New Testament evidence tends to confirm a "right" of private property, over against enforced collectivism by church or state. To be sure, converting one's personal possessions into common property, held in partnership with other believers, was not a requirement for entrance into Jesus' holy community. But Luke's definition of fellowship challenges our attitude toward, and use of, private property. One tangible example of the Spirit's renewal in the early Christians was their *attitude* of partnership, their *bias toward sharing* with needy Christians. Their instinctive expression of family love

was to give over their own resources into the service of others; and this reaction displayed the grace that "was upon them all" (Acts 4:33).

In some ways, mandatory communalism would be easier. Enforcement
would be more feasible, since compliance could be monitored by external
observation. While the leaders (if they were conscientious) would feel a
heavy responsibility to administer the group's resources equitably and com-
passionately, for the average member pure communalism would simplify
struggles of conscience over money and what it can buy. Having turned over
their money to the leaders, members could turn over the hard decisions as
well: "How much is enough? How do I weigh my family's needs against
those of others? Should I save prudently or give to the poor until there is
no more to give?"

Acts, however, points to a more difficult form of financial fellowship,
which probes our motives and never lets us shift responsibility to others.
The concepts of enforcement and compliance don't fit into Luke's portrait,
for the generosity he extols is prompted not by external coercion or peer
pressure, but by the inner compulsion of grateful love. This focus on heart
attitude has its dangers, to be sure.[20] Hypocrisy, pride, and a pinched and
calculating spirit are constant threats. Compassion can be counterfeited,
either in a boldfaced lie such as Ananias's and Sapphira's (see below) or in
the subtle self-deception that talks "faith" and "love," but turns a closed
heart toward needy sisters and brothers (1 John 3:17; James 2:15–16).

In its preoccupation with heart attitudes, Luke's portrait of early Christian κοινωνια is a discomforting challenge to economically comfortable
Christians, relentlessly probing our motives. When confronted with another person's need, is our first impulse to help or to edge away, to find a
way to meet the need or to find an excuse for avoiding involvement? When
brothers and sisters are in need, the normal response of people touched by
God's Spirit is to share together as members of a family do. How normal is
the evangelical church today?

Luke sums up the result of the Christian sense of family partnership:
"There was not even a needy person among them" (Acts 4:34). His words
deliberately echo the Lord's ancient promise of blessing toward Israel, if Israel were to prove faithful:

> There will not be a needy person among you, for the Lord your God
> will greatly bless you in the land that the Lord your God is giving
> you to inherit as your portion, if you listen intently to the voice of
> the Lord your God, to keep and to do all these commands that I
> am commanding you today (Deut. 15:4–5).[21]

This promise assured Israel of God's blessing in material prosperity if Israel proved faithful to the Lord and his law (see Deut. 28:1–14; Mal. 3:8–12). Israel disobeyed and received curse rather than blessing, but now God's promise of a blessing that erases want is coming to fulfillment in the church, not through abundant harvests, but through open hearts. The fulfillment of God's promise through hearts turned inside out, from protective selfishness to risky liberality, is a more marvelous work of God than ample rainfall and bumper crops from Palestinian soil would have been. The practical κοινωνια in the church is the *fruit* of the Spirit who removes the curse, making dry ground fertile once again.[22]

Financial Fellowship in a Global Dimension

The church's financial partnership to meet physical needs was not limited to a local setting, where the needs of brothers and sisters could be seen by all. When prophets at Antioch in Syria announced a coming famine, the response in that predominantly Gentile church was immediate: "Insofar as any of the disciples had financial means, each designated [an amount] for ministry, to send it to the brothers living in Judea" (Acts 11:29). Their gift illustrates the logic of mutual fellowship in God's gifts that Paul explained in connection with a later collection of Gentile contributions for needy Jewish believers: "For since the Gentiles have become partners [κοινωνεω] in the Jewish saints' spiritual things, they in turn should serve [Jewish believers] in material things" (Rom. 15:27). Spiritual life had come to the Gentiles through Israel, through the gospel of Jesus the Messiah. How fitting it was, then, that believing Gentiles acknowledge their debt by giving to sustain the physical life of their spiritual benefactors! Across the miles and the differences between Jew and Gentile, there was an exchange of God's gifts in fellowship, a circulatory system of grace in the body of Christ, as its members met each other's needs through all the resources that God had showered on his people.

This international dimension of the early church's fellowship in material resources calls us to lift our eyes and to see ourselves as part of the whole church. On the one hand, we need the gifts that Christ has given to the church in other parts of the world; on the other hand, we are accountable for our stewardship of resources that we enjoy in abundance, which are needed by other parts of the body in other corners of the earth. These resources are not only material wealth and what it can accomplish, but also such riches as opportunities for pastoral training and biblical education for all the people of God. When we learn to think, pray, and care for the family of God globally, what needs of unseen brothers and sisters will we discover and hurry to fill?

THE SPIRIT'S FELLOWSHIP SCORNED

The sobering account of Ananias and Sapphira strikes a sour note in Luke's otherwise upbeat account of the church's earliest days. The severity of their punishment offends many modern scholars, who vent their resentment either on Luke the storyteller or (if they accept the historicity of the incident) on Peter, the inflexibly authoritarian apostle. Is this an outburst of the old Simon Peter, who sheathed his sword only because of Jesus' stern rebuke (John 18:10–11)?

Such suspicions show how far our thinking is from the New Testament's sense of the terrifying holiness of God. If the deaths of Ananias and Sapphira shock us, we ourselves may have fallen into their sin!

The nature of their sin must be grasped in order to understand the severity of their punishment and the message of this somber incident. We have seen that mandatory collectivism was not the norm in the church in Acts, and so Ananias's sin was not simply a refusal to relinquish control over his finances to the apostles. Nor was it simple greed. Rather, the issue is one of integrity in the very presence of the God of truth, who searches hearts. Ananias failed to realize that where the Spirit is, God is—God, the consuming fire, who destroys deception on contact.

Luke shows us Ananias's and Sapphira's intent to deceive even before we read Peter's indictment in Acts 5:3–4. Barnabas's gift (4:36–37) is an introduction to the incident of Ananias and Sapphira, as well as an illustration of the preceding summary (in vv. 32–35).[23] The parallel between Barnabas and Ananias is unmistakable: both sold (πωλεω) property (αγρος, κτημα) and brought (ηνεγκα, aorist of φερω) an amount of money (χρημα, τιμη/μερος) and placed (τιθημι) it at the apostles' feet (προς/παρα τους ποδας των αποστολων). Barnabas was recognized by the apostles as a "son of encouragement,"[24] and the reader infers that Ananias's motive was to gain similar recognition.

There was, however, one crucial difference between Barnabas and Ananias. Barnabas, out of a heart set on serving others, gave the full purchase price of his property. Ananias, performing his deed of mercy for human eyes (Matt. 6:2–4), brought part of his profit, claiming it was the whole. He "pilfered part of the money" (Acts 5:2). Luke's choice of the verb *pilfer* (νοσφιζομαι, also in v. 3), points back to the only passage in the Greek Old Testament in which νοσφιζομαι appears: the account of the sin of Achan, who "pilfered" some of the things devoted to the Lord at the destruction of Jericho (Josh. 7:1).[25] Achan embezzled from his Master, secreting away for himself some of the spoils of war that the Lord, Israel's champion, had claimed for himself. In so doing, Achan showed his contempt not only for the knowledge of the Lord (thinking to deceive the Searcher of hearts), but also for the holiness of the Lord (daring to touch what was devoted to the Lord, to be consumed to purge the land from pagan pollutions). Through his scorn for the God of Israel, Achan defiled Israel. Consequently, when Israel's soldiers advanced against the tiny town of Ai, expecting easy triumph, their holy champion displayed his displeasure by turning them back in defeat (Josh. 7:12). When Achan's sin was uncovered, he and his household had to be treated as things devoted to the Lord for destruction—not only stoned, but also consumed in flames (vv. 15, 25–26).

The verb νοσφιζομαι is only one of the links between Achan and Ananias. In both cases, the withholding of wealth belonging to the Lord brought the punishment of death. But had Ananias, in fact, imitated Achan's sin of embezzling the Lord's property? Did Peter not say that the property and its proceeds were under Ananias's authority, to do with as he chose? The central sin, the crucial parallel that makes Ananias a replica of Achan, then, is their deception. When Ananias claimed, in the presence of the Holy Spirit, who indwells Christ's church, that he was offering to God the entire sum of money he had received for his property, that whole amount became the Lord's possession. Ananias and Sapphira precisely imitated the heart of Achan's sin, scorning both the knowledge and the holiness of the Lord in the midst of his people: "You have lied to the Holy Spirit . . . not to men, but to God" (Acts 5:3–4). "Why was it agreed among you to test [πειραζω] the Spirit of the Lord?" (v. 9).[26] This couple, like their Old Testament counterpart, dared to deceive in the presence of the Holy One of Israel.

The judgment that fell immediately on Ananias and Sapphira was a sign foreshadowing the full and final judgment of deceivers at the Messiah's coming, just as the lame man's leap previewed the full resurrection healing that the Messiah will bring when he appears from heaven. Because that final day has not come, we do not yet see the full blessing and cursing to which these signs testify. Physical affliction is sometimes God's instrument to discipline and purify his people (1 Cor. 11:30–32). Physical healing may flow from the confession and forgiveness of sins (James 5:14–16). On the other hand, selfish liars may appear to go on prospering, while for humble believers adversity persists despite intense prayer, reminding them to rest in God's sufficient grace (2 Cor. 12:7–10). From the warnings of the New Testament epistles, we see that serious sins in the church did not regularly meet with instantaneous divine execution. Not everyone who profaned the temple of the Holy Spirit through sexual immorality (1 Cor. 6:15, 19), or who grieved the Spirit through bitter anger (Eph. 4:30–31), or even who lied in the Spirit's presence (v. 25) was struck dead in the early church—or today. The patience of God gives room for repentance (2 Peter 3:9). In this age of God's long-suffering, people appear to get away with big lies and small fibs without facing the immediate judgment that Ananias and Sapphira experienced. But God is not mocked: what one sows, one will eventually reap (Gal. 6:7)!

The judgment on Ananias and Sapphira, in its suddenness and severity, warns the church down through the generations. Although Luke records other miracles of judgment (Acts 9:8; 12:23; 13:11), this is the only one on people within the community of Jesus. It reminds us that the Spirit who brings joy (13:52; 8:39) also brings danger to any who would take lightly his purity and power.

The appropriate response to the burning glory of the Spirit is fear: "And great fear came on all who heard" (Acts 5:5). "Great fear came on the whole church and all who heard these things" (v. 11).[27] "Of the others, no one dared to join them, but the people magnified them" (v. 13). Fear is the appropriate response when God's presence and power are revealed in the midst of frail human beings, whether through angels (Luke 1:12; 2:9) or through the miracles of Jesus (5:8–10, 26; 7:16; 8:25; 9:34) or of the apostles (Acts 2:43). Following the Old Testament (e.g., Ps. 103:17; Prov. 1:7), Luke can sum up the whole life of faith and piety in the phrase "the fear of the Lord" (Acts 9:31; Luke 1:50).

In contrast to the abject terror evoked by some pagan conceptions of capricious and malevolent deities, the fear of the Lord is rooted in the assurance of his holiness, constancy, and justice. Those who fear the Lord rejoice in his grace, but are vividly aware that to violate his holiness is dangerous. If we feel that heartfelt joy and awestruck fear are incompatible emotions, we have not fully grasped what it means to stand in the presence of the Lord of glory, who is "good and terrible at the same time."[28]

THE HOLY COMMUNITY TODAY

How things have changed, you may be thinking. Foreign to many churches today is the vibrant fellowship with God that we have observed in Acts: the joy, the confident expectation of prayer answered, the tangible expression of family care, the fear in the face of the awful holiness of God. But what has really changed? I see indications in the New Testament that the miraculous signs of blessing and cursing, foretastes of full and final healing and judgment at Jesus' return, had their proper place in the ministry of the apostles. But the heart of Luke's description of Jesus' holy community should be seen in every church in every generation.

If we do not see in our churches the fellowship of the Spirit, drawing diverse people together into a family of God, eager to share with one another —food, time, funds, encouragement—what has changed? It could be as simple as this: We have *lost sight of the church* as God shows it to be in Acts. It is easy to lapse into viewing the church in terms of its externals— organizational routine and structure—and to think of our fellow members only in terms of their aggravating habits and frustrating failures. When little seems to be happening in the church, when nothing seems to change, it becomes easy to expect little or nothing to change.

But God challenges us to "fix our gaze not on what is seen, but on what is unseen" (2 Cor. 4:18). What would happen if, in the face of all the "evidence" that our senses present, we took God at his word when he describes his church—not free from sin's infection yet, but on the way to healing through the presence of his Spirit? How would the church look different if we recognized and treated that obnoxious or needy member as a sister or brother, bound together with us forever in the love of the family of God? What healing would result if, acutely aware that we stand in the presence of the One who searches hearts, we were to drop façades and "speak truth to each other" as members of one body (Eph. 4:25)? Changes in the way we treat one another in the community of Christ flow from changes in the way we see each other—and our ability to see the holy presence of Christ the Lord among us.

Notes

[1] On the Day of Atonement, the scapegoat, symbolically carrying Israel's guilt, was banished into a solitary, deserted place (Lev. 16:20–22).

[2] F. C. Baur and his disciples of the "Tübingen School" in the nineteenth century alleged that Acts intentionally softens the harsh theological conflict that actually occurred between Paul and Peter concerning the place of the Gentiles and the role of the law of Moses in the church, in order to motivate the rival factions of the author's own, postapostolic era to set aside their differences and emulate the (artificially fabricated) harmony of the apostles' days. Baur's suggestions, sprinkled somewhat randomly in various essays, were developed more consistently by his disciple Albert Schwegler in his two-volume *Das nachapostolische Zeitalter in den Hauptmomenten seiner Entwicklung* [The Postapostolic Age in the Main Features of Its Development] (1846). See W. Ward Gasque, *A History of the Interpretation of the Acts of the Apostles* (Peabody, Mass.: Hendrickson, 1989), 21–54.

[3] As we saw in the first chapter, "the problem of historical precedent" is best resolved by comparing what is *described* in Acts with what is *prescribed* in the New Testament epistles.

⁴ Later summaries (6:7; 9:31; 12:24; 19:20; etc.) can be brief, since the texture of the early congregations' life together has been conveyed in the early summaries we are considering.

⁵ Luke uses a periphrastic construction (the Greek verb ησαν, "they were," plus the participle προσκαρτερουντες, "devoting"), when an imperfect form of "devote" would have said essentially the same thing. This construction emphasizes slightly the continuous character of their devotion. "Devote" (προσκαρτερεω) itself expresses the idea of consistent, long-term attention to someone (Acts 8:13; 10:7) or something. In the New Testament, prayer is often the activity to which Christians are "devoted" in long-term, concentrated commitment (Acts 1:14; 2:42; 6:4; Rom. 12:12; Col. 4:2).

⁶ Joseph A. Fitzmyer, *Luke the Theologian: Aspects of His Teaching* (New York: Paulist, 1989), 138–39, suggests that "community" is the closest English equivalent of κοινωνια in Acts 2:42.

⁷ Greek: η κοινωνια του αγιου πνευματος (2 Cor.); κοινωνια πνευματος (Phil.). In Phil. 2:1, Paul may be referring to the Spirit as our partner and the initiator of our fellowship (Gerald F. Hawthorne, *Philippians* [WBC; Waco: Word, 1983], 66; Moisés Silva, *Philippians* [Wycliffe Exegetical Commentary; Chicago: Moody, 1988], 103), or possibly to our mutual partnership with one another as recipients of the Spirit (Ralph P. Martin, *Philippians* [NCB; Grand Rapids: Eerdmans, 1976], 87).

⁸ Επι το αυτο expresses physical proximity: "in the same place" (BAG, 123) (Luke 17:35; Acts 1:15; 2:1, 47; 4:26 [quoting Ps. 2:2]). Ernst Haenchen (*The Acts of the Apostles: A Commentary* [Philadelphia: Westminster Press, 1971], 192) notes that it is an expression found frequently in the Psalms (LXX): see, e.g., 34:3 ("Magnify the Lord with me; let us exalt his name *together*"); 55:14 ("you who sweetened foods *together* with me"); 102:22 ("when the peoples were gathered *together*, and the kingdoms to serve the Lord"); 133:1 ("How good and pleasant it is when brothers dwell *together*"). Ομοθυμαδον expresses unity of purpose and intention. In Acts it refers six times to unity within the church (1:14; 2:46; 4:24; 5:12; 8:6; 15:25) and four times to the unified (hostile) purposes of non-Christian groups (7:57; 12:20; 18:12; 19:29). Its only other use in the New Testament is in Rom. 15:6: "so that *with one accord*, with one mouth you may glorify the God and Father of our Lord Jesus Christ."

⁹ Acts 1:15; 9:30; 10:23; 11:1, 12, 29; 12:17; 14:2; 15:1, 3, 22, 32, 33, 36, 40; 16:2, 40; 17:10, 14; 18:18, 27; 21:7, 17; 28:14, 15.

¹⁰ Αγαπαω does appear in Luke's gospel, but only with reference to love for enemies or God.

¹¹ See Acts 2:46, where "bread" is indefinite, lacking the article (κλωντες . . . αρτον).

¹² "Bread" in Acts 20:7 lacks the definite article, but in v. 11 it is definite: "Having gone up and broken *the* bread (κλασας τον αρτον) and tasted and spoken a long time until daybreak, in this way he departed." That this is the Lord's Supper and not a normal meal is indicated by the fact that *before* the bread was broken, Paul had already discoursed deep into the night.

¹³ Paul's correctives in 1 Cor. 11 imply that in Corinth the common meal preceded the observance of the Lord's Supper. Abuses at the common meal, such as drunkenness and the neglect of needy fellow believers, were rebuked by Paul, who came close to forbidding the common meal in order to emphasize the spiritual significance of the New Covenant memorial meal (v. 34).

¹⁴ The words "This is my blood of the covenant" (Mark 14:24; Matt. 26:28) closely resemble Moses' words in Ex. 24:8: "This is the blood of the covenant that the Lord has made with you in accordance with all these words."

¹⁵ This translation reflects the LXX translators' apparent reluctance to produce a text that stated explicitly that human beings saw God—even though that is what the Hebrew text says! So, the NIV correctly reads, "They saw God, and they ate and drank."

¹⁶ Thus, the Philippians' "partnership for the cause of [εἰς] the gospel" (1:5) was not simply their having shared in its benefits by faith, but rather their sharing in its propagation through their financial support. See Martin, *Philippians*, 65.

¹⁷ The noun κοινωνια ("fellowship, partnership") appears eighteen times in the New Testament besides Acts 2:42, and in five of these (all in Paul's letters) it is associated with the sharing of material resources. The verb κοινωνεω ("share, have partnership with") appears eight times in the New Testament, and in four (again, all in Paul) it has financial connotations. Another noun of this word group, κοινωνος, appears only once in Luke-Acts, describing James and John as Simon's "partners" in the fishing industry (Luke 5:10).

¹⁸ Note the parallel summary (with κοινος) at Acts 4:32.

¹⁹ Entry into the membership of the monastic community of Essenes at Qumran was a prolonged process. The Manual of Discipline (1QS) prescribes an initial examination, followed by a year of probation and instruction. If, after this period, a second examination is approved by the community, the applicant's "property and earnings shall be handed over to the Bursar of the Congregation who shall register it to his account and shall not spend it for the Congregation." Then, after another year of probation and a further examination, "he shall be inscribed among his brethren in the order of his rank for the Law, and for justice, and for the pure Meal; his property shall be merged and he shall offer his counsel and judgement to the Community" (1QS 6:13–23). (The translation is that of G. Vermes, *The Dead Sea Scrolls in English*, 3d ed. [London: Penguin, 1987], 70.) But the Damascus Document (CD) and other Qumran documents suggest that some Essenes who looked to Qumran for leadership nevertheless lived in Israelite towns, married, raised children, and did business with "outsiders" (Vermes, *Dead Sea Scrolls*, 9). These less pure members of the sect presumably were not included in the pooling of financial resources of the "men of holiness," who lived celibate lives of simplicity and meditation on the Torah at the Qumran settlement itself.

²⁰ Note the consistency with which Jesus and his apostles made a point of their indifference to the amount that people give to God, in view of God's focus on the hidden motive of the giver. A widow's pittance outdoes the largess of the rich, in Jesus' accounting (Luke 21:1–4). To Paul, the poverty-stricken Macedonians provide the ideal example for Corinthian giving: "For if there is a readiness [to give], [God finds the gift] acceptable in relation to what [the giver] has, not what he does not have" (2 Cor. 8:12; cf. 9:7).

²¹ The wording in Acts echoes that of the Septuagint. Acts 4:34: ουδε γαρ ενδεης τις ην εν αυτοις. Deut. 15:4 LXX: οτι ουκ εσται εν σοι ενδεης. Luke often speaks of Christ's compassion for the "poor" (πτωχος, ten times in Luke's gospel), but "needy" (ενδεης) appears only in Acts 4:34. Its single appearance here—together with the construction "not to be among you/them" (ουκ/ουδε εσται/ην εν σοι/αυτοις)—signals an allusion to Deut. 15:4.

²² Paul likewise moves from an Old Testament form of the Lord's provision for Israel to a new, Spirit-produced form in the church. In Ex. 16:18 NIV, the wisdom of the Lord's provision of manna is shown in its sufficiency without wasteful surplus: "He who gathered much did not have too much, and he who gathered little did not have too little." In 2 Cor. 8:15, Paul applies these words to the balance of resources through the Gentile churches' contributions to the church in Judea. This redistribution of resources to meet needs is not a human

plan but a divinely orchestrated distribution, for the Gentiles' gifts are the product of God's grace (2 Cor. 9:8–11).

[23] The verbs shift from the imperfect tense in the summary to the aorist tense in the account of Barnabas (4:36–37) and on through the narrative of Ananias and Sapphira (5:1–11).

[24] The relationship between the name Barnabas and its interpretation as "son of encouragement/exhortation" (υιος παρακλησεως) is not transparent. The two most probable suggestions are: (1) Barnabas is derived from נביא בר ("son of a prophet"), that is, one having a prophetic gift, an exhorter, a preacher. (2) Barnabas represents the Aramaic expression נחה בר ("son of consolation"), and reflects Joseph's supportive and encouraging character. This explanation fits Luke's characterization of Barnabas elsewhere in Acts. See especially Acts 11:23–24 NIV: "When he arrived and saw the evidence of the grace of God, he was glad and *encouraged* [παρακαλεω] them all to remain true to the Lord with all their hearts. He was a good man, full of the Holy Spirit and faith." See David J. Williams, *Acts* (Good News Commentary; San Francisco: Harper and Row, 1985), 79.

[25] Νοσφιζομαι is used only once elsewhere in the New Testament, in Titus 2:10: Slaves should not *embezzle* from their masters.

[26] Peter's words to Sapphira may allude to Israel's testing of the Lord in the wilderness through their complaints at Massah (Ex. 17:1–7) and Meribah (Num. 20:1–13). Faith in the Lord's presence with Israel is the point at issue in Ex. 17, while recognition of the Lord's holiness is the focus of Num. 20. When Jesus was tested (πειραζω) by the Devil in the wilderness (Luke 4:12), he quoted Deut. 6:16: "You shall not test (εκπειραζω) the Lord your God [Deuteronomy continues:] as you did at Massah."

[27] Likewise after Sceva's sons, having frivolously and faithlessly used Jesus' name in exorcism, received judgment: "This became known . . . and fear fell upon them all" (Acts 19:17).

[28] C. S. Lewis, *The Lion, the Witch and the Wardrobe* (New York: Macmillan, 1950), 103, describing the lion Aslan, the symbol of Christ. See also pp. 64–65. Another picture of the mingling of joy and fear is in the scene of the Rat's and the Mole's meeting with the god Pan in Kenneth Grahame's *The Wind in the Willows* (London: Methuen, 1908), chapter 7: "Then suddenly the Mole felt a great Awe fall upon him, an awe that turned his muscles to water, bowed his head, and rooted his feet to the ground. It was no panic terror —indeed he felt wonderfully at peace and happy—but it was an awe that smote and held him and, without seeing, he knew it could only mean that some august Presence was very, very near. . . . 'Rat!' he found breath to whisper, shaking. 'Are you afraid?' 'Afraid?' murmured the Rat, his eyes shining with unutterable love. 'Afraid! Of *Him*? O, never, never! And yet—and yet—O, Mole, I am afraid!' "

SIX

DIVERSITY IN UNITY

OUR KIND OF PEOPLE, ALL KINDS OF PEOPLE

"Variety is the spice of life." So we say, and in many ways it's true. Differences make life interesting: even your favorite menu will become tedious if served three times a day, seven days a week, fifty-two weeks a year. Different kinds of foods, books, friends, and experiences (travel, sports, music, art, drama, hard labor, and relaxation) bring richness to our lives.

Differences between cultures do not always produce pleasant experiences. Submerged in a culture and language foreign to our own, we may be overwhelmed by "culture shock" or, over an extended period, "culture fatigue." Everything seems strange and intimidating: words, gestures, what you eat, how you greet, traffic laws, table etiquette, clothing styles, sights, sounds, and smells. Too much variety becomes overpowering, exhausting, paralyzing.

When different kinds of people—different in language, nationality, tradition, economic status, or religious belief—rub against each other, friction is generated. Friction can heat people to the ignition point, producing misunderstandings, suspicion, prejudice, pride, anger, and even violence. We think of Arab and Jew in the Middle East, Catholic and Protestant in Ireland, black and white in South Africa, and black, white, Hispanic, and Asian in North America.

Christ's church is no stranger to the heat of culture friction. Although the Spirit of Jesus is creating a holy community in which believers readily part with their property to relieve each other's need, the renovation of our attitudes and behavior is far from complete. The counterfeit compassion

87

of Ananias and Sapphira proved that paradise had not yet arrived. Even genuine believers grumbled about each other when some widows' daily needs were overlooked, so that a practice that should have displayed Christian unity threatened to disrupt that unity (Acts 6:1). The cultural boundary between two kinds of people, "Grecian Jews" and "Hebraic Jews," was the crack that could have become a chasm.

These two groups had much in common: (1) Both were Jewish.[1] Together they confessed that the God of Israel is the only true and living God. (2) Both were Christian. Together they confessed that Jesus is the Messiah, the Son of God, who died and was raised to redeem people from sin and death. (3) Both shared in the great outpouring of the Spirit by which Jesus imparts his resurrection power to all who trust in him. With these shared convictions and experiences, the unity of this Christian community had a lot going for it. But an inefficient grocery delivery system—a minor problem like a speck of sand in a hiking boot—became the irritant that could have split the church.

These early Christians found, however, that the differences that threaten division can be God's prod to look beyond oneself, beyond the circle of "our kind of people," to see the rich diversity of people "from every nation, tribe, people, and language," being woven by the Spirit into a multicolored, many-textured tapestry (Rev. 7:9–10). If we try to keep the peace by filtering out folks who are not "like-minded," or who will not or cannot adjust themselves to our comfort zone, then the artificial and superficial unity that results will rest on the shifting sands of culture, tradition, and familiarity. God has a way of unsettling this comfortable "fellowship," challenging us to pursue the real thing instead: "He himself is our peace, who made both [Jew and Gentile] become one, dismantling the dividing wall, the enmity, in his flesh . . . in order to create the two [Jew and Gentile] into one new man in himself, making peace, and to reconcile both [Jew and Gentile] to God in one body through the cross, by which he killed the enmity" (Eph. 2:14–16).

The friction that results when different kinds of people have contact with each other is an inevitable by-product when churches try to be faithful to the Great Commission. A church that only touches "our kind of people" (in language, culture, social status, and background) is a shrunken distortion of Christ's "holy *catholic* [universal] church."

The crucial question is, How will we handle the friction? Luke's commentary on the early church's wrestling with these issues points the way. Luke traces the skillful strategy of the all-wise God, who solved a food problem among Jewish Christians in Jerusalem in a way that spread the word of Jesus out from Jerusalem, north to Samaria, west to the coastal towns, northeast to Damascus, northwest to Antioch, and on across the great sea to distant lands at "the ends of the earth."

THE SEVEN SERVERS

Diverse Kinds of Diversity

Several types of diversity among people are important to Luke's narrative of the Seven Servers (Acts 6:1–7).[2] Most obvious is the difference in language between "Hellenists" and "Hebrews." Although both groups were Jewish in heritage and faith (and, to a large extent, in genealogical descent from the patriarchs), Hellenists were used to thinking and speaking in Greek, while Hebrews normally spoke a Palestinian Semitic language, Hebrew or Aramaic.[3]

Many Hellenistic Jews had originally been part of the Dispersion, the "scattering" of Israelites outside Palestine that had begun with the Assyrian and Babylonian conquests in earlier centuries. Even Jews who lived in Palestine were influenced by Hellenism (the spread of the Greek language and culture),[4] but Jews living among the Gentile peoples elsewhere in the Roman Empire were immersed in Greek language and lifestyle daily. Dispersion Jews constantly confronted the questions, What are the limits of involvement in Hellenistic culture for a Jew who seeks to be faithful to God's covenant? How much must Gentiles change their lifestyle if they wish to join us in service to our God? How does a Jew or a proselyte worship the Lord while living far from the temple in Jerusalem?

Although Dispersion Jews spoke Greek, they were divided among themselves regarding the other cultural influences of Hellenism. Some (such as Philo of Alexandria) tried to build bridges to Greek thought and find common ground with their Gentile neighbors. For Philo, this involved interpreting the Torah according to the categories of Neoplatonic philosophy. Other Dispersion Jews zealously maintained Judaism's distance from the pagan world, opposing all compromise with Greek culture.[5] This group would have included the parents of Saul of Tarsus, who were Hebraic Jews, and who brought him to Jerusalem for rabbinical training, although they had lived in Tarsus of Cilicia and possessed Roman citizenship (Phil. 3:5; Acts 22:3, 28). Stephen's opponents, whose zeal for temple and Torah led to their accusations and execution of Stephen, were Jews from the Dispersion—from Cyrene and Alexandria in northern Africa and from Cilicia and Asia in Asia Minor (Acts 6:9). While jealously defending the

traditions of the fathers, such Greek-speaking Jews would have found it difficult to worship and receive instruction in Hebrew or Aramaic, so they
had their own synagogues even in Jerusalem itself.[6]

This division of language and culture within Judaism was carried over
into the church. By this time, believers in Jesus numbered in the thousands,
and official persecution made their large gatherings in the temple courts
difficult.[7] No doubt some of the many house churches in which the Christians met daily carried on their instruction in Hebrew or Aramaic, while
others used Greek. It is little wonder, then, that some house groups were
overlooked as food was distributed to widows in need.

Acts 6 also reveals a diversity of need and ministry in the church. After
Pentecost, the presence of God's Spirit in the church not only reconciled
people to God through the gospel, but also reconciled believers to each
other and filled them with a commitment to fellowship. As a result, material needs were met through the grateful generosity of more affluent
Christians. Christ's saving work not only overcomes the alienation between
sinful humans and the holy God, but also sets in motion antidotes to the
"toxic waste" of that alienation—financial want, sickness, sorrow, suffering, hostility, and death. Although these two aspects of God's salvation and
the church's ministry cannot be separated from each other, the apostles recognized that they had to be distinguished from each other. Therefore, each
ministry of God's grace was entrusted to leaders who could give it their un-
divided attention.

Consequently, the apostles spoke of two types of ministry, applying related words to both: "*serve* tables" (διακονειν, Acts 6:2) and "*service* of the
word" (διακονια, 6:4). Whether meeting the physical hunger of widows
or the spiritual hunger for the word, leadership in the church is the work
of servants, "for even the Son of Man did not come to *be served*, but to *serve*
[διακονεω]" (Mark 10:45). Gifts of God's Spirit equip believers to serve others, whether through spoken words that declare God's truth or through serving deeds that display God's compassion (1 Peter 4:10–11). Thus, in Acts
6, public recognition is given to a second group of leaders alongside the
apostles, so that each area of need in the ever-growing church receives the
attention it warrants.[8]

God's Gateway to Diverse Peoples

The Seven Servers are God's gateway for the gospel to even more diverse
peoples. Luke skillfully emphasizes this theme:

(1) In the list of the Servers (v. 5), emphasis is placed on the first and
the last by the addition of descriptions. Stephen, the first on the list, is

described as a man "full of faith and of the Holy Spirit," and the aptness of his description will become evident in the account that follows. Through Stephen's Holy Spirit–full witness, the church will be pried loose from the temple and Jerusalem itself. Nicolas, the last named, is described in two significant terms: "a proselyte" and "an Antiochene."[9] He is a foretaste of things to come: (a) He is a proselyte, a Gentile who converted to the Jewish faith before believing the message of the Messiah— a foretaste of the Gentiles at the ends of the earth. (b) His home city is Antioch in Syria, which will be the site of the first Gentile church mentioned by Luke (11:19–21) and the sending point of Paul's Gentile mission to the West (13:1–3).

(2) These seven are not only compassionate servants of widows, but also the vanguard of the gospel's invasion into Gentile territory. Echoes of Numbers 27 in Acts 6:1–7 suggest a parallel between the appointment of Joshua as Moses' successor and that of Stephen and his fellow servants.

(a) The unusual use of ἐπισκέπτομαι in the apostles' instruction to the church, "*Choose*, brothers, seven men attested [by others], full of the Spirit and wisdom," recalls Moses' prayer, "Let the Lord, the God of spirits and of all flesh, *choose* [ἐπισκέπτομαι] a man over this assembly" (Num. 27:16 LXX).[10] This word choice is noteworthy because Luke typically uses other word groups to express choice and selection (ἐκλέγομαι, Acts 1:2, 24; χειρο-τονέω, 14:23). The Lord's answer to Moses' prayer is Joshua, just as the Lord's answer to the church's need in Acts 6 is the appointment of the Seven.

(b) Joshua is qualified to succeed Moses because "he has *the Spirit* in himself" (Num. 27:18); similarly, the Seven must be men "full of *the Spirit*" (Acts 6:3).

(c) Joshua was set apart for his leadership when Moses *laid his hands on him* (Num. 27:23); likewise, the Seven were set apart as the apostles *laid hands on them* with prayer (Acts 6:6).[11]

Through these points of contact with the story of Joshua's appointment, the reader who knows the Old Testament is alerted to expect that the Seven, like Joshua, will take the lead in carrying God's dominion into new, Gentile territory. Joshua led Israel *into* the Canaanite territory of Palestine, a land full of spiritual pollution (Gen. 15:16; Lev. 18:27–28), but promised to Israel as their inheritance. Under Joshua, this land was purged to become God's holy territory. Now the Seven Servers lead as God's new Israel is scattered out of Jerusalem *into* Judea and Samaria and, through Antioch, to the ends of the earth. They will carry the conquering light of God's kingdom into the regions of Gentile darkness, claiming the whole earth as God's holy territory.

STEPHEN, OPENING THE DOOR OF
GOSPEL DISPERSION

Despite the brevity of his ministry, Stephen was the most prominent of the Seven. Not only is he first in Luke's list and one of only two to receive further description, but also his description shows him to be a prime exemplar of the leadership qualifications set forth by the apostles: "full of the Spirit and wisdom." Stephen was "full of faith and of the Holy Spirit" (Acts 6:5), but also "full of grace and power" (v. 8)—indeed, so powerful in his witness that his opponents could not withstand "the wisdom and the Spirit with which he was speaking" (v. 10). In fact, his preaching anticipated the spread of the gospel into the Gentile world, for his opponents were Dispersion Jews from northern Africa (Cyrene, Alexandria) and Turkey (Cilicia, Asia) (v. 9).

Stephen's speech (Acts 7:2–53) makes him a central figure, not only among the Seven, but also in the book of Acts as a whole. It is unique among the samples of Christian preaching reported by Luke. The longest address in Acts, it contains only one mention of Jesus, a veiled reference to the "Righteous One" (v. 52). It abounds in references to the Old Testament, yet omits the messianic testimonia quoted in the other sermons (e.g., Ps. 16:8–11; Acts 2:25–31; 13:35). Its indictment of Israel's rebellion, past and present, leads not to a call for repentance and a promise of forgiveness, as in other sermons (Acts 2:38; 3:19; cf. 5:31), but to a pronouncement of condemnation reminiscent of the ancient prophets' oracles of doom.

Yet Stephen's message played a pivotal role in the spread of salvation to the ends of the earth. Through the persecution provoked by Stephen's witness, the Lord scattered other witnesses, bearing good news, out through Judea and Samaria in the second stage of the church's development (Acts 8:4).[12] Stephen's message also anticipated Paul's later confrontations with Jewish audiences (13:44–48; 28:23–28). Most importantly, Stephen's speech laid the theological foundation for the dispersion of the believers, the scattering of the New Israel.

The Assault on Temple and Torah

Stephen's speech was a response to the accusations that had been made against him. It was alleged that he had spoken "blasphemous words against Moses and against God" (Acts 6:11), and words "against this holy place and against the law" (6:13), claiming that Jesus "will destroy this place and change the customs Moses handed down to us" (6:14). In each case we see the same two accusations: Stephen was challenging the permanence of the *temple* and of the *Torah*.

Although geographical distance from Jerusalem made the local syna-gogue the site of most Jews' weekly practice of their faith, the temple con-tinued to be the true center of Judaism until its destruction in A.D. 70. In the synagogues, the Torah was taught and prayer was offered each Sabbath, but only in the Jerusalem temple could legitimate sacrifices be offered, for only in Jerusalem had the Lord caused his Name to dwell (Deut. 12:5-7, 11-14; 1 Kings 8:27-30). Among the most heinous crimes that the Seleu-cid king Antiochus IV (175-163 B.C.) committed against Judaism was his order to offer sacrifices of swine to idolatrous images erected in the temple in Jerusalem, provoking the Maccabean liberation movement. With An-tiochus's "abomination of desolation" (167 B.C.) and a later desecration of the temple by the Roman general Pompey (63 B.C.) fresh in Jewish mem-ories, it is understandable that Jesus' announcement that the temple would be destroyed (Mark 13:2) was seized upon by his accusers as blasphemous treason against the God of Israel (14:58; see John 2:19-20).

The Torah was even more fundamental to Jewish experience and prac-tice. As the disclosure of the Lord's will for his chosen people, it was Is-rael's "life" (Deut. 32:46-47; Rom. 7:10; cf. 2:17-20). A tractate in the Mishnah (a collection of rabbinical teachings compiled around A.D. 200) compares the law to a "medicine of life," which, like a plaster on a wound, protects the Israelites from the infection of their evil inclination (*Kiddushim* 30b). Supplementing the written Torah, at least for the Pharisees, was the oral law, an ongoing accumulation of traditions concerning the applica-tion of the law to the changing conditions of Jewish life. Jesus' correction of and disregard for rabbinical tradition led his opponents to charge him with advocating disregard for the law itself (Mark 2:24).

The God Who Travels and the People Who Spurn Their Savior

Stephen's speech addressed both of the charges that had been leveled against him. In response to the implication that his announcement of the temple's impending destruction was a blasphemous attack on God, Stephen surveyed Israel's history to demonstrate that the Lord's presence with his people was not limited to Mt. Zion, Jerusalem, or even the land of promise. The God of glory appeared to Abraham in Mesopotamia (Acts 7:2), was "with Joseph" in Egypt (v. 9), and sent his angel to Moses in the Sinai desert (vv. 30, 38, 44)—declaring the site of the burning bush to be *"holy land"* (γη αγια, v. 33). Although at last Solomon built a "house" for the Lord,

Stephen paraphrased Solomon's dedicatory prayer in his statement that "the Most High does not live in houses made by men" (vv. 47–50; cf. 1 Kings 8:27).

Israelite history was full of comings and goings from the Land of Promise, from the time that Abraham "went out from the land of the Chaldeans" to Haran, and from there relocated to "this land in which [Stephen's accusers] now live" (εξερχομαι, μετοικιζω, Acts 7:4). Abraham's arrival in the land was not really a homecoming, for "God gave him no inheritance in it, not even a footstep," but only a promise of future possession by Abraham's descendants—although he was childless (v. 5). After suffering as an "alien in a foreign land" (παροικον εν γη αλλοτρια), Abraham's seed would come out (εξερχομαι, vv. 6–7). And, in fact, Moses, after being an "alien in the land of Midian" (παροικος εν γη Μιδιαμ, v. 29), did later lead them out (εξαγω, vv. 36, 40). Joseph was sold into Egypt (v. 9), to which Jacob sent out his other sons when famine struck (εξαποστελλω, v. 12) and came himself in response to Joseph's summons (καταβαινω, v. 15). Upon his death, Jacob and his sons were transported back to the land for burial in the tomb that Abraham had purchased (further testimony to their tenuous residence in the land) (μετατιθημι, v. 16). Even before rehearsing the fathers' being led into the land with Joshua (εισαγω, v. 45), Stephen introduced a prophetic citation foretelling the exile, when God would "transport you beyond Babylon" (μετοικιζω, v. 43, citing Amos 5:27). God's presence with the fathers as they entered and exited the land, making holy even the wilderness of their sojourning, should have convinced Stephen's accusers that God's presence among his people cannot be confined to one "holy place" (land, city, or temple) on this earth.

To the charge that he had opposed Moses, God's chosen leader and lawgiver, Stephen answered that it was not he but his accusers who had fallen into the pattern so typical of their ancestors, rejecting the deliverer sent by God. Previous generations had repudiated Joseph (Acts 7:9) and Moses (vv. 22, 27, 35, 39), through whom God preserved life and gave liberty. They had persecuted the prophets who announced the righteous Rescuer to come (v. 52). Now this generation, proud to have the law but refusing to keep it, had killed the Righteous One,[13] to whom the prophets pointed (vv. 52–53). So it was Stephen's opponents who failed to follow the law of Moses. They were the rebellious, the stiff-necked, the uncircumcised in heart of whom Moses had spoken (Ex. 32:9; 33:3, 5; Lev. 26:41). Moses stands preeminent among the prophets who predicted the coming righteous Servant, as Peter had declared (Acts 3:23–26; cf. John 5:45–56). Therefore, only Stephen and those like him who listened to Jesus were heeding Moses.

Stephen's overview of Israelite history, with its attention to the themes of the locale of worship and the leaders appointed by God, provides a theological transition in the narrative of Acts to the dispersion of the church among the Gentile nations. Soon persecution would bar most Christians (certainly the Hellenistic wing of the church) from access to the temple on Mt. Zion in Jerusalem.[14] In the Old Testament, such a scattering was God's curse against rebellious people, excluding them from his presence and his land (Deut. 28:64; Ezek. 36:19).[15] But with the saving achievement of the Messiah Jesus, Herod's temple had become obsolete. Exclusion from the edifice that dominated Zion was no longer exclusion from the courts of the Lord, for Jesus was the new temple as well as the final Deliverer.[16] The tongues of fire, miniature glory-clouds, resting on each disciple of Jesus at Pentecost, sealed the presence of the Spirit of glory and of God wherever believers might be scattered (see 1 Peter 4:14).[17] The God who was with Abraham in Mesopotamia, with Joseph in Egypt, and with Moses in the Sinai goes with his scattered messengers.

The Light Dispersed to Antioch

As Luke's narrative unfolds, the truth of Stephen's insight is revealed: The living God is not locked inside Herod's stone sanctuary on Mt. Zion, but rather travels with his scattered messengers. One example:

> Those who had been scattered from the affliction that arose over Stephen made their way as far as Phoenicia, Cyprus, and Antioch, speaking the word to no one but Jews. But there were some of them, men from Cyprus and Cyrene, who, having come to Antioch, were speaking also to Greeks. . . . And the Lord's hand was with them. (Acts 11:19–21)

Antioch in Syria, which two centuries earlier had been the capital of that notorious temple profaner Antiochus IV, now became a site of the Lord's new "temple." Christians from the Jewish Dispersion, from Cyprus and Cyrene, broke through the ethnic-religious barrier to announce God's good news to uncircumcised Gentiles, and God's power accompanied their announcement. To encourage these new Gentile believers, the Jerusalem church sent a Dispersion Jew from the tribe of Levi, Barnabas from Cyprus (4:36; 11:22). Barnabas seems to have been a second Stephen, "full of the Holy Spirit and faith" (11:24; cf. 6:5), but it would be Paul, enlisted by Barnabas to assist in teaching the fledgling Antiochene church, who would face violence from the same group of unbelieving Hellenists who had opposed Stephen (9:29).

The church at Antioch was therefore an extension of Stephen's life, theology, and martyrdom. Although increasing diversity now characterized the church, a deep unity remained among those who trusted Jesus. This unity was expressed not only in the preaching ministry of prophets from Jerusalem to the church in Antioch (11:27), but also in the offering sent from Antioch to Jerusalem for the relief of the poor (vv. 28–30). This exchange of gifts reflected the two ministries, word and tables, which the apostles had distinguished when Stephen and his fellow servers were appointed (6:2, 4).

Yet Antioch was also the gateway to even greater diversity, for from there the Holy Spirit would send out Barnabas and Saul to carry the message of God's salvation to the distant islands and to peoples far away (13:1–4). Although Herod's temple in Jerusalem would survive a few more years, its function had become obsolete in the purposes of God. The time had arrived in which the holy presence of the Lord would travel along with his pilgrim people wherever they might go, as in the days of the patriarchs and of the Exodus.

PHILIP, SAMARIA, AND THE FOREIGN EUNUCH

Philip, another of the Seven Servers, is Luke's prime example of a "dispersed Christian," driven from Jerusalem by the persecution that had been ignited by Stephen's speech (Acts 8:1, 4). The dispersion of the church could be seen as a judgment on Jerusalem, which lost many witnesses of the Lord. But it also brought blessing to the nations, for "those who had been scattered traveled along, announcing the good news of the word" (v. 4). Philip's witness was central, for through him old ethnic and religious walls were broken down and two new kinds of people were welcomed into Christ's church.

Samaria Receives the Word and the Spirit
The Samaritans (8:5–25) may have been the product of intermarriage between the tribes of the northern kingdom of Israel and Gentile peoples who had been transported into the regions of Israel by the conquering Assyrians (2 Kings 17:24–41; Ezra 4; Neh. 4). Under the Assyrians, worship in this region combined the idolatrous paganism of the expatriate Gentiles and their attempts to placate the Lord, whom they viewed as the local deity (2 Kings 17:25–26). "They feared the Lord and they served their own gods according to the decree of the nations from which they had been forced to

emigrate" (2 Kings 17:33). A temple was built to the Lord on Mt. Gerazim in the fourth century B.C., but to please Antiochus IV of Syria in 167 B.C., the same year that the Maccabees resisted his imposition of Greek religion on Judea, the Samaritans readily rededicated their temple to the Greek god Zeus.[18] Samaritans accepted only the books of Moses as scripture, so their hoped-for Messiah/"Restorer" was not a Davidic king, but a prophet like Moses (Deut. 18:15–19; see John 4:25). Although respected by some Jewish rabbis for their adherence to the law,[19] Samaritans were usually classified with Gentiles as outsiders to the "house of Israel" (Matt. 10:5–6). Jews did not share eating or drinking vessels with Samaritans (John 4:9), considering them "unclean."

In view of the background and status of Jewish-Samaritan relations, Philip's preaching in Samaria marked more than a geographical expansion of the church's witness. The deep chasm of religious hostility and exclusion that had separated Jews and Samaritans for generations was bridged by Philip's announcement that the kingdom of God had arrived through Jesus the Messiah, as many Samaritans believed this good news.

There was, however, something odd about the Samaritans' entry into messianic salvation. Peter had promised at Pentecost, "Repent, be baptized, and you will receive the Holy Spirit" (Acts 2:38), but Luke calls attention to the fact that this order was interrupted in Samaria: "[The Spirit] had not yet fallen upon any of them; but they had only been baptized into the name of the Lord Jesus" (8:16), even though their baptism had been accompanied by faith (v. 12). The separation of conversion (faith with baptism) from the reception of the Spirit's power was so abnormal that Luke singles it out for special comment. Why was the reception of the Spirit delayed in Samaria?

The answer does not lie in viewing the Samaritans' abnormal experience as a precedent for a "second blessing" theology of Christian experience: first trusting in Jesus as Savior, and later receiving the Spirit's power to serve him as Lord. Rather, the solution is found in the Samaritans' history and peculiar relationship to Israel's covenant community, for the Samaritans occupied a sort of covenantal "no man's land"—not belonging to Israel, but not quite pagan Gentiles either. The movement of the Spirit and the word of God across this major religious frontier had to be witnessed by none other than apostles commissioned by Jesus himself, so Philip's ground-breaking evangelism was confirmed by the testimony of Peter and John (v. 14). The Spirit was abnormally delayed in Samaria in order to allow for the arrival of prominent apostles, Peter and John, from the Jerusalem church.[20] Apostolic witnesses were needed to confirm that God had signified his reception of the Samaritans by giving them his Spirit. Therefore, the Spirit did not come in eschatological power until Peter and John were present, and until they placed their hands on the Samaritan believers to symbolize these believers' solidarity with the mother church in Jerusalem.

Samaria linked the Spirit baptism of the Jewish church at Pentecost, on the one hand, with the Spirit baptism of Cornelius and his fellow Gentiles, on the other. The coming of the Spirit on Samaritan believers was a *second installment* of the enthroned Jesus' outpouring of the Spirit of promise. As the apostles had believed in Jesus before the Spirit came on them in power at Pentecost, so also the Samaritans believed before the Spirit came on them—not because it is normal for people to come to faith without receiving the Spirit in power, but because these groups lived on *the edge between the ages*. Their experience spanned the redemptive epoch of anticipation, when "the Spirit was not yet, because Jesus had not yet been glorified" (John 7:39), and the epoch of fulfillment, the "last days" in which the risen Lord pours out the Father's promise (Acts 2:33). The Spirit's coming in Samaria also anticipates his falling on the Gentiles at Cornelius' house. Luke signals this connection by using similar phrasing in the two accounts: "*The apostles* in Jerusalem, *having heard* that Samaria *had received* [δεχομαι] *the word of God* . . ." (8:14), and, "*The apostles* and the brothers who were throughout Judea *heard* that even the Gentiles *had received* [δεχομαι] *the word of God*" (11:1).

As the Spirit awaited the arrival of apostolic witnesses before bestowing his gifts to signify the Samaritans' inclusion among the people of God, so also when Cornelius and his friends received the Spirit, God provided an apostolic witness, Peter, who (with other Jewish believers, 11:12) could testify before the church that God had indeed lavished on uncircumcised Gentiles the treasured gift of his Spirit (11:17; 15:7–9). Thus, the apostles' role as witnesses was not only to evangelize unbelievers, but also to attest to the church that God was now welcoming Samaritans and Gentiles through faith in Jesus. Jewish Christians had to heed the testimony of Christ's witnesses: God gives repentance and his Spirit not just to people linked by history and heredity to the patriarchs and promises, but to outsiders as well.

Good News to a Pilgrim-Alien from the Ends of the Earth
The conversion of the Ethiopian eunuch whom Philip met on the road to Gaza provides further demonstration of God's intention to include former outcasts as full participants in his holy community (Acts 8:26–39).

Through parallels of action and wording, Luke implies that the conversion of the eunuch, like that of the Samaritans, was a preview of the conversion of Cornelius. In each encounter (Philip with the eunuch, Peter with Cornelius), the Lord's messenger was supernaturally directed to his intended Gentile audience. Philip was directed by an angel and by the Spirit (8:26, 29), and Peter was directed by a vision and by the Spirit (10:10–16, 19–20; an angel also spoke to Cornelius, v. 3). In both incidents, the rhetorical question was asked, whether anything could or should prevent their receiving baptism (8:37; 10:47).[21] Philip brought the gospel to the Samaritans, and Peter followed, bringing apostolic confirmation of this extension. Now Philip broke through the last barrier, carrying the gospel into Gentile territory—and Peter's apostolic role again was to testify that God had welcomed even the Gentiles by giving them his Spirit.[22]

Philip met the eunuch in Gentile territory, on the way to the ancient Philistine stronghold of Gaza. (At the end of this account, Philip is "found" at Azotus, the site of the ancient Ashdod, another of the five Philistine cities. Cf. 1 Sam. 6:17; Zeph. 2:4–7.) The man to whom the angel directed Philip was a Gentile foreigner. Although he had made a pilgrimage to the temple in Jerusalem and had procured a scroll of the prophet Isaiah, he was not Jewish but Ethiopian, an administrator from the court of the queen. Nor could he have become a proselyte, a complete convert to Judaism, for he was a eunuch. He was twice excluded from the worshiping community of Israel, not only as a Gentile, but also as a eunuch, for the Torah commanded: "A eunuch [LXX: θλαδιας] and one emasculated by cutting shall not enter the assembly of the Lord" (Deut. 23:1). His status could have been no more than "one who fears God," denied the opportunity to convert to Judaism and therefore excluded forever from the Court of Israel in the temple complex.[23]

But the pilgrimage of this Ethiopian official to the house of God in Jerusalem—and, even more so, his faith in the good news about Jesus— signaled the beginning of the international expansion of God's kingdom, predicted by ancient psalmists and prophets:

> Ambassadors will come from Egypt; *Ethiopia* will extend her hand to God [in allegiance]. (Ps. 68:31)

> Glorious things have been spoken about you, O city of God: "I will remember Rahab [Egypt] and Babylon among those who know me; and behold, foreigners and Tyre and *the people of the Ethiopians.*" (Ps. 87:3–4)

> And in that day the Root of Jesse will be, even the one who arises to rule the nations; upon him the nations will hope. . . . In that day it shall be that the Lord will show his hand again to be zealous for the remnant of his people, whatever is left from Assyria and from Egypt and from Babylonia and from *Ethiopia* and from Elam and from the East [sunrise] and from Arabia. (Isa. 11:10–11)

When the Messiah, the descendant of Jesse, would come, the rule of the Lord would extend as far south as the Ethiopian kingdom, which would send tribute and worshipers to the Lord's royal throne in Jerusalem. The foreigner from a distant land whom Philip now instructed was a sign that these ancient promises were coming to fulfillment.

But this man was not only a foreigner from Ethiopia, but also a eunuch, perpetually unfit for the holy community according to the laws of the earthly sanctuary. Yet the prophetic Scriptures had spoken a special word of hope to eunuchs and foreigners:

> Let no foreigner who is devoted to the Lord say, "The Lord will exclude me from his people." And let no eunuch [LXX: ευνουχος] say, "I am a dry tree." For the Lord says this: "To the eunuchs who keep my Sabbaths, who choose what I will and cling to my covenant, I will give in my house and within my walls a place of note[24] better than sons and daughters; I will give them an everlasting name that will not pass out of existence. And to foreigners who are devoted to the Lord, to serve him and to love the Lord's name and to become his slaves, . . . I bring them into my holy mountain and make them glad in my house of prayer. . . . For my house will be called a house of prayer for all the nations." (Isa. 56:3–7)

The ancient law excluding uncircumcised Gentiles and castrated eunuchs from the community of the Lord was tied to a physical sanctuary that was now obsolete. Peter would soon learn that the ancient law distinguishing "clean" and "unclean" meats—symbolizing an ethnic distinction between "clean" and "unclean" people—had likewise served its purpose and dissolved into a deeper definition of holiness. It was no longer to be understood in terms of externals such as diet or racial descent, but rather in terms of internal allegiance to Jesus Christ. When the heavenly voice said, "Things that God has declared clean, you must not call unclean," Peter rightly concluded, "God has shown me that I must not call any person unclean" (Acts 10:15, 28). The "house of prayer for all nations" was not the product of Herod's construction in Jerusalem. It was located (among other places) at a wadi beside a wilderness road in old Philistine territory, where a castrated Ethiopian was cleansed for priestly service through faith in the Lamb of God, who "was led like a sheep to the slaughter" (8:32, quoting Isa. 53:7).

THE SPIRIT'S UNITY IN TODAY'S CHURCH OF MANY CULTURES

Sunday school children sing, "Red, brown, yellow, black and white, they are precious in his sight." We know that's true. But that does not make it easy for people of different races or cultures to live together in the church in mellow harmony. We experience frictions and tensions, misunderstandings and frustrations, when we try to practice the unity of Christ's body, not just among "our kind of people," but among all kinds of people.

In cities like Los Angeles, it is rare for a church facility to be used by only one language group. One church sign after another announces services in English and Spanish; or Korean and English; or Spanish, Vietnamese, and English; or Mandarin and Cantonese; and so on. Those signs send a fitting message about Christ's church, but behind them are real struggles to work out in practice a loving unity that only God can create. Nothing but the oil of his Spirit can enable believers from different cultures to rub elbows without friction. What Luke tells us about the Seven Servers offers encouragement and wise insight as the church wrestles with the stresses of internal culture shock:

(1) Frustration and misunderstanding are not abnormal when different kinds of people live and work together. There is nothing automatic about expressing Christ's love in a multicultural or multiracial situation. The unity of the Spirit in the church is God's creation, but Scripture also commands: "Make every effort to keep the unity of the Spirit through the bond of peace" (Eph. 4:3 NIV). Preserving and expressing our oneness in Christ demands strenuous effort.

(2) The solution to the tensions is not to reduce the variety in the church. When a congregation begins to reach out and draw in people from a different cultural or social group, comfortable routines and long-held assumptions will be disturbed. Why create a children's church for newly converted single-parent families, when our own children sat with us in the pew since they were toddlers? Why sing new songs, rather than our old Fanny Crosby favorites? The temptation to segregate ourselves into distinct, homogeneous fellowships, each at home in its own comfort zone, is very strong.

But Acts points in the opposite direction: the apostles did not send the Hellenists off to start a "separate but equal" church structure in which they could care for their own widows without disturbing Hebrew-speaking Christians with their complaints. The solution to the tensions was not segregation, but selfless love. The apostles acknowledged the problem without defensiveness or impatience. They acknowledged their own limitations, admitting that they could no longer oversee both the ministry of tables and the ministry of the word. They also invited the members of the church to recognize the leaders whom they would trust in this ministry.

(3) Leaders who have the Spirit's wisdom are vital to the growing unity of the multicultural church. The problem that threatened the church in Acts 6:1 had several layers: *physical*, for widows were going hungry; *organizational*, for the food was not getting to them; and *interpersonal*, for the result was misunderstanding, discontent, and complaints. This complex problem demanded selfless love, unquestionably. But it also required *wisdom*—divine wisdom.

The apostles exhibited such wisdom in untangling the snarled strands of the problem, identifying the source, and proposing a solution. The Seven were noteworthy for the fullness of the Spirit and his wisdom in their lives. Because they had received a share in Messiah's anointing with the Spirit of the Lord, "the Spirit of wisdom and understanding," they reflected the wisdom of Jesus the Messiah, to do justice for the poor (Isa. 11:2, 4). The complex problems posed by the church's mission to embrace all kinds of people demand leaders who can wisely analyze the problems and formulate just and compassionate solutions.

(4) Diverse peoples and diverse needs call for diverse ministries. The apostles humbly recognized that the needs of the church had outstripped their own abilities to oversee every ministry. This was not merely because of the numbers involved, but also because of the church's linguistic diversity and the difference in character between word ministry and table ministry. Both are important administrations of God's multifaceted grace (1 Peter 4:10–11). But no one can focus on every form of ministry. Each member makes its unique contribution to the health of the Body, so that the variety in the Body promotes its unity (1 Cor. 12:14–26). Different people have different needs, and so the church must identify among its members the spiritual gifts to meet each need.

God alone has the wisdom, power, and grace to weave the tangled threads of different people, with different cultures, customs, and languages, into a single tapestry of glorious beauty. But he does it through the self-giving love he has placed in his children and the Spirit-guided wisdom he has given to the leaders of his flock.

Notes

¹ Some were probably *proselytes*, Gentile converts to Judaism (Acts 2:11; 6:5).

² Were the seven men appointed to "serve tables" in Acts 6 the first deacons (mentioned elsewhere in the New Testament as an *office* only in Phil. 1:1; 1 Tim. 3:8–13; and probably Rom. 16:1)? The verb that describes their activity is διακονεω, a cognate of διακονος (which often in the New Testament means "servant" in an unofficial sense, but does designate a recognized church office, "deacon," in the passages listed above). Another related noun, διακονια, is applied to the apostles' *"ministry* of the word" in Acts 6:4—illustrating how flexibly this word group can be used. The Seven carried on a ministry of deeds, showing compassion for physical needs, while the apostles were to concentrate on teaching, addressing spiritual needs. Thus, the division of labor in Acts 6 seems at least to anticipate the later distinction between the roles of elder/overseer and deacon/servant.

³ From the time of the Assyrian conquest, Aramaic or Syriac seems to have become the most commonly used language in the ancient Near East, although there is evidence that among Palestinian Jews, Hebrew persisted as a living language in everyday usage. See Robert H. Gundry, "The Language Milieu of First-Century Palestine: Its Bearing on the Authenticity of the Gospel Tradition," *JBL* 83 (1964): 404–8, citing the findings of such archaeologists as J. T. Milik, N. Avigad, E. L. Sukenik, and Y. Yadin, confirming the use of Hebrew in the first century. Luke's term "Hebrew" (εβραιος, only here in Acts; cf. "Hebraic dialect" in Acts 21:40; 22:4; 26:14) is broad enough to refer to either Semitic language. The significant point is that the Hellenist/Hebrew distinction in Acts 6:1 is a linguistic/cultural one within Jewish Christianity.

⁴ Martin Hengel, *Judaism and Hellenism: Studies in Their Encounter in Palestine During the Early Hellenistic Period*, trans. John Bowden, 2 vols. (Philadelphia: Fortress, 1974), 1:58–78.

⁵ Ibid., 247–54.

⁶ Joachim Jeremias, *Jerusalem in the Time of Jesus: An Investigation into Economic and Social Conditions During the New Testament Period* (London: SCM, 1969), 65–66, cites Talmudic references to a synagogue of the Alexandrians and a synagogue of the Tarsians (which Jeremias takes to be one and the same), confirming the natural implication of Acts 6:9, that the Synagogue of the Freedmen was composed of Dispersion Jews from Egypt and Cilicia.

⁷ At this point, the church numbered well over five thousand persons (Acts 4:4; 5:14). It is unlikely that believers' homes in Jerusalem, where Christians shared their meals, could accommodate large gatherings, so it is probable that one hundred or more of these home fellowships were meeting. Cf. B. Blue, "Acts and the House Church," in *The Book of Acts in Its First Century Setting*, ed. Bruce W. Winter, vol. 1: *The Book of Acts in Its Graeco-Roman Setting*, ed. D. W. J. Gill and C. Gempf (Grand Rapids: Eerdmans, 1994), 119–222, especially 130–44.

⁸ The church's growth is the context for the appointment of the Seven Servers, as Luke shows by summarizing the situations before and after this event in almost identical words: "as the disciples were *multiplying* [πληθυνοντων των μαθητων]" (Acts 6:1) and "the number of the disciples *was multiplying* . . . exceedingly [επληθυνετο ο αριθμος των μαθητων . . . σφοδρα]" (v. 7). The cognate noun "multitude" (πληθος) also appears twice in this text: "the multitude of the disciples [το πληθος των μαθητων]" (v. 2) and "the whole multitude [παντος του πληθους]" (v. 5).

⁹ Greek: προσηλυτον Αντιοχεα.

¹⁰ In using επισκεπτομαι, the LXX is reflecting a similarly unusual usage of the Hebrew word פקד, which normally means "oversee, visit, intervene (to judge or deliver)," but which in Num. 27:16 seems to express the idea of selection, based on close attention to qualification.

¹¹ Num. 27:23 LXX: επεθηκεν τας χειρας αυτου επ᾽ αυτου; Acts 6:6: επεθηκαν αυτοις τας χειρας.

¹² The mention of "Judea and Samaria" in Acts 8:1 is the first appearance of "Judea and Samaria" since Jesus' promise in Acts 1:8.

¹³ The "Righteous One" (צדיק) is the title of the Servant of the Lord in Isaiah 53:11. Earlier in this Servant Song, the rejection of the Servant by the people he came to rescue is foretold (Isa. 53:4).

¹⁴ Martin Hengel, Acts and the History of Earliest Christianity (Philadelphia: Fortress, 1980), 74, may be correct when he infers from Acts 8:1 ("except the apostles") that the persecution led by Saul and others focused on the Greek-speaking Christians to whom the Seven particularly ministered.

¹⁵ The verb in these passages in the LXX is διασπειρω, as in Acts 8:1, 4; 11:9. The noun Dispersion (διασπορα) refers to Jews living outside Palestine in John 7:35 and James 1:1, whereas in 1 Peter 1:1 it is used metaphorically of Gentile Christians who, living on this earth, have not yet entered their heavenly inheritance (v. 4).

¹⁶ Edmund P. Clowney, "The Final Temple," WTJ 35 (1973): 156–89.

¹⁷ Dennis E. Johnson, "Fire in God's House: Imagery from Malachi 3 in Peter's Theology of Suffering (1 Pet 4:12–19)" JETS 29 (1986): 285–94. See also M. G. Kline, Images of the Spirit (Grand Rapids: Baker, 1980), 35–42.

¹⁸ Josephus, Antiquities 12.258–61. See K. Haacker, "Samaritan," in NIDNTT, 3:452.

¹⁹ Babylonian Talmud tractate Berakot 47b, cited in J. Jeremias, "Σαμαρεια," TDNT, 7:89.

²⁰ The prominence of Peter and John within the circle of the apostles is not only implied in such passages as Acts 3–4, but also explicitly affirmed by Paul when he calls them, together with James, "those reputed to be pillars" (Gal. 2:9).

²¹ Acts 8:37: "Behold, water! What prevents my being baptized? [τι κωλυει με βαπτισθηναι]." Acts 10:47: "Can anyone prevent water, that these should not be baptized? [μητι το υδωρ δυναται κωλυσαι τις του μη βαπτισθηναι τουτους]."

²² The church's struggle to understand the implications of the inclusion of the Gentiles by faith will be discussed in chapter 8.

²³ Some scholars think it unlikely that a God-fearer would have had a biblical scroll in his possession. They propose that "eunuch" is a governmental title, without the implication of physical castration (Ernst Haenchen, The Acts of the Apostles: A Commentary (Philadelphia: Westminster Press, 1971), 314). But since another word ("important official," δυναστης) identifies his governmental position, "eunuch" does refer to his physical condition. So Hans Conzelmann, Acts of the Apostles, ed. E. J. Epp, trans. J. Limburg, A. T. Kraabel, and D. H. Juel (Hermeneia; Philadelphia: Fortress, 1987), 68; Hengel, Acts and Earliest Christianity, 79.

²⁴LXX: ονομαστον, normally "noteworthy, famous," but here perhaps "a place to preserve their name [ονομα]," since eunuchs would not have descendants ("sons and daughters") to do so.

SEVEN

AN ENEMY CONQUERED

GOD'S VICTORY OVER HIS ENEMIES

A psalmist sings in hope, "God will crush the heads of his enemies, the hairy crowns of those who proceed in their faults" (Ps. 68:21). Another confesses his allegiance to the Lord: "Do I not hate those who hate you, O Lord, and waste away [in anguish] over your enemies? With complete hatred I hate them; they have become my enemies" (139:21–22). In another psalm, applied often to Jesus in the New Testament, we hear the Lord's promise to his Messiah: "Ask me, and I will give you the nations as your inheritance, and the corners of the earth as your possession. You will shepherd them with an iron scepter; you will shatter them like an earthen pot" (2:8–9).

The psalmists' rejoicing over the slaughter of the enemy is echoed in the New Testament, especially in the book of Revelation. A heavenly voice pleads for the destruction of Babylon the prostitute, who has drunkenly celebrated the martyrdom of Christians (Rev. 17:6): "Give back to her as she gave back [to others], double¹ according to her deeds. . . . As much as she glorified herself and lived in luxury, to that extent give her torture and mourning. . . . Rejoice over her, O heaven and saints and apostles and prophets! God has judged her for the judgment you received from her" (Rev. 18:6–7, 20). The champion of God's armies is the word of God, from whose mouth proceeds "a sharp sword with which to strike down the nations. 'He will rule them with an iron scepter.' He treads the winepress of the furious wrath of God Almighty" (19:15). It is hard to avoid the impression that God wants his oppressed people to feel a rush of adrenaline, even celebration, as they envision his enemies "getting what's coming to them"!

Such violent antipathy toward enemies does not set well with moderns, for whom tolerance and pluralism are treasured qualities. J. S. Semler in the eighteenth century contended that a humane reader, enlightened to eternal moral truths, cannot be blamed for finding the book of Revelation "unpleasant and repulsive" when it celebrates the extermination of the heathen, for this perspective is in conflict with the enlightened ideal of "divine, all-inclusive love and charity for the restoration of men."[2] Vernard Eller, in arguing a case for pacifism from the Bible, takes pains to emphasize, "Man is not the enemy."[3] C. S. Lewis, troubled by the vindictiveness of the psalmists, proposes a kinder, gentler approach to God's enemies today (although he laments our loss of righteous indignation).[4] Remembering that "when we were God's enemies, we were reconciled to him through the death of his Son" (Rom. 5:10 NIV), who are we to ask God to blast those who are still his enemies?

Nevertheless, in an important respect humankind *is* the enemy of God —not irredeemably perhaps, but voluntarily, deliberately, and persistently. While Satan and his influence over humanity are real, we cannot portray ourselves as hapless victims, shrugging off our guilt with "The devil made me do it." When we harm others, when we betray the good that we know, such evil discloses something amiss deep within us. How, then, should we treat the real enmity toward God in ourselves and others? How does God deal with his enemies?

Part of the answer is found in God's treatment of Saul of Tarsus, who was (in his own words) "a blasphemer and a persecutor and an insolent aggressor" (1 Tim. 1:13), and who (in the words of his teacher Gamaliel) was "fighting against God" (Acts 5:39). Throughout his life, Paul remembered his hostility toward Christ and his church, but those memories impressed on him the marvel of God's grace, of which he became a prime beneficiary and a herald. Paul had no doubt that, despite his zeal for the God of Israel, he had been an enemy of Israel's Messiah; his hatred and aggressiveness could not be minimized or excused.[5] Yet *this* enemy was conquered, vanquished, condemned, and even executed in a way very different from what we might have anticipated, in a conquest leading through judgment to resurrection and a new life of loyalty to the Lord he had once opposed.

The story of Saul's conversion is familiar: the purpose of his trip (to arrest and bring back Christian believers for trial and punishment), the bright light and heavenly voice at midday, the speaker's identification as "Jesus, whom you are persecuting," Saul's blindness, Ananias's mission of healing and commissioning, and Saul's initial preaching in Damascus. Familiarity may be our biggest obstacle to understanding, for we need to learn from Luke not only the facts of Paul's call, but also its significance.

We have noticed that the importance of Paul's conversion is underscored by its being narrated three times in Acts: first by Luke the narrator (Acts 9:1–31), then by Paul, answering the disturbance of a Jewish mob in the temple precincts (22:1–21), and finally by Paul as part of his speech before King Agrippa II (26:12–20). Variations between the three accounts fit each to its context. In Acts 9, Luke, in his role as omniscient narrator, describes the vision granted to Ananias (vv. 10–16), a detail omitted in Paul's later reports. Thus, a twofold revelation—Christ's appearance to Saul and the vision to Ananias—confirms God's initiative in calling the Apostle to the Gentiles, just as in the next section a twofold revelation (Peter's vision of the sheet and Cornelius's vision of an angel) confirms God's initiative in granting faith and the Spirit to the Gentiles. In Acts 22, Paul, accused of defiling the temple, emphasizes his heritage, training, and zeal in Judaism (vv. 3–5). He narrates a vision of the Lord Jesus that he received while worshiping *in the temple* (vv. 17–21). In Acts 26, Paul places special emphasis on the promises of God spoken to Israel through the prophets, particularly the hope of the resurrection (vv. 6–8, 22–23). This emphasis is tailor-made for Agrippa, whom Paul challenges in conclusion, "King Agrippa, do you believe the prophets? I know you do" (v. 27).

Other variations between the three accounts amplify and reinforce biblical themes that come to expression in Paul's call and conversion: his blindness as covenant curse, his continuity with ancient prophets called by God, and his mission to the Gentiles. On closer examination, then, this familiar story in threefold form yields rich insights into Paul's mission and message.

God's Enemy

Saul first appears on the pages of Acts as a young man who served as the approving cloak attendant for Stephen's accusers as they prepared to stone him (Acts 7:58; 8:1). Saul approved so heartily of their action that he immediately took the lead in a "great persecution" against the church at Jerusalem, including house-to-house searches and arrests of believers (8:1, 3). His efforts served to disseminate the Nazarene cult rather than obliterate it, so he gained authorization to travel to the Dispersion, to Damascus in Syria, and to arrest and bring back any followers of "the Way" whom he might find there (9:1–2).

The Source of Saul's Enmity

What inflamed Saul's white-hot hatred of a group that had enjoyed the favor and high regard of their non-Christian Jewish neighbors (Acts 2:47; 5:13)? Perhaps he endorsed the accusations that Stephen had been speaking against the temple and the Torah, blaspheming God (6:9–14). Saul may have even visited the Synagogue of the Freedmen in Jerusalem, along with other former residents of Cilicia.[6] But the source of Saul's antipathy toward the followers of Jesus is explicitly identified only in Paul's own accounts of his activities (Acts 22 and 26).

Paul's speech to the temple crowds in Acts 22 strategically stresses his fidelity to Judaism, both before and after his coming to believe that Jesus is the Messiah. Paul had come to the temple on this occasion for the very purpose of silencing rumors that he had urged Jews in the Dispersion to abandon their observance of the law (21:20–26). Paul's credentials in Judaism were impressive. Although born among the Dispersion, he was brought to Jerusalem by his family as a young child. There he was brought up in his parental home, and then trained under Gamaliel II, son or grandson of Hillel, founder of one of the two great rabbinical schools of first-century Judaism (22:3).[7]

His rabbinical training was "strict" (κατα ακριβειαν, 22:3), for he was affiliated with the Pharisees, "the strictest sect of our religion" (την ακριβεστατην αιρεσιν, 26:5), as were his parents before him (23:6). The Pharisees' allegiance to the Torah and its contemporary application to Jewish life was so well known that Paul could sum up the measure of his devotion simply by stating his affiliation with this sect: "in regard to the law, a Pharisee" (Phil. 3:5; see also Acts 15:5). Paul's encounter with the risen Jesus would compel him to reevaluate this aspect of his legacy in a most radical way. On the other hand, the same encounter would confirm his Pharisaic hope for the resurrection of the dead (23:6; 26:6–8).

Paul also spoke of himself as "God's zealot [ζηλωτης]" (Acts 22:3). This zeal manifested itself in his devotion to the law and the rabbinical traditions that interpreted and applied it, for he speaks elsewhere of having been "extremely zealous [ζηλωτης] for the traditions of my fathers" (Gal. 1:14 NIV; see Acts 21:20). In its essence, zeal refers to a passionate jealousy on behalf of God, his authority and his honor, a jealousy that motivates strenuous, even violent resistance to anyone who threatens God's glory or the holiness of his people.

Zealous champions of the past exemplified wholehearted commitment to the Lord and resistance to foreign religious influences. Preeminent among these was Phinehas, grandson of Aaron, whose zeal moved him to slay an Israelite man who flagrantly violated Israel's religious and sexual purity by having relations with a Midianite woman, apparently as an expression of worship toward Baal of Peor. God commended Phinehas's action:

> Phinehas, son of Eleazar, son of Aaron the priest, caused my fury to rest from the Israelites; for he was zealous [LXX: ζηλόω] with my zeal among them, and I did not utterly destroy them in my zeal. Thus I said, "I am giving him a covenant of peace, and a covenant of eternal priesthood will belong to him and his seed with him, because he was zealous for his God and atoned for the sons of Israel." (Num. 25:11–13)

A later psalmist celebrated Phinehas's zeal, saying, "This was credited to him for righteousness for endless generations to come" (Ps. 106:31).

Closer to Paul's time were the Maccabees, who resisted the defiling of temple and Torah initiated by the Seleucid monarch Antiochus IV in the second century B.C. Judas Maccabeus, his brothers, and their successors eventually succeeded in their guerrilla warfare against Antiochus's forces, securing Judah's political independence under their (Hasmonean) dynasty for a century. In Saul's own lifetime, a definable group within Judaism resisted Roman rule, and the name Zealots was applied to this group by Josephus and others.[8] According to Josephus, Judas the Galilean was the first leader of this sect, which was committed to the violent overthrow of the Roman occupiers (6 B.C.).[9] The zeal of the Jewish conspirators who later bound themselves on oath not to eat until they had slain Paul (Acts 23:12–14) was typical not only of Zealots but also of deeply committed members of other Jewish sects.

Against this background, the source of Saul's antipathy for Stephen and other followers of Jesus is not hard to deduce: To a "strict" and "zealous" Pharisee, the proclamation of a Messiah who had been condemned by Judaism's leaders and executed in disgrace, and especially the view (attributed to Stephen) that this Messiah would destroy the temple and change the Torah, would sound like apostasy from the God of Israel. Josephus reports that some Dispersion Jews were alarmingly lax about calling converting Gentiles to undergo circumcision.[10] Stephen and other adherents to "the Way" no doubt appeared to Saul as Hellenizing compromisers, threats to the purity of Israel's allegiance toward the living God. As a faithful servant of God, Saul was obligated to heed the command: "You must purge the evil from among you" (Deut. 17:7 NIV).

Later, having become a servant of Jesus, Paul would call attention to Deuteronomy 21:23 as showing that Jesus' crucifixion was a sign of God's curse: "Cursed is everyone who is hanged on a tree" (Gal. 3:13). Once he recognized Jesus as the Messiah, Paul could see that Jesus underwent that curse on behalf of others. However, if Saul had made the connection between the form of Jesus' execution and the sign of the curse in Deuteronomy 21 before his encounter on the road to Damascus, he could only have seen Jesus' shameful death as a sign that Jesus deserved God's curse and therefore could not be the Lord's Anointed.[11] Since the form of Jesus' death itself "proved" that Jesus was a false Messiah and an enemy of God, Saul the Pharisee would have seen himself as waging holy war against the enemies of God.

Judgment on the Enemy

Burning with zeal, but blinded by ignorance, Saul had things backwards. He was to discover that those whom he was hunting down as enemies of God were in fact the beloved and chosen people of God, friends of the Messiah. He was to spend a lifetime amazed that his own zeal for the Torah had made him into "a blasphemer and a persecutor and an insolent aggressor," an enemy and persecutor of God, God's Messiah, and God's church.

On the road leading to Damascus, Saul was confronted by a figure resplendent with divine glory, brighter than the sun overhead. The suddenness and sheer power of the radiance sent Saul and the others in his caravan falling to the ground, cringing in terror. His fellow travelers saw the light (Acts 22:9), but discerned no form in its midst (9:7).[12] Saul alone saw the light's source, the Son of God. Saul's companions heard a terrifying sound (9:7), but they did not discern the voice of the speaker, whose words were meant for Saul's ears alone (22:9).[13] In other words, as we pay attention to the details of Paul's two reports of what was seen and heard by him and his fellow travelers, the narratives are seen not to contradict, but to complement one another. They establish that the revelation was given to Saul alone, yet was not merely subjective. Others could testify that *something* remarkable had taken place, but Saul alone perceived the specific content that the Lord intended to communicate.[14]

The glorious figure accused Saul: "Why do you persecute me?" (9:4; 22:7; 26:14).[15] Whoever this was, Saul knew that he was to be addressed as "Lord" with great respect, even obeisance[16]—and that he considered Saul his enemy. When the speaker identified himself as "Jesus, whom you are persecuting," it became apparent that the purpose of Saul's present journey was the reason for the enmity between him and this One whose glory outshone the sun. Saul had seen himself as a zealot for God, hunting down those who sowed seeds of apostasy among the Dispersion, but now, to his shock, he learned that he was persecuting the glorified Messiah himself!

The way people treat God's servants expresses their attitude toward God himself. For example, Moses told complaining Israelites, "Your murmuring is not against us, but against God" (Ex. 16:8). Similarly, the Lord comforted Samuel, "They have not rejected you, but they have rejected me so that I should no longer be their king" (1 Sam. 8:7). And Jesus commissioned disciples for a preaching mission with the assurance, "He who hears you hears me, and the one who rejects you rejects me. But the one who rejects me rejects him who sent me" (Luke 10:16). In pursuing and destroying the servants of Jesus, Saul was persecuting Jesus himself. The identification of the Lord with his servants, so forcefully impressed upon Paul through Jesus' challenge, would be revealed even more fully through Paul's later expositions of union with Christ and of the church as the body of Christ.[17]

This violent enemy of the Lord and his people had brought himself under divine judgment. Paul himself would later write, "If anyone destroys God's sanctuary, God will destroy this person; for the sanctuary of God is sacred, which [sanctuary] you are" (1 Cor. 3:17). The blinding light from heaven at last brought Paul's actions into clear focus: "I was persecuting the church of God and trying to destroy it" (Gal. 1:13).

Blind at Midday

Saul's spiritual blindness had brought him under God's covenant curse, as his physical blindness, resulting from the display of Christ's glory, attests. In chapter 3, we noticed the connection between the healing of Paul's blindness and the healing of the Lord's blind servant in Isaiah 42. Now we need to trace the symbolism of blindness back to the covenant treaty between the Lord and Israel.[18] In recounting his experience before the crowds in the temple, Paul says that the brilliant light that left him sightless came "about midday"[19] (Acts 22:6). This recalls Moses' prophecy that this covenant curse (among others) would fall upon a disobedient Israel: "The Lord will strike you with madness, blindness, and distraction of mind. You will grope about at midday,[20] as a blind man gropes about in the dark" (Deut. 28:28–29). The physical blinding of Zedekiah, the last king of Judah, marked a representative fulfillment of this curse for covenant infidelity. Zedekiah "did evil in the eyes of the Lord," bringing upon Jerusalem and Judah the Lord's anger and expulsion from his presence (1 Kings 24:19–20). The Babylonian conquerors killed Zedekiah's sons before his eyes, and

then put out his eyes, leaving that last horrible image scalded into his memory (25:7). But the blindness spoken of in Deuteronomy 28 is more than
physical, as we see from its association with madness and mental distraction. Isaiah lamented the coming fulfillment of this curse because of Israel's
disloyalty to the Lord of the covenant: "We will grope like blind men
along a wall, and like those having no eyes we will grope. And we will fall
at midday [LXX: μεσημβρια], as if at midnight" (Isa. 59:10). Having turned
from the light of God's word, Israel would be helpless, "like those having
no eyes."

This Old Testament symbolism of judgment illumines the scene of Saul
of Tarsus, blinded by divine glory, groping in darkness despite the midday
sunlight, in need of others to lead him by the hand into Damascus. About
Saul's three days in Damascus before his sight was restored we are told only
that they were spent in fasting and prayer (Acts 9:9, 11). It may well be
that his meditation turned to the sign of the curse that he had experienced,
and how it symbolized his misdirected zeal. "I acted ignorantly in unbelief,"
he would later write (1 Tim. 1:13). Concerning fellow Jews who were continuing to reject Jesus the Messiah, as Paul had done, he would write: "I
testify about them that they have zeal for God, but not according to knowledge" (Rom. 10:2). Again, regarding Jews and Gentiles: "The god of this
age blinded the minds of unbelievers, so that they do not see the light of
the gospel of the glory of Christ, who is the image of God" (2 Cor. 4:4).
The contrast between the darkness/blindness of rebellion and seeing the
light of divine glory is a pervasive biblical theme, but Paul experienced this
graphic metaphor in a direct and intense way. Despite his strenuous zeal,
Saul the persecutor was the climax of Israel's rebellion against the Lord.
Stephen's indictment of Israel's stubbornness perfectly sets the stage for
Saul's entrance:

> "Which of the prophets did your fathers not *persecute?* They even
> killed those who announced beforehand the coming of the Right-
> eous One, whose betrayers and *murderers* you have become. . . ."
> And Saul was there, approving [Stephen's] murder. On that day
> a great *persecution* broke out against the church at Jerusalem. . . .
> Saul was trying to destroy the church. . . . Saul was still breath-
> ing out threats and *murder* against the Lord's disciples. (Acts 7:52;
> 8:1, 3; 9:1)[21]

At the start of his mission to the Gentiles, Paul would encounter a fellow Jew, Elymas Bar-Jesus, who would oppose the spread of faith in Jesus,

just as Paul had done (13:6–12). This Jewish false prophet, whom Paul called an "enemy of all righteousness" (v. 10), was likewise struck blind with the covenant curse-sign at a word from the Lord (v. 11)—now spoken through Paul![22] Just as "the hand of the Lord was against" Israel in its periods of rebellion (Judg. 2:15; 1 Sam. 12:15), so Paul introduced the judgment on this Israelite opponent of Christ with the words, "The hand of the Lord is against you" (Acts 13:11). Elymas groped about in his self-inflicted darkness, helplessly seeking someone to lead him by the hand, just as Paul had needed guides to lead him into Damascus.[23] Saul of Tarsus and Elymas Bar-Jesus of Cyprus epitomize the darkness and confusion that unbelievers have brought upon themselves through their rejection of Jesus the Messiah. The Lord has judged his enemies by plunging them into blindness.[24]

SAUL, GOD'S MESSENGER

Alongside the theme of judgment on the Lord's enemy, there emerges from these accounts a second theme—the commissioning of the Lord's messenger—as the spotlight is turned from what Paul has been to what he will be.

In Paul's apostolic call there are echoes linking it to God's enlistment of prominent Old Testament prophets. As the Lord calls Moses' name twice at the burning bush, "Moses! Moses!" (Ex. 3:4), and Samuel's name twice to awaken and commission him (1 Sam. 3:10), so Paul's divine call begins with the repetition of his name: "Saul! Saul!" (Acts 9:4). Moses' call comes as he watches the "sight" (ὅραμα) of the burning bush (Ex. 3:3 LXX; Acts 7:31); so also, Paul's call is associated with a "vision" (ὅραμα) that comes to Ananias (Acts 9:10) and then one that comes to Paul himself (v. 12). As Moses and Samuel respond to the Lord's summons with the servant's expression of readiness to obey, "Here I am" (literally, "Behold, I [am here]") (Ex. 3:4; 1 Sam. 3:4), so Ananias responds to the Lord's summons, "Yes, Lord" (literally, "Behold, I [am here], Lord") (Acts 9:10), indicating his readiness to hear and obey the Lord's word.[25] As the Lord reveals to Moses that his name is "I am" (Ex. 3:14), so Jesus answers Paul's question, "Who are you, Lord?" with an echo of the divine name: "*I am* Jesus, whom you are persecuting" (Acts 9:5).[26] As the Lord instructs Moses to tell the Israelites, "The God of your fathers . . . has sent me to you" (Ex. 3:15), so Ananias informs Paul that "the God of our fathers" has commissioned him to be a witness (Acts 22:14–15). The LXX records Moses' plea,

"I ask, Lord, *choose* [προχειριζομαι] another person, an able person, whom you will send" (Ex. 4:13). Using the same word, which is rare in biblical Greek, Ananias announces to Paul, "The God of our fathers *chose* [προχειριζομαι] you" (Acts 22:14; 26:16).[27] Through these multiple allusions, Luke invites us to recognize Paul's conversion as a prophetic call like that of Moses, the preeminent prophet with whom God spoke face-to-face (Num. 12:8), and that of Samuel, the founder of the prophetic tradition subsequent to Moses (see Acts 3:24).[28]

Further correspondences tie Paul's call to the commissioning of later prophets. Paul's traveling companions witnessed the overpowering presence of God in bright light and a thunderous sound, but were not given access to the content of the revelatory vision, which was intelligible only to Paul. Similarly, when Daniel received a vision of a glorious messenger from God, he reports, "I, Daniel, alone saw this great vision, and the men who were with me did not see this vision, and strong fear fell upon them and they fled quickly" (Dan. 10:7). The flight of Daniel's companions implies that, although the content of the vision was not made clear to them, they had experienced phenomena of terrifying power and splendor. Saul's call also resembles Ezekiel's, for when the latter fell to the ground at the appearance of the Lord's glory, he was commanded, "Stand on your feet!" (Ezek. 2:1).[29] Likewise, Paul, having fallen to the ground, heard the command, "Rise and stand on your feet!"[30] And he, like Ezekiel, was told of his mission to proclaim God's word (Acts 26:16).

The prophets' commissioning visions sometimes predicted their sufferings or promised protection from the hostile reactions of those whose evil would be exposed by God's word. Because God called Jeremiah not only to a constructive ministry of "building and planting," but also to speak words of judgment, "to uproot and tear down" (Jer. 1:10), the Lord assured him, "Do not be afraid of them, for I am with you and will rescue [LXX, εξαιρεομαι] you" (v. 8; see v. 19; Ezek. 2:6; 3:9). To Paul the Lord Jesus says, "I will rescue [εξαιρεομαι] you from your own people and from the Gentiles" (Acts 26:17).[31]

The call of the prophets involved their being brought into the heavenly courtroom of the Lord, to hear God's purposes and to be purified, being conformed to God's holiness.[32] Like the prophets, Paul was summoned into the glorious presence of the Lord for an audience with the sovereign who commissioned him. He was called by name and chosen for this task. By divine grace, he was made a confidant of the Lord "to know his will and to see the Righteous One and to hear a voice from his mouth" (Acts 22:14). His prophetic call was a call to suffering (9:16), but it came with a reassurance of the Lord's protective presence (26:17). Paul was the Lord's servant, sent to lead the nations out of darkness and into the light.

GOD'S FORGIVENESS

Was Paul God's enemy or God's servant? Was he a blind man who needed a guide, or a guide who led the blind? The answer lies at the very heart of Paul's apostolic mission and message. It is God's grace in Jesus Christ.

On Pentecost, Peter had quoted the promise given through Joel, "Everyone who calls on the name of the Lord will be saved" (Acts 2:21; Joel 2:32). He had urged his hearers, "Repent and undergo baptism, each of you, upon the name of Jesus Christ for the forgiveness of your sins" (Acts 2:32). The "name of the Lord," of which Joel had spoken, is Jesus Christ. Those whom Saul had been pursuing were "those who call on the name" of the Lord Jesus (9:14, 21, also alluding to Joel 2:32). Thus, when the devout Ananias of Damascus had completed the healing of Saul's physical blindness, he went on to exhort Saul, "Arise, be baptized, and wash your sins away, *calling on his name*" (Acts 22:16). Saul needed to see himself as a person in desperate need of rescue from his own sins and their consequences, and he had to call on the name of Jesus. That name, which Saul had tried to eradicate, was his only hope.

Just as Isaiah could speak God's message only after a burning coal from the altar of God touched his lips to purify them and remove his guilt (Isa. 6:7), so Saul could carry Jesus' gospel only after his sins were "washed away"[33] (Acts 22:16). Saul was now to speak for God to the Gentiles, "to open their eyes, to turn them from darkness to light, and from Satan's authority to God, so that they may receive *forgiveness of sins* and a place among those who are sanctified by faith" in Jesus (26:18). To declare this message of grace, he had to be gripped to the core by the greatness of his own need and of God's astounding mercy. Reflecting on his own history of hostility to Jesus the Messiah, Paul would later write:

> For this reason I was shown mercy, so that in me, the preeminent [sinner], Christ Jesus might display his comprehensive patience as a prototype for those who were to believe on him, resulting in their eternal life. (1 Tim. 1:16)

As a Pharisee, of course, Saul had believed that forgiveness was needed and possible through God's mercy.[34] First-century Judaism confessed that the Lord's grace, not Israel's merit, was the source of Israel's status as the chosen people of God. To be "blameless according to the law" (Phil. 3:6) was not to have achieved sinless perfection, but only to have avoided deliberate sins and to have offered appropriate sacrifices for inadvertent transgressions. But it was only through the revelation on the road to Damascus that the depth of Saul's need for forgiveness became clear to him: his zeal for the law had provoked him to persecute God's Anointed One! Forgiven apart from (in spite of!) his efforts to keep the law, Saul was now uniquely prepared to announce God's forgiving grace to the Gentiles apart from their efforts to the keep the law.

GOD'S WITNESS TO THE NATIONS

Closely tied to the gracious forgiveness that transformed Saul's status from God's enemy to God's herald was the fact that his mission would be directed toward the Gentiles. This appears in all three accounts of Saul's call:

(1) In Acts 9, the Lord Jesus reveals to Ananias that Saul is a chosen instrument to carry Jesus' name before the Gentiles (v. 15).

(2) In Acts 22, Paul recounts that Ananias informed him that he would be the witness of the Righteous One "to all men" (v. 15), and that he himself later received a vision in the temple in which the Lord warned him that his testimony, like that of Stephen, would be rejected by the people of Jerusalem (v. 18), but that he would be sent "far away to the Gentiles" (v. 21). On Pentecost, Peter had cited the prophetic promise that the Lord would bring his peace to "those far away" (Isa. 57:19) as being fulfilled in Jesus Christ (Acts 2:39). The repetition of the adverb "far away" (μακραν) in Acts 22:21 implies that Paul was the chosen witness through whom God's peace would reach the faraway Gentiles.[35]

(3) In Acts 26, Paul's Gentile mission is described in echoes of the Servant's role in Isaiah: "to open their eyes and to turn them from darkness to light" (v. 18; Isa. 42:6–7, 16). Paul, the once-blind servant (Isa. 42:19), now not only sees "the light of the gospel of the glory of Christ" (2 Cor. 4:4), but also bears this light, by which God's salvation pierces the Gentiles' darkness.

CONCLUSION: FROM ENEMY TO AMBASSADOR

Jesus' "conquest" of Saul of Tarsus is of central importance in Luke's portrait of what Jesus continued to do and teach after his enthronement in heaven. Saul (Paul) is not only the Apostle to the Gentiles, commissioned to carry salvation in Jesus' name to "outsiders" such as Theophilus. He is also the crucial exhibit of the gospel of grace, living the message he proclaims.

He preaches that those whose relation to God is based on law are under a curse (Gal. 3:10), for his own zeal for the law had made him a cursed persecutor of Christ. He announces reconciliation as a gift from God for Gentiles who have been enemies (Col. 1:21–22), for he himself has received God's mercy and peace—even though he had been God's enemy, destroying God's church and persecuting God's Messiah. Paul stands as the prime example, to his own day and ours, of the futility of human religious effort and of the surprising mercy of God.

What has become of the justice of God, the divine wrath that avenges Saul's insults to God's honor and his assaults on God's people? It has been satisfied by the one event that (probably) had convinced Saul for so long that Jesus could not be the Messiah: "the tree." If the crucified Jesus is indeed the Anointed One who is pleasing to God, the risen One who confronted Saul in blinding glory on the Damascus road, then the tree of curse can be explained only as Paul does in writing to the Galatians: "Christ became a curse for us" (Gal. 3:13). How can the God of justice declare the "worst of sinners" to be "the righteousness of God," unless he has also "made [Jesus], who had no sin, to be sin for us" (2 Cor. 5:21)?

The union between Christ and his people that Saul first glimpsed in Jesus' rebuke, "Why do you persecute *me?*" operates in two directions. Jesus counts his people's sufferings as belonging to himself. And he counts his own suffering and death as belonging to his people: "I have been crucified with Christ and I no longer live, but Christ lives in me" (Gal. 2:20 NIV). "All of us who were baptized into Christ Jesus were baptized into his death" (Rom. 6:3 NIV).

A time is coming when the Lord Jesus will destroy those enemies who persist in hostility toward him and his people: "It is just for God to repay affliction to those who afflict you, and relief to you, the afflicted, together with us" (2 Thess. 1:6–7). But Paul also proves to us, in his words and his own experience, that at the present time God is conquering his enemies in a surprising way, condemning them to death for their sin and then executing them on the cross in Jesus, their substitute, and raising them with him to behold his glory and bear witness to his grace.

Many Christians have not shared Paul's experience of a violent hatred for Jesus being brought to a sudden reversal by God's arresting grace. But every child of God can see in Paul's example God's severe judgment on his or her own sin, and God's abundant mercy in removing that sin through Christ's cross. Saul the persecutor is a vivid portrait, embedded in real history, of what each of us, pious or profligate, would be apart from the Spirit of God, who alone can shatter human pride so that we "call on the name of the Lord." Paul, the prophet and messenger of the New Covenant, who was caught up into the radiance of God's heavenly court on the way to Damascus, declares that all believers have a share in the beatific vision he received that day: "And we all, with unveiled faces reflecting the Lord's glory, are being transfigured from glory into glory. This is from the Lord, the Spirit" (2 Cor. 3:18).

Notes

¹ M. G. Kline, "Double Trouble," *JETS* 32 (1989): 171–79, argues that the Greek word translated "double" (διπλοω), like its Hebrew counterpart in such Old Testament texts as Isa. 40:2, means "an equivalent amount," a "doublet," or exact reflection of the harm that the harlot Babylon has caused to others. Thus, such texts are an appeal to the *lex talionis*, "life for life, eye for eye, tooth for tooth" (Ex. 21:23–24).

² J. S. Semler, *Treatise on the Free Investigation of the Canon* (1771–75), quoted in W. G. Kümmel, *The New Testament: The History of the Investigation of Its Problems* (Nashville: Abingdon, 1972), 63–64.

³ Vernard Eller, *King Jesus' Manual of Arms for the 'Armless* (Nashville: Abingdon, 1973), 60.

⁴ C. S. Lewis, *Reflections on the Psalms* (New York: Harcourt, Brace & World, 1958), 22: "I feel sure . . . that we must not either try to explain them away or to yield for one moment to the idea that, because it comes in the Bible, all this vindictive hatred must somehow be good and pious. We must face both facts squarely. The hatred is there—festering, gloating, undisguised—and also we should be wicked if we in any way condoned or approved of it." Lewis speaks of our living "in a milder age" than that of the psalmists (p. 23).

⁵ Even his comment, "I acted unknowingly in unbelief" (1 Tim. 1:13), is not to excuse his behavior but to show that his rebellion was not irreversible apostasy in the face of full understanding.

⁶ Saul was born in Tarsus in Cilicia (Acts 22:3), and some members of the Freedmen's Synagogue were Jews from Cilicia (6:9). As one born a Roman citizen (22:28), he would not himself have been a freedman (a former slave who had achieved freedom). But it is not unlikely that other Jews from the Dispersion would have found such a synagogue in Jerusalem linguistically inviting. On the other hand, because Paul was a "Hebrew born of Hebrews," raised in a Hebrew- or Aramaic-speaking home (Phil. 3:5), he would have had no difficulty attending the Hebrew/Aramaic-speaking synagogues in Jerusalem.

⁷ W. C. van Unnik, *Tarsus or Jerusalem: The City of Paul's Youth* (London: Epworth, 1962), 17–45, thoroughly surveys the use of the terms "bring up" (ανατρεφω) and "train" (παιδευω) in ancient biographical materials, showing that "bring up" refers to a child's early nurture in the parental home prior to the start of formal education.

[8] Josephus, *Antiquities* 18.6; *Jewish War* 2.170–71. See Luke 6:15; Acts 1:13.

[9] Josephus, *Jewish War* 2.118; see Acts 5:37.

[10] Josephus, *Antiquities* 20.2, reports that when King Izates of Adiabene sought to become a full proselyte to Judaism, the Jewish merchant through whom he had learned the faith of Israel, fearing for his own and the king's safety, sought to dissuade Izates from submitting to circumcision—in the end, unsuccessfully, Josephus reports with evident satisfaction.

[11] Luke records an allusion to Deut. 21:23 in the apostles' early preaching: "Jesus . . . whom you had killed by *hanging* him on a *tree*" (Acts 5:30). G. B. Caird has noted that this allusion to Deut. 21:23 testifies to the apostles' early conviction that Jesus' death was vicarious suffering, "that Jesus had borne the curse on behalf of others" (*The Apostolic Age* [London: Duckworth, 1955], 55). This allusion to Deut. 21 may also be indirect evidence that the Jewish opponents of Christianity had employed that text to refute Christians' claims for Jesus' messiahship.

[12] Acts 9:7: "hearing the voice, but seeing *no one* [μηδενα δε θεωρουντες]." Note that Paul does not say "seeing *nothing* [μηδεν]."

[13] "Those with me beheld the light, but did not hear *the voice of the one who was speaking* to me [την δε φωνην ουκ ηκουσαν του λαλουντος μοι]" (Acts 22:9).

[14] Similarly, when Daniel once received a vision, those who were with him perceived phenomena that struck them with terror, yet only Daniel himself received the content of the revelation (Dan. 10:7).

[15] Of the nine uses of *persecute* (διωκω) in Acts, eight refer to Saul as persecutor. In the other instance, Stephen reminds his accusers that their ancestors persecuted all the prophets (7:52)—only a few sentences before Saul is introduced into the narrative (v. 58). The related noun, *persecution* (διωγμος), appears twice in Acts: in 8:1, where Saul takes the lead in persecuting Christians, and in 13:50, where he and Barnabas are the victims of persecution.

[16] Although κυριος ("Lord") can be used simply as a title of polite address, like our "sir" (John 12:21; Acts 16:30), in the context of such a display of divine glory, Saul would have expressed awareness of the supernatural power and authority of the One who spoke to him.

[17] Seyoon Kim, *The Origin of Paul's Gospel* (Grand Rapids: Eerdmans, 1982), 252–56.

[18] M. G. Kline, *Treaty of the Great King* (Grand Rapids: Eerdmans, 1963), 124–29.

[19] Greek: περι μεσημβριαν. Noon or *midday* (μεσημβρια) is used only once elsewhere in the New Testament (Acts 8:26). In Acts 26:13, a synonymous construction (ημερας μεσης) is used to describe the time of the Damascus-road revelation.

[20] The LXX has μεσημβρια, as in Acts 22:6.

[21] Note that "persecute" (διωκω) and "murderers" (φονεις) in Stephen's speech are repeated in the descriptions of Saul in 8:1 ("persecution" [διωγμος]) and 9:1 ("threats and murder" [απειλης και φονου]).

[22] "Filled with the Holy Spirit" (πι[μ]πλημι in an aorist form, with πνευματος αγιου, v. 9) is Luke's formula to prepare us for a prophetic pronouncement that comes from God, bearing his authority and power. For other examples, see Luke 1:15–17, 41–42, 67; Acts 2:4; 4:8, 31; 9:17 (see v. 20).

[23] The words are χειραγωγεω (Acts 9:8; 22:11) and χειραγωγος (Acts 13:11).

[24] Second Mac. 3:24–40 claims to report a divine appearance that has superficial simi-

larities to the call of Paul. Heliodorus, chancellor of the Syrian king Seleucus IV (who ruled 186–175 B.C.), was sent by Seleucus to seize the treasures in the temple at Jerusalem. Upon entering the temple treasury, Heliodorus was struck down by a supernatural rider of terrifying glory and power, plunged into blindness, muteness, and a mortal illness that was reversed only through the intercessory prayers of the Jewish high priest Onias III. Restored to health (according to the account), Heliodorus made a sacrifice and vows to the Lord, and subsequently testified to all of the acts of the Lord that he had seen. The conversion of Paul, however, is directly related to such biblical themes as the curse of blindness in Deut. 28, the healing of the Servant in Isa. 42, and the calling of the great prophets (see the next section).

²⁵ The LXX in 1 Sam. 3:4 reads ιδου εγω, as in Acts 9:10. The underlying Hebrew expression, *hineni*, likewise appears in the call of Moses (Ex. 3:4), but the LXX translates it "What is it [τι εστιν]?"

²⁶ "I am" (εγω ειμι), used in Jesus' self-identification in Acts 9, 22, and 26, is fuller than is grammatically required in Greek, since the form of the verb itself indicates the person and number of the subject—making the inclusion of the pronoun εγω redundant. This fuller formula in John's gospel (especially 8:58) and possibly in the Synoptic Gospels (e.g., Mark 6:50; 14:62) links Jesus' reference to himself to Yahweh's self-designation in Ex. 3:14 (cf. Isa. 43:10). See D. E. Johnson, " 'I Am': Intimations of Eternity in John's Gospel," in *The Gospels Today: A Guide to Some Recent Developments*, ed. J. H. Skilton (Philadelphia: Skilton House/Sowers, 1990), 132–49; D. M. Ball, " 'My Lord and my God': The Implications of 'I Am' Sayings for Religious Pluralism," in *One God, One Lord in a World of Religious Pluralism*, ed. A. D. Clarke and B. W. Winter (Cambridge: Tyndale House, 1991), 53–71. For a different view, see P. B. Harner, *The "I Am" of the Fourth Gospel* (Facet Books, Biblical Series, 26; Philadelphia: Fortress, 1970).

²⁷ Προχειριζομαι appears only twice elsewhere in the canonical Old Testament books (in Josh. 3:12, of the tribal representatives selected to carry stones from the Jordan riverbed; in Dan. 3:22, of the soldiers selected to cast the three faithful Hebrews into the fiery furnace) and once elsewhere in the New Testament (in Acts 3:20, of Jesus, the chosen Messiah). In the LXX, the verb also appears three times in 2 Maccabees. Its infrequency of use in biblical Greek strengthens the likelihood of an intentional allusion to Ex. 4:13 in Acts 22 and 26.

²⁸ Paul himself compares his apostolic ministry to the ministry of Moses in the institution of the Old Covenant. Paul's New Covenant ministry, which brings righteousness and the Spirit, is superior to that of Moses in glory and permanence (2 Cor. 3:6–18).

²⁹ LXX: στηθι επι τους ποδας σου.

³⁰ Greek: αναστηθι και στηθηι επι τους ποδας σου.

³¹ In a later vision, the Lord reassured Paul in words reminiscent of Jer. 1:8: "Do not be afraid, but rather speak and do not be silent. For I am with you, and no one will set upon you to harm you" (Acts 18:9–10). See also Josh. 1:9; Isa. 43:1–2.

³² M. G. Kline, *Images of the Spirit* (Grand Rapids: Baker, 1980), 57–58.

³³ "Wash . . . away" (απολουω) is used only once elsewhere in the New Testament: in 1 Cor. 6:11, Paul reminds the Corinthians that they have been washed from their sinful background in sexual immorality, idolatry, etc.

³⁴ A balanced evaluation of the recent discussions of Jewish and Pauline soteriology

(since E. P. Sanders's *Paul and Palestinian Judaism* [Philadelphia: Fortress, 1977]) is Stephen Westerholm, *Israel's Law and the Church's Faith: Paul and His Recent Interpreters* (Grand Rapids: Eerdmans, 1988).

[35] See Eph. 2:17–18 for a Pauline application of Isa. 57:19 LXX, including the key term "far away" (μακραν), to the mission to the Gentiles. Gentiles were "far away," not in terms of geographical distance, but in terms of exclusion from God's covenant with Israel (Eph. 2:12). In Christ the barrier that kept Gentiles at a distance, barred from God's sanctuary, was dismantled. Aliens now have access to God's holy place "through the blood of Christ" (Eph. 2:13).

EIGHT

ILLEGAL ALIENS WELCOME

DISBAND THE BORDER PATROL

I write these words within sixty miles of the U.S.-Mexico border, a boundary notorious for the tensions evoked by the attempts of Mexican men, women, and children to find work at a living wage across the border and by the attempts of U.S. immigration officials to halt their quest. The Berlin Wall, the symbol of the Germany's Cold War division, has fallen. The Soviet Union is fractured to pieces as smaller republics (now "independent states") have reinstituted the boundaries that once marked them off from Mother Russia. The lines that separate nations and peoples are unavoidable realities.

Not all groupings of people appear on maps. Language, race, religion, culture, gender, and age can divide neighborhoods or families. They can also bind people together across vast distances and the artificial lines drawn by governments. In "Mending Wall," Robert Frost observes, "Something there is that doesn't love a wall." But his New England neighbor is ready with the adage, "Good fences make good neighbors," as they repair the barrier that keeps the poet's apple orchard from invading the neighbor's pine grove.

From a biblical perspective, one border throughout history has dwarfed all others in importance: the boundary separating faithful loyalty to God from unbelieving rebellion against him. Down through the centuries of promise, that boundary virtually coincided with the line marking off Israel from the Gentile nations. To be an Israelite was to be in covenant with God; to be non-Israelite was to be among God's enemies. There were exceptions on both sides, of course. Israelites broke covenant, prostituting their devotion before idols, and Gentile aliens (such as Rahab, Ruth, and Naaman) were mysteriously drawn to embrace the God of Israel. Nonetheless, the generalization can stand: the borders of Israel were the borders of God's kingdom; the boundaries of Jacob's family were the boundaries of God's people.

Boundary markers distinguished the holy "territory" of God's covenant from the common sphere of the nations. Gentiles wishing to change allegiance needed to submit to these boundary markers: circumcision, dietary laws, the temple with its sacrifices, and the ritual calendar, especially the Sabbath.[1] In the Judaism of the apostles' time, Gentiles who underwent ceremonial washing, were circumcised, and sent a sacrifice to Jerusalem had "shouldered the yoke of the Torah" and were to be regarded as members of Israel's community. They had committed themselves to keeping the Lord's covenant and were to be regarded as Jews in every respect, according to leading rabbis of the New Testament period. On the other hand, some Gentiles were merely "those who fear God,"[2] attracted to the synagogue by Judaism's ethical monotheism, but unwilling to cross the boundary marked by the demand of circumcision, remaining outsiders to the covenant community.[3]

The dividing wall between Jew and Gentile, rooted in God's election of Israel as his own people, was higher and more impregnable than the differences between Hellenistic and Hebraic Jews. Yet Philip's evangelization of Samaritans and of an Ethiopian eunuch were the first fissures in that massive wall of division between Jew and Gentile.

In the conversion of Cornelius, his friends, and his household, the hand of God himself detonated the charge that dismantled the great wall once and for all. Moreover, the erasure of the ethnic, cultural, and religious boundary between Jewish insiders and Gentile outsiders disclosed with new clarity the only reason why insiders or outsiders could approach the holy presence of God. At the apostolic council of Acts 15, Peter rehearsed his role in God's call to the Gentiles, declaring the universality of divine grace: "We believe it is through the grace of our Lord Jesus that we are saved, just as they are" (v. 11 NIV). Only God's own mercy, unsought and undeserved by its recipients, can explain the inclusion of Gentiles in the people of God. But the same must be said of Jews, Abraham's natural descendants! "God imprisoned all [Jew and Gentile] to disobedience, so that he may have mercy on all [Jew and Gentile]" (Rom. 11:32).

THE SIGNIFICANCE OF CORNELIUS

Luke's account of Cornelius conveys the mystery of mercy to insider and outsider alike, the grace that crosses boundaries and makes them obsolete, bringing light to the Gentiles and salvation to the ends of the earth. Luke emphasizes the importance of this event in four ways:

Repetition. The whole sequence of events is told twice, first by the narrator (Acts 10:1–48) and then by Peter upon his return to Jerusalem (11:1–18). Within these two accounts, Cornelius's vision is described four times, not only by the narrator (10:3–7) and Peter (11:13–14), but also by Cornelius's servants (10:22) and Cornelius himself (10:30–32). The threefold repetition of Peter's vision is mentioned in both accounts (10:16; 11:10).

The conversion of the Gentiles at Cornelius's house is mentioned a third time, when the apostolic council hears Peter describe how he first preached the gospel to uncircumcised Gentiles, as God had planned (15:7–8).

Parallel Reports in Jerusalem. The connection between the conversion of Gentiles in Cornelius's house and the earlier conversion of Samaritans through Philip's preaching is shown by the parallel wording used by Luke to summarize the reports that reached Jerusalem (8:14; 11:1).

Both reports that reached the apostles in Jerusalem called for further investigation or discussion, since in both cases the word of God had broken through the traditional boundaries of the people of God to evoke faith in people who were outside the community of God's covenant. The conversion of the Samaritans was a foreshadowing of the conversion of the Gentiles.[4]

Parallel Questions About Baptism. Not only the faith of the Samaritans, but also that of the Ethiopian eunuch, foreshadows the world-shaking event in Cornelius's home. This parallel is indicated by the similarity of the questions that are posed after the gospel has been presented to the eunuch and to Cornelius. After hearing the good news about Jesus, the Ethiopian asks, "What *prevents* me from *being baptized?*" (Acts 8:36).[5] After the Holy Spirit descends upon Cornelius and those with him, Peter asks, "Can anyone *prevent* water, so that these people, who have received the Holy Spirit as we did, should not *be baptized?*" (10:47).[6] The same verb *prevent* (κωλύω) reappears on Peter's lips in the question that concludes his report of God's grace toward Cornelius and the other Gentiles: "Who was I to be able to *prevent* God?" (11:17).

Thus, in the Ethiopian's question we hear the first strains of a motif that Luke will develop in the account of Cornelius: no one can prevent the baptism of Gentiles who have faith in Jesus. Probably the theme is phrased negatively ("not prevent") in answer to the assumption of some Jewish Christians that Gentiles should be forbidden to undergo Christian baptism until they had also embraced the covenantal "badges" of Judaism—circumcision, Torah (diet, calendar, etc.), and temple. But when God himself welcomes Gentile outsiders, cleansing them for his holy community through faith in Jesus, who dares to stand in his way?

Introduction to Antioch. Finally, the conversion of Cornelius and his friends is the prelude to the planting of the church at Antioch in Syria (11:19–30). Formerly the capital of the Hellenistic kingdom of the Seleucids, Antioch was the third largest city in the Roman Empire (after Rome itself and Alexandria).[7] As a trade and transportation center joining land routes from the East with the sea lanes of the Mediterranean, Antioch was ethnically cosmopolitan, a crossroads of cultural influences.

Antioch's significance in Acts is consistent with these characteristics. Here Jewish Christians from the island of Cyprus and from Cyrene in North Africa broke through the historic barrier between Israel and the Gentiles, declaring the message of Jesus the Lord not only to fellow Jews (v. 19), but also to Greeks (v. 20)—and their witness to the Gentiles was under the obvious blessing of the Lord (v. 21). This church grew impressively (vv. 21, 24, 26) and soon gained the attention of its pagan neighbors, who attached to it the name Christians—meaning "Christ's adherents or servants."[8] At Antioch, Paul and Barnabas were set apart by the Holy Spirit and sent over the Mediterranean to the Gentiles in regions west (13:1–3), and to Antioch they returned (14:26–27).[9] Thus, Antioch was both the initial site and the symbol of Paul's mission as the Apostle to the Gentiles. Cornelius was the prelude to Antioch, the gateway to the ends of the earth.

A GOD-FEARER, YET UNCLEAN

Cornelius is introduced as a centurion (a commander of one hundred soldiers) from the Italian regiment. No doubt his troops were based at Caesarea Maritima because this port city, which had been created by Herod the Great, functioned as the provincial capital under the Roman governors of Judea.[10] Like a centurion described in Luke's gospel, Cornelius was noteworthy for his kindness to the Jewish people. The earlier centurion had donated funds sufficient to build a Jewish synagogue in Capernaum, on the northwestern shore of the Sea of Galilee (Luke 7:5). Cornelius was note-

worthy for his charitable gifts to the poor, as well as his constant prayer
(Acts 10:2, 4). Thus, his conscientious response to God's word displayed
itself both in compassion toward fellow humans and in devotion to God.
He was, in short, "devout and God-fearing" (v. 2).

The term *God-fearing*[11] has a special significance in this religious setting.
It designates a special category of Gentiles who were adherents to Jewish
synagogues, but who had not become full converts (proselytes) to Judaism
(Acts 13:16, 26; 16:14; 17:4, 14; 18:7).[12] The status (or lack of status) of God-
fearers in first-century Judaism was largely defined by their hesitation to
undergo proselyte conversion. That required submission to the rite of circumcision, to the dietary restrictions in the Levitical commands and other
regulations pertaining to ritual cleanness, and to the centrality of the temple in Jerusalem, as well as adherence to the monotheism expressed in the
Shema' (Deut. 6:4–5) and to the law's ethical demands. The conversion
ritual included the presentation of a burnt offering (some rabbis allowed
exceptions in cases of hardship), the circumcision of males, and a ceremonial washing.[13]

Many Gentiles, although they admired Israel's worship of one God and
the ethical standards of the law, hesitated to undergo circumcision, which
was viewed by non-Jews as a foreign and repugnant mutilation of the body.
Josephus recounts the example of Izates, prince of Adiabene (along the
northern Tigris River, between Armenia and Parthia). Izates learned of Judaism from a Jewish merchant named Ananias. When Izates sought to become a proselyte through circumcision, his mentor, Ananias, fearing for
his own safety as well as the prince's status among his subjects, sought to
dissuade him, arguing that he "might worship God without being circumcised, even though he did resolve to follow the Jewish law entirely; which
worship of God was of a superior nature to circumcision," and that God
would forgive the omission of circumcision, since this omission was a political necessity. Later, however, a scholar in the law from Galilee rebuked
Izates, arguing that the law of circumcision was the first among the commandments by which a Gentile must express his willingness not only to
read but also to do what is written in the law. Izates submitted to circumcision and (through God's providence) suffered none of the adverse consequences that Ananias had feared.[14] The social pressure against full conversion to Judaism that would have been felt by powerful and prominent
Gentiles made the commitment of a proselyte like Izates all the more ad-
mirable in Josephus's eyes.

The status of the God-fearers, who were "not quite" proselytes, was
more ambiguous. Cornelius's messengers reported to Peter that their com-

mander was "respected by all the Jewish people" (Acts 10:22), no doubt particularly for his contributions to the poor (vv. 2, 4, 31). His schedule of prayer was attuned to the worship in the temple, for he received the angelic vision during his prayer at three in the afternoon (vv. 3, 30)—the "time of prayer," as Luke has told us (3:1), coinciding with the offering of the evening sacrifice. Nevertheless, in the eyes of Jewish Christians, such credentials could not outweigh the decisive defect in his commitment and, hence, his status vis-à-vis the covenant community: he was a "man who has uncircumcision," unfit for table fellowship with observant Jews who followed the Messiah Jesus (11:3). Peter himself would have taken this view, had God not shown him otherwise in his own preparatory vision (10:14, 34–35). Cornelius represented a class of Gentiles whom Paul and his colleagues would encounter repeatedly in the synagogues of the Dispersion.

PREPARATORY VISIONS

An Angel Sent to Cornelius

The four summaries of the angel's words move from an emphasis on Cornelius's piety to a focus on Peter's message of salvation, which Cornelius needs to hear. In the first report, the angel reassures Cornelius in terms reminiscent of the Old Testament: "Your prayers and gifts to the poor have come up [αναβαινω] as a memorial offering [μνημοσυνος] before God" (Acts 10:4 NIV). The Israelites' cry in Egyptian slavery "went up [αναβαινω] before God" (Ex. 2:23), and the grain offering was to be offered as a memorial (μνημοσυνος), an aroma pleasing to the Lord (Lev. 2:2). Thus, Luke's description of Cornelius is confirmed by the angelic witness, who has observed the divine favor that met Cornelius's expressions of worship in the heavenly court of God. The angel's commendation of Cornelius's prayer and almsgiving is repeated in Cornelius's account of the vision upon Peter's arrival (Acts 10:31). The briefer summaries of the vision given by Cornelius's servants to Peter (v. 22) and by Peter upon his return to Jerusalem (11:13–14) do not mention Cornelius's prayers and deeds of mercy.

On the other hand, the importance of the message that Peter was to speak becomes more prominent in the retellings of the vision. In Luke's initial narrative, the angel simply directs Cornelius to send for Simon, called Peter (10:5). In the servants' report, we learn that Cornelius expected to hear words from Peter (v. 22). The importance of Peter's message is stressed more when Cornelius recounts his vision to Peter: "Now we are all here in the presence of God to listen to everything the Lord has commanded you to tell us" (v. 33 NIV). Cornelius's insight that Peter is a messenger of God who speaks in the presence of God indicates that in Cornelius the promise of Isaiah 45:14 is reaching fulfillment: Gentiles from afar bow before Israel (as Cornelius bowed before Peter, Acts 10:25), confessing, "Surely God is with you."[15] When Peter defends himself before the church in Jerusalem, he summarizes the angel's message, as relayed by Cornelius: "[Simon Peter] will bring you a message through which you and all your household will be saved" (11:13–14 NIV).[16]

Thus, as Cornelius's vision is told and retold, our attention is focused first on the sincerity of his piety, manifested in gifts of compassion and in prayer. Gradually, however, Luke shifts our gaze to the message of salvation that God himself was sending to Cornelius through Peter. At the beginning, Cornelius is living proof "that God is not one to show favoritism, but in every nation (ἔθνος) the one who fears him and does right is acceptable to him" (10:34–35). But by the end, we see that Cornelius too needs the salvation that comes only through the gospel that Peter brings —forgiveness of sins to those who believe in Jesus' name (v. 43), and repentance leading to life, which God grants through the Spirit (11:18).

A Meal Sent to Peter

While Cornelius had his vision, God also used a vision to prepare his messenger Peter to associate with Gentiles, and so to bring them "the good news of peace through Jesus Christ" (Acts 10:36 NIV). If Jewish Christians would greet with suspicion a Gentile's claim to have been visited by God's angel, the vision granted to Peter would confirm that the initial breach in the wall between Jew and Gentile was the work of God himself.

A similar set of two visions laid the groundwork for the baptism of Saul: in the three days following the revelation on the Damascus road, Saul saw a vision of a man named Ananias, who would restore his sight (9:12),[17] and Ananias himself received a vision in which the Lord confirmed that Saul was indeed a vessel chosen to bear Christ's name (v. 10). In both cases, an unlikely outsider (Saul the persecutor, Cornelius the Gentile) received a vision in which the messenger of Christ who would bring deliverance was identified by name (Ananias, Simon Peter), and then in a second vision each messenger was sent by the Lord to bring God's word of welcome. By his own initiative, God brought in the Apostle to the Gentiles (Saul) and the firstfruits of the Gentiles (Cornelius).

Peter's vision focused on food because he was hungry, awaiting the midday meal (10:9–10). But his vision had spiritual depth because matters of diet, for the Jew, had profound implications for one's relationship to God and his covenant. Detailed regulations in the law distinguished clean animals, approved by God for Israel's consumption, from unclean animals: land animals had to both chew the cud and have a split hoof; sea creatures had to have fins and scales; winged insects had to have jointed legs to hop; birds of prey, reptiles, and other crawlers were off-limits (Lev. 11).

Why were there such precise regulations? Some have speculated that Israel's divinely selected, kosher menu was a means of protection from food-borne diseases in an age before refrigeration, but God's own explanation goes deeper than physical hygiene:

> I am the Lord your God; you shall be sanctified and be holy, because holy am I, the Lord your God. Do not defile your souls by all the reptiles [ερπετον] that move on the ground. Because I am the Lord who led you up out of the land of Egypt to be your God, you also shall be holy, because holy am I, the Lord. (Lev. 11:44–45)

Israel's distinctive diet was a visible sign of its holiness, its separateness as the people of God. To eat meat from forbidden animals or meat prepared in forbidden ways was to defile oneself in the presence of the holy God by disregarding the boundary he had marked around his holy people. We see the depth and strength of this conviction in Daniel, who resolved not to defile himself with the royal food and wine in the court of Nebuchadnezzar, requesting only vegetables and water (Dan. 1:8).

Since ceremonial defilement was contagious through touch, observant Jews cautioned that eating with Jews known to be indifferent to the kosher laws could easily lead to one's own ritual pollution. This was the theological rationale of those who criticized Jesus for eating with tax collectors and sinners who, despite their Jewish heritage, were lax about the Torah's commands and casual about contact with Gentiles (Luke 5:30; 15:2; cf. Mark 7:4–5). How much more, then, should Jews who were serious about holiness avoid eating with the unclean Gentiles themselves! It was Peter's eating with the uncircumcised men of Cornelius's circle that would prove to be most troubling to certain Jewish Christians (Acts 11:3).

In his vision, Peter saw a container (σκευος) like a sheet being lowered by its four corners from heaven. It was like Noah's ark (though made of cloth, not wood), for inside were all kinds of (domesticated) four-footed animals, reptiles (ερπετον), and birds of the air (10:12; 11:6). The same three categories—domesticated animals, crawling animals, and birds—

were specified in the instructions given to Noah (Gen. 6:20).[18] There was, however, an important difference between Noah's ark and Peter's tarp: in the ark, a distinction was drawn between clean and unclean animals (7:2–3), symbolizing the separation of Noah from the wicked of his generation (v. 1). Among the animals Peter saw in the tarp, however, God made no distinction; instead, he commanded Peter to kill and eat anything that he saw.

Understandably, Peter was shocked and protested strongly in language reminiscent of Ezekiel's objection when the Lord commanded him to eat food prepared in an "unclean" manner:

> And I said [ειπα], "Surely not [μηδαμως], Lord [κυριε] God of Israel. Behold, my soul has not been defiled by uncleanness [ακαθαρ-σια] . . . no unclean meat has entered [εισερχομαι] my mouth [εις το στομα μου]." (Ezek. 4:14)[19]

Ezekiel had been commanded to prepare mixed-grain cakes and cook them over human excrement in order to signify the Lord's judgment on Judah. Ezekiel's priestly sensitivities were shocked, particularly at God's command to use human excrement as fuel to cook food, for the law's command that such waste be disposed of outside the camp implied that it was ceremonially unclean (Deut. 23:12–13). But now Ezekiel's diet was to be a prophetic portrait of the destruction of the wall separating Judah from the pagan Gentiles, for the Lord said, "In this way the people of Israel will eat defiled things among the Gentiles" (Ezek. 4:13).

God's command to Peter, "Kill and eat," likewise announced the destruction of the wall between Israel and the Gentiles. But now the connotation was very different. Peter's protest was answered by the heavenly voice: "Do not call anything impure [κοινοω] that God has made clean [καθαριζω]" (Acts 10:15; 11:9 NIV). Instead of symbolizing Israel's pollution along with the Gentiles', as Ezekiel's unclean diet was to do, Peter's diet was to symbolize the Gentiles' purification along with Israel. The command that shocked Ezekiel announced the defilement and rejection of Israel, but the command that shocked Peter announced the cleansing and reception of the Gentiles. Peter made it clear that this was the meaning of the vision when, having reminded Cornelius that the law forbids Jews' close association with Gentiles, he stated, "But God has shown me that I should not call any man impure [κοινον] or unclean [ακαθαρτον]" (10:28 NIV). The reminder of the customary Jewish scruples (which had been exhibited by Peter during the vision) and the repetition of the terminology of impurity and (un)cleanness show that Peter's words here were Spirit-taught commentary on his vision. In erasing the boundary between clean and unclean animals, God erased the boundary between clean and unclean peoples.

A distinction remains between that which is pure and fit for God's holy presence, on the one hand, and the evil and pollution that are excluded, on the other. But the surface boundaries dividing the clean from the unclean are erased so that the depth of the cleft dividing sin from holiness might be shown. In God's sight, our true beauty—or ugliness—is more than skin-deep. What defiles is not superficial contact with disease or death, or a diet of forbidden foods. Nor can the cleansing remedy for defilement be found in physical ceremonies that touch only the surface of life. Jesus said,

> "Do you not understand that nothing from outside that enters into a man can defile him, because it does not enter his heart but his stomach, and goes out into the latrine?" [With this statement he was] cleansing [καθαρίζω] all foods. And he was saying, "What comes out of a man is what defiles him. For from within, out of men's hearts, evil thoughts proceed." (Mark 7:18–21)[20]

If the source of defilement lies in the depths of the human heart, the cleansing must permeate as deeply. This is what the conversion of Cornelius demonstrates, for Peter would later recall that when he preached to Cornelius and his friends, God made no distinction between Jews and Gentiles, "for he purified [καθαρίζω] their hearts by faith" (Acts 15:9 NIV).

The vision left Peter wondering "what this vision that he had seen might be" (10:17). God's threefold repetition of the vision made evident both the importance and the certainty of its message, for this is the significance of repetition in earlier prophetic visions, such as the Egyptian Pharaoh's twofold dream, which was interpreted by Joseph.[21] Peter had to seek to understand this revelation of an event so certain and so central to the plan of God. But his understanding of its meaning would become clear only as he obeyed the words that were spoken to him by the Spirit (10:19; compare the Spirit's command to Philip, 8:29). When Cornelius's messengers arrived, Peter could not hesitate to go with them (10:20). At this point, had it not been for the Spirit's instruction, Peter might still have had misgivings about accompanying this Gentile party back to the Gentile who commissioned them.[22] But the Spirit is to be obeyed, and when Peter descended to greet Cornelius's messengers, the Spirit's word was confirmed by their report of Cornelius's piety and obedience to an angel's instruction to send for Peter.

PETER'S MESSAGE FOR THE GENTILES

When the travelers arrived at Cornelius's home, Peter proclaimed the good news of Jesus, customized to address the destruction of the wall between Jew and Gentile (Acts 10:34–43).

As Cornelius recounted his vision of an angel, Peter came to a more profound understanding of a theme revealed in the Old Testament Scriptures: "God is not one who plays favorites, but in every nation the one who fears him and does right is acceptable to him" (v. 34). On the plains of Moab, Moses had declared to the Israelites that the Lord their God was the sovereign owner of heaven, earth, and all they contain. "For the Lord your God is God of gods and Lord of lords, the great and strong and fearsome God, who shows no favoritism and accepts no bribe" (Deut. 10:14, 17). The Lord demonstrates his impartiality especially in his love for the alien, the Gentile dwelling in the midst of Israel (v. 18). The God of Israel is the Lord of all creation, and therefore his compassion extends beyond the boundaries of Abraham's family.

The rabbis of Judaism saw this connection between Israel's monotheistic faith and the ultimate inclusion of the Gentiles in the kingdom of God. The *Sifre to Deuteronomy*, a loosely structured anthology of rabbinical comment, contains a comment that interprets the *Shema'* (Deut. 6:4–5), Israel's central monotheistic confession, as a prophecy of the Lord's rule over the Gentile nations in the future. Taking their lead from Zechariah 14:9 ("The Lord will be king over the whole earth. On that day there will be one Lord, and his name will be one"), the rabbinical commentator(s) take "the Lord our God" to refer to the Lord's rule over Israel in the present age, and "the Lord is one" to refer to his rule over all the nations in the age to come.[23]

Paul offers a similar argument, reinforcing his statement that God is the God of Gentiles as well as of Jews with a summary of the *Shema'*: "since there is only one God" (Rom. 3:29–30). God's unity and uniqueness demand that his dominion include not merely Israel, but also the Gentile nations. Now, Paul announces, the "age to come" has dawned with the revelation of God's righteousness through faith in Christ (vv. 21–22). The time has arrived for the one Lord to extend his kingdom over the Gentiles.

This background explains the title that Peter attributes to Jesus in the introduction to his sermon (Acts 10:36). That title stands out as an unexpected insertion in the syntax of the Greek sentence, separating the direct object ("word," with its relative clause) from the subject and verb ("you know"): "The word that he sent to the sons of Israel, proclaiming peace through Jesus Christ—*this one is Lord of all*—you know." Jesus Christ is the preacher of peace from God (Isa. 52:7; cf. Eph. 2:17) because he is Lord of all. On Pentecost, Peter declared that Jesus is enthroned as the Lord spoken of in Psalm 110 (Acts 2:33–36). Now, in Cornelius's house, Peter enriches the title: Jesus is not simply "Lord" (κυριος), but "Lord of all" (παντων κυριος). His peaceable kingdom includes not only Israel, but also the Gentiles.[24]

In Deuteronomy 10, Moses moves from the premise that Israel's Redeemer is Lord of lords to the conclusion that he does not show favoritism (v. 17), but rather loves the (non-Israelite) alien (v. 18) even as he has loved Israel in the patriarchs (v. 15). There is even a hint that in the eyes of God, the physical rite of circumcision does not distinguish Israel from the Gentiles, for the Israelites themselves need a deeper surgery than that performed on the body: "Be circumcised in your hard heart, and do not stiffen your neck any longer" (v. 16).[25] The cleansing must permeate to the deep root of Israel's impurity—to the heart. If external circumcision does not exempt Israelites from the need for internal circumcision, must the lack of external circumcision exclude Gentiles from the possibility of internal circumcision?

Through his meeting with Cornelius, the answer was made clear to Peter and, in turn, to the church. Peter saw that God accepts people from every nation who fear him and express that reverence in action (Acts 10:34). This is not to say that pious Gentiles such as Cornelius are "noble savages," unspoiled and innocent, for Peter knows that they too need forgiveness of sins (v. 43). Peter was shown that Gentiles receive that forgiveness through faith in Jesus, apart from circumcision and becoming Jews: "All the prophets testify about [Jesus] that everyone who believes [παντα τον πιστευοντα] in him receives forgiveness of sins through his name [ονομα]" (v. 43 NIV). The Lord of all bestows forgiveness on all who have faith in him.

Peter's mention of the prophets suggests that he would have gone on to cite Old Testament promises of forgiveness to those who trust in the name of the Lord.[26] Although apostolic preachers typically did not cite Scripture when speaking to pagan Gentiles (see Acts 14:14–18; 17:22–31), the ancient prophecies would have been meaningful to a God-fearer such as Cornelius, who even scheduled his prayers according to the sacrificial ritual of the temple. Perhaps among these promises would have been Joel 2:32, which Peter cited at Pentecost: "And everyone [πας] who calls on the name [ovoμα] of the Lord will be saved" (Acts 2:21 NIV). The comprehensiveness of the promise ("everyone") and the mention of the name of the Lord suggest that this promise from Joel may have been in Peter's mind as he introduced the prophets' words promising forgiveness in Jesus' *name* to *everyone* who believes in him.

THE GENTILE PENTECOST

Peter's preaching was interrupted by God's initiative. The Spirit "fell upon" (επιπιπτω) and "was poured out upon" (εκχεω) all those who heard the message (Acts 10:44–45).[27] The verbs link this event with the "pouring out" (εκχεω) of the Spirit at Pentecost (2:17, 33) and with the "falling" (επιπιπτω) of the Spirit upon the Samaritan believers through the ministry of Peter and John (8:16).

The connection with Pentecost is reinforced in other ways. Recipients of the Spirit spoke in tongues—both the Gentiles with Cornelius (10:46) and the original disciples at Pentecost (2:4, 8, 11). They magnified God (μεγαλυνω, 10:46)—that is, they declared his wonders (μεγαλεια, 2:11). As a result, those who heard them, both the Jewish believers with Peter in Caesarea (10:45) and the residents from the Dispersion in Jerusalem (2:7, 12), were amazed (εξιστημι). Baptism in the name of Jesus Christ followed both bestowals of the Spirit (2:38; 10:48). Peter's report upon his return to Jerusalem draws the most explicit parallel between the two bestowals of the Spirit: "The Holy Spirit came on them *as [he had come] on us at the beginning*. And I remembered the Lord's word, how he would say, 'John baptized with water, but you will be baptized with the Holy Spirit.' . . . God gave them *the same gift as he gave us*" (11:15–17). The baptism with the Spirit promised by Jesus and poured out by him on Pentecost now flowed into Gentile hearts through faith in Jesus.

How was the church to know that the inclusion of the Gentiles was God's idea and not Peter's? When the Samaritans received the Spirit, two apostolic witnesses were present and could confirm what God had done. In Cornelius's house there was but one apostle. While Peter's integrity is reliable,[28] the biblical principle stands that matters of moment must be confirmed by a plurality of witnesses (Deut. 19:15; Matt. 18:15). This was the role of the Jewish Christian "brothers" who had accompanied Peter from Joppa to Caesarea (Acts 10:23). "The believers from the circumcision who had come with Peter were astonished [εξιστημι], because even on the

Gentiles [και επι τα εθνη] the gift of the Holy Spirit had been poured out" (v. 45).[29]

The astonishment of these disciples enhanced their credibility as witnesses, since their testimony to the Gentiles' reception of the Spirit certified an event contrary to their expectation.[30] Luke emphasizes their status as "believers of the circumcision" (οι εκ περιτομης πιστοι, v. 45). Is not this description gratuitous? From Luke's narrative to this point, would we not assume that all believers (except the Ethiopian, who has returned to his country) were "of the circumcision," either as ethnic Jews or as proselytes to Judaism (2:11; 6:5)?[31] Yet Luke, rather than leaving their circumcised status a tacit assumption, calls attention to it. Nothing less than God's miraculous initiative could have convinced them that God had cleansed and welcomed Gentiles by faith in Jesus, apart from circumcision. When "those from the circumcision" (οι εκ περιτομης) criticized Peter for his table fellowship with uncircumcised men (11:2), these brothers stood ready to support the apostle and confirm the astonishing welcome of God, extended "even to the Gentiles" (v. 12).

But, of course, the things that Peter and the six brothers with him had seen and heard in Cornelius's house were signs of God's own testimony. Peter made that clear when addressing the apostolic council (Acts 15). It was God who made the choice (εκλεγομαι) that Gentiles should hear the gospel through Peter's lips and believe (v. 7). It was God who bore witness (μαρτυρεω) to the Gentiles' faith by giving them his Holy Spirit (v. 8). It was God, who knows hearts (v. 8; cf. 1 Kings 8:39), who cleansed the Gentiles' hearts by faith (v. 9). Therefore, just as Peter would have been opposing (κωλυω) God if he had refused to baptize Cornelius and the other Gentile believers (11:17), so those who would impose circumcision on Gentile believers *after* their baptism were now guilty of wanting to test (πειραζω) God (15:10). Testing God, we remember, was the sin of the wilderness generation (Ex. 17:2) and of Ananias and Sapphira (Acts 5:9) —lethal evil![32] Misguided zeal for the law of Moses had placed opponents of the Gentile mission in league with those who despised the holy presence of the God of grace among his people!

CONCLUSION: FALLEN WALLS, OPEN DOORS

God himself brought the great wall down. Over Peter's protests, to the astonishment of his six companions from Joppa, and despite the opposition

of some from the Pharisees' party in the church (Acts 15:5), God dismantled the barrier separating Jew and Gentile once for all. Gentiles were not
to be judged in terms of the boundary markers or badges of ancient Israel
—circumcision, diet, and calendar—for such surface things, while they had
their place until the Messiah came, could not reach to the heart of the issue.
The heart of the issue is, in fact, the heart, and it is in the depths of our
thoughts and motives that genuine cleansing, separation from pollution,
must transpire. God makes no distinction, cleansing the heart of the Jew
by faith in Jesus and the heart of the Gentile by the same faith in the same
Jesus.

What does this tell us about all the other walls that so easily divide people? The early church did not find it easy to "catch up" with what God had
done at Cornelius's home. Differences of perspective persisted between Jew
and Gentile, vegetarians and meat eaters, observers of special days and
those who did not, and so on. Yet God's direction was clear: none of these
cultural differences—not even the cultural distinctives that God himself
had imbedded in the Torah as a symbolic wall of separation between the
holy and the "unclean"—can stand as a wall segregating those who are one
with each other in Christ Jesus.

Evangelism must lead with the gospel, not with a call to cultural conformity or moral reformation. Repentance is not adopting the evangelist's
clothing style, speech patterns, or taste in music. It is seeing the horror of
one's sin and receiving the forgiving grace of Christ, embracing the Savior in faith for washing from sin's guilt and liberation from its tyrannical
control.

In dealing with other Christians, we must be especially careful to distinguish what God's word says about the lifestyle that "fits" faith, on the one
hand, from what we find culturally comfortable, on the other. Christians
find it too easy to pass judgment on each other or to lay obligations on each
other in areas where God's word gives us freedom: clothing, music, types of
relaxation, use of money, etc. "Who are you to judge someone else's servant?"
challenges Paul (Rom. 14:4 NIV). Peter's warning about testing God soberly
alerts us to the consequences of arrogant judgmentalism (Acts 15:10).

As we apply the abiding standards of holiness and justice revealed in
God's law, we must learn to distinguish the peripherals from the spiritual
heart issues, especially in nurturing new Christians. They will struggle
with patterns of external behavior that do not fit their new nature in
Christ, as we all do. But the first and most important thing is to focus on
the heart of the matter. Reflecting on what he himself had discovered in
a new way at Cornelius's home, Peter said, "We believe it is through the

grace of our Lord Jesus Christ that we are saved, just as they are" (15:11 NIV). Christ's grace destroys self-trust and pride. As we depend on Christ's grace, purification from lust, gluttony, greed, deceit, and bitterness will follow.

Now that the wall is down, the servants of Christ are called to crawl over the rubble with the message of salvation. It is comfortable to stay in the sphere of people like ourselves, seeking refuge in a familiar ghetto of Christian contacts. But we cannot wait for non-Christians to cross the culture gaps, to scale the walls to get to know us well enough to see Christ's grace in our lives. The gospel speaks with power in every culture, to every people under heaven. When the gospel touches a new culture, it does not leave that culture unchanged. Yet God does not demand that people leave their culture in order to hear of his grace in Christ. We who have experienced this grace are the ones who must climb the walls, build the bridges, and suffer the stresses of culture shock. People who know Jesus must pay the price to pierce the barriers between peoples. And as they do, Jesus spreads his salvation to the ends of the earth.

Notes

[1] James D. G. Dunn, "The New Perspective on Paul," *BJRL* 65 (1983): 96–122, describes the ceremonial distinctives of Judaism as "identification markers" (p. 108) or "badges" (p. 110).

[2] Greek: φοβουμενοι τον θεον or σεβομενοι τον θεον. The title is probably from such Old Testament texts as Pss. 115:11; 118:4; 135:20, where, however, the title was probably given to Gentiles who had become full proselytes to the faith of Israel and thus participated in the temple worship.

[3] Although some recent scholars have questioned whether early Judaism recognized a category of "God-fearing" Gentiles who fell between mere paganism and proselyte conversion, a third-century stele recently discovered at Aphrodisias seems to establish the distinction clearly. See Conrad H. Gempf, "Appendix 2: The God-Fearers," in Colin J. Hemer, *The Book of Acts in the Setting of Hellenistic Historiography*, ed. Conrad J. Gempf (WUNT, 49; Tübingen: J. C. B. Mohr, 1989), 444–47.

[4] Similarly, when a large number of Gentiles turned to the Lord at Antioch in Syria, "the report concerning them reached the ears of the church at Jerusalem, and they sent Barnabas to Antioch" (Acts 11:22).

[5] Greek: τι κωλυει με βαπτισθηναι;

[6] Greek: μητι το υδωρ δυναται κωλυσαι τις του με βαπτισθηναι τουτους;

[7] F. F. Bruce, *Paul: Apostle of the Heart Set Free* (Grand Rapids: Eerdmans, 1977), 130.

[8] F. F. Bruce, *New Testament History* (Garden City, N.J.: Doubleday, 1972), 267.

[9] Acts 14:26 NIV, "where they had been committed to the grace of God for the work [εις το εργον] they had now completed," recalls the Holy Spirit's words in 13:2 NIV: "Set

apart for me Barnabas and Saul for the work [εις το εργον] to which I have called them."
The mission begun at Antioch had to end there, with the report of God's opening a door
of faith to the Gentiles.

¹⁰ Roman governors also maintained a headquarters in the Antonia fortress, overlooking the temple courts in Jerusalem. They traveled to Jerusalem during the great feasts in
order to be able to give immediate attention to social unrest or uprisings that arose from
the concentration of zealous Jewish pilgrims during such times. Caesarea was preferred by
Romans not only for its milder weather, but also because of its more Greco-Roman cultural
atmosphere.

¹¹ Greek: φοβουμενος τον θεον.

¹² Luke also speaks of Gentiles who have become full proselytes as "the proselytes who
reverence [God]" (των σεβομενων προσηλυτων) in Acts 13:43.

¹³ "Proselytes," Encyclopedia Judaica (Jerusalem: Keter, 1972), 13:1182–83.

¹⁴ Antiquities 20.2.

¹⁵ The same Greek word (προσκυνεω) is found in Isa. 45:14 LXX and Acts 10:25. Note
that Paul also alludes to Isa. 45:14 in 1 Cor. 14:25. I am grateful to Edmund P. Clowney for
bringing this connection to my attention, as well as raising my awareness of the richness
of the New Testament's use of the Old Testament in general.

¹⁶ The angel's promise looks back to Peter's words on the day of Pentecost, explaining
the promise of Joel ("Everyone who calls on the name of the Lord will be saved," Acts 2:21)
in terms of the forgiveness of sins and the gift of the Holy Spirit (2:38), and then assuring
his hearers, "The promise is for you and your children and for all those far away, as many as
the Lord our God will call" (2:39). Cornelius and his household were "far away," not geo-
graphically but covenantally. The angel's promise also looks forward to the apostles' words
to the jailor of Philippi: "Believe in the Lord Jesus, and you will be saved—you and your
household" (16:31 NIV). Note the parallel wording in Acts 11:14 (σωθηση συ και παν ο
οικος σου) and 16:31 (σωθηση συ και ο οικος σου).

¹⁷ Several early and reliable textual witnesses (p74, ℵ, A) do not contain the words "in
a vision" (εν οραματι) here, but other early manuscripts (B, C) as well as the vast majority of later witnesses include them, as do the NIV and the standard editions of the Greek
New Testament (UBS, NTG).

¹⁸ The LXX also mentions "wild beasts" (θηρια, Gen. 6:19), which are included in
Peter's report of the vision in Acts 11:6.

¹⁹ Note the wording derived from Ezek. 4:14 LXX in Acts 11:8: "But I said [ειπον], 'Surely
not [μηδαμως], Lord [κυριε], because something common or unclean [ακαθαρτον] has
never entered [εισερχομαι] my mouth [εις το στομα μου].' "

²⁰ Only Mark's gospel, which is traditionally associated with Peter's ministry, contains
the commentary on Jesus' statement that foods that enter a person do not make the person unclean, "In saying this, Jesus cleansed [καθαριζω] all foods" (Mark 7:19).

²¹ See Joseph's words in Gen. 41:32 NIV: "The reason the dream was given to Pharaoh
in two forms is that the matter has been firmly decided by God, and God will do it soon."
So also, Peter's thrice-given vision underscores God's firm purpose to cleanse the unclean,
and to do so soon. Another suggestion, less plausible to me, is that the threefold vision corresponds to Jonah's three days inside the great fish, as part of a larger typological correspondence between the prophet Jonah and Simon Peter bar-Jonah. Robert W. Wall, "Peter,
'Son' of Jonah: the Conversion of Cornelius in the Context of Canon," JSNT 29 (1987):
79–90. Other parallels between Jonah and Peter that Wall points out (association with

Joppa, commissions to proclaim God's word to Gentiles, initial hesitation on the messenger's part, verbal parallels, etc.) are more persuasive.

²² The Greek word translated "hesitate" in 10:20 (διακρινω) is woven throughout the Cornelius narrative and is used in a number of different senses. In the middle voice, it typically means "dispute," and sometimes particularly "dispute with oneself, doubt, hesitate," as in this verse. It reappears in the middle voice in 11:2, where the believers from the circumcision disputed with Peter over his table fellowship with Cornelius. In the active voice, it means "differentiate, make a distinction, discriminate." Despite the NIV's translation of 11:12 ("hesitate," imitating 10:20), the best manuscripts at 11:12 have διακρινω in the active voice: "The Spirit told me to accompany them without *making any distinction*" (over the fact that they were Gentiles). In 15:9, διακρινω is again in the active voice when Peter declares that God "*made no distinction* between us and them." To *dispute* with oneself or others over welcoming Gentile believers is to oppose God, who does not *discriminate* between Jew and Gentile.

²³ Jacob Neusner, *Sifre to Deuteronomy: An Analytical Translation*, 2 vols. (Atlanta: Scholars' Press, 1987), 1:85, translates Sifre to Deut. 31.4 (on 6:4) as follows:

"The Lord, our God":—for us.

"the Lord is one":—for everyone in the world.

"the Lord, our God":—in this world.

"the Lord is one":—in the world to come.

And so Scripture says, "The Lord shall be king over all the earth. In that day shall the Lord be one and his name one" (Zech. 14:9).

Neusner indicates that it is impossible to date the origination of particular sayings in Sifre to Deuteronomy, but he does find some of its material to date from late antiquity (*Sifre to Deuteronomy*, 1:5). The similarity between Paul's reasoning in Rom. 3:29–30 and the reasoning in Sifre to Deuteronomy 31.4 supports the antiquity of a Jewish connection between God's unity and his eschatological rule over the nations.

²⁴ The title "Lord of all" is a crucial element in Paul's argument that God impartially includes Jew and Gentile alike in the salvation that Christ has brought: "For there is no difference between Jew and Gentile—the same one is Lord of all [ο γαρ αυτος κυριος παντων], being rich toward all who call on him" (Rom. 10:12). Note the allusion to Joel 2:32 (which Paul cites in v. 13) in "all who call on him" (cf. Acts 2:21).

²⁵ Cf. Deut. 30:6; Lev. 26:41; Jer. 4:4; Rom. 2:28–29 on the motif of circumcision of the heart. Note especially Deut. 30:6, in which Moses predicts that after Israel's disobedience and exile, the Lord will regather Israel and he himself will circumcise their hearts.

²⁶ Thus, Ernst Haenchen is not reading the text carefully when he asserts that "10.34–43 is somewhat contradicted by the statement of 11.15 that the Spirit fell on the hearers the moment Peter *began* to speak" (*The Acts of the Apostles: A Commentary* [Philadelphia: Westminster Press, 1971], 355). Haenchen believes that 10:34–43 is presented as a finished speech. Comparison with Peter's speech in Acts 3, however, suggests that 10:43 is an introduction to what would have been another phase of Peter's sermon. In Acts 3, Peter's call to repentance and the promise of forgiveness (v. 19) do not conclude that sermon, but instead are followed by reference to the eschatological promises "God spoke through the mouth of his holy prophets" (v. 21). This mention of the prophets introduces Old Testament *testimonia* (vv. 22–23, 25). It is therefore reasonable to suppose that the Spirit's descent on the Gentiles at Cornelius's house occurred near the beginning of what would have

been a longer discourse, including quotation of the prophetic promises to which Peter alluded (10:43).

[27] The description of those who received the Spirit as "all who heard [ακουω] the message [λογος]" emphasizes the importance of Peter's preaching. See v. 33 ("to hear [ακουω] everything the Lord has commanded you to tell us") and v. 36 ("You know the word [λογος]").

[28] Peter Smuts has suggested to me that the accounts of the healing of Aeneas and the raising of Tabitha (Acts 9:32–43) may prepare the reader for Peter's role in the conversion of the Gentile Cornelius by underscoring the divine authority that had been entrusted to him. Particularly through the restoration of Tabitha to life, Peter is attested as a messenger of God, after the pattern of the confirmation of Elijah's prophetic authority through the resurrection of the (Gentile!) widow's son at Zarephath (1 Kings 17:17–24, alluded to in Luke 7:11–17).

[29] This motif, "even the Gentiles" (και τα εθνη), reverberates through the succeeding narrative: "The apostles and the brothers throughout Judea heard that *even the Gentiles* had received the word of God" (11:1). "God has granted *even to the Gentiles* repentance unto life" (v. 18). At Antioch, some disciples "were speaking *even to the Greeks* [και προς τους Ελληνιστας], telling the good news about the Lord Jesus" (v. 20).

[30] Similarly, the apostles' initial unbelief and amazement when confronted by the risen Lord (Luke 24:24, 37, 41) show the irrefutability of the "many convincing proofs" of his resurrection that he showed them (Acts 1:3: Luke 24:40–43). They are more credible as witnesses because their doubt was overcome by the incontrovertible demonstration of God's action.

[31] It is possible that "those from the circumcision" could indicate that these brothers not only were circumcised themselves, but also advocated the circumcision of Gentiles. But would this not be the assumption of the whole church at that point?

[32] Ex. 17:2 LXX: τι πειραζετε κυριον; Acts 15:10: τι πειραζετε τον θεον;

NINE

THE GROWING WORD

How Grows the Church?

Church growth research seems to show that unchurched, suburban North Americans are more likely to return to a church after an initial visit if: (1) their children are well cared for; (2) the music is contemporary; (3) friendly people welcome them; and (4) the preaching is crisp in pace and relevant to their felt needs. Now, the book of Acts does not mention church nurseries or musical styles. Acts does describe a community of believers who not only loved each other, but also welcomed new disciples, so we may conclude that early Christians were friendly and welcoming. But Acts focuses on the role of preaching, more than any other factor, in the growth of the church.

It is surprising that preaching still counts for something in late twentieth-century America. Oratorical skill has receded from the place of prominence it once held in public life. If someone uses words *too* skillfully, we suspect that we are being manipulated—or we smile in amusement at the speaker's verbal snobbery. Television has shrunk our attention spans and lowered our threshold of patience for the spoken word. Sound bites and video images are the media to which we entrust our important messages—leaving us vulnerable, of course, to new, more sophisticated forms of manipulation.

Christians from Africa, Asia, and Latin America could well pity their brothers and sisters in North America, who have been impoverished mentally and spiritually by these technological luxuries. Even American culture is not utterly desensitized to preaching. The African-American community still respects leaders who speak with eloquence and power. Preaching-centered superchurches show how the effectiveness and content of preaching can influence a church's whole ministry. Preaching, the avenue along which God's grace traveled to the ends of the ancient world, still brings grace today to people who hardly hear it over the drone of their own busyness. Preaching, the Spirit's scalpel, still cuts through our mental clutter and distracted impatience to remove infection of the heart and to bring healing.

But what is Christian preaching? What message should we preach? How should we preach it? The book of Acts is a unique resource for us as we search out these questions. Luke emphasizes the theme of preaching by speaking of the "growth" of the word in his transitional summaries (Acts 6:7; 12:24; 13:49; 19:20) and by devoting a large proportion of Acts to particular apostolic speeches. The speeches in Acts give us a window on an aspect of Christian preaching that we find nowhere else in the New Testament. The Gospels give us samples of Jesus' preaching during his earthly ministry, but Acts shows us how the gospel was preached *after* his death, resurrection, ascension, and bestowal of the Spirit. Paul's letters summarize the gospel he preached (1 Cor. 15:3–4; Rom. 1:18–8:39), but they were addressed to congregations that were already confessing faith in Jesus. Thus, they provide only indirect access to Paul's *evangelistic* proclamation at the cutting edge of Christianity's invasion of the Greco-Roman world. Only Acts gives us multiple examples, in a variety of settings and to a variety of audiences, of the message that called people initially to faith in Jesus.[1]

On the other hand, the New Testament does not draw a sharp line between the *evangelistic* message that calls non-Christians to faith and the *nurturing* message that builds committed Christians in their faith. Paul's letters, for example, show us that the gospel of Christ is not simply a port of entry to be passed through and left behind as we grow to maturity in Christian truth and living. Rather, *the whole Christian understanding of reality and ethics flows from the message of Christ's death and resurrection.* Christian maturity involves the working out of that gospel in our thought and behavior with more and more consistency.

For this reason, Luke included evangelistic sermons in his second volume to Theophilus, even though Theophilus had already "been taught"[2] the Christian message (Luke 1:4). Theophilus and new believers like him need to hear the apostles preach the gospel. Thus, although the sermons in Acts are focused on calling unbelievers to faith, they also nurture the confidence of believers in the things they have been taught.[3]

Luke's gospel itself is an extended summary of the apostles' teaching to young Christians. In his prologue, Luke announces his purpose to transmit accurately things that "were handed down[4] to us by those who from the first were eyewitnesses and servants of the word" (Luke 1:2 NIV). The contents of Luke's gospel show that this teaching demonstrated that Jesus is the promised Messiah, explained the significance of his death and resurrection, called for faith in him, and defined the response that Jesus commanded his disciples to give to God (e.g., Luke 11:1–13; 12:22–34) and each other (e.g., 22:24–30).[5]

This story of Jesus, taught by the apostolic eyewitnesses, was a primary focus of attention for Jesus' new disciples (Acts 2:42). This message had been the Spirit's instrument to create this new community of faith. Convinced that Jesus was Lord and Messiah (Acts 2:36), these new believers naturally looked to those who had been with Jesus for instruction in the implications of their faith. Acts opens with Jesus *teaching*, as recorded in Luke's "former book" (1:1), and it closes with Paul preaching the kingdom of God and *teaching* about the Lord Jesus (28:31).

CENTRAL THEMES OF THE PREACHING IN ACTS

In the preaching in Acts, we hear one story again and again, yet each repetition casts the story in a new light. The central themes of "the word of this salvation" (Acts 13:26) are constant, whether spoken by Peter or by Paul, whether announced in the Jerusalem temple, a Dispersion synagogue, or among Greek intellectuals. But as we move from one sermon to the next, we find these themes tailored to suit the situation, background, and assumptions of the audience. Luke shows us not only *what* the apostles preached, but also *how* they preached their message to reach the diverse peoples of the Roman world. We will survey four central themes woven throughout the sermons in Acts, and then sample one of Paul's sermons to illustrate the adaptation that builds bridges of understanding to different kinds of people.

The apostles' message could be summarized by four themes: (1) Jesus, crucified and risen to life, is the Messiah and Savior promised in the Scriptures, who has brought the kingdom of God among us. (2) Jesus the Messiah bestows the blessings of the kingdom. (3) Jesus the Messiah will come to judge and to deliver. (4) People must repent and trust in the name of Jesus for salvation.[6] Let us consider each one in detail.

1. *Jesus the Messiah Has Brought the Promised Kingdom*

The Last Days and the Messiah. The last days, promised through the prophets, have dawned—days of relief and restoration, but also of crisis, in which the proud and stubborn are separated from those who humbly hope in God. We have seen this theme in Peter's sermons in Acts 2 and 3, and it continues throughout the book. Jesus is the proclaimer of peace to the sons of Israel, as Isaiah foresaw (Acts 10:36; Isa. 52:7). Jesus is the descendant of David who brings salvation to Israel (Acts 13:23, 27, 32). Even when Paul addressed a pagan audience, his thought reflected the biblical contrast between the age of promise and the age of fulfillment: "The times of ignorance God overlooked, but now he is commanding all people everywhere to repent. For he has set a day when he will judge the world with justice by the man he has appointed" (17:30–31; compare Rom. 3:25–26). History is in God's hands, and the appearance of his Messiah has brought it to this moment of blessed opportunity and solemn decision.

Testimonies to the Messiah. The apostles appealed to testimonies from God to support their claim that Jesus is the Messiah. These testimonies were crucial because Jesus' death in shameful circumstances seemed to contradict the claim that he is the champion for whom God's people have hoped.

God testified on Jesus' behalf through the miraculous signs accomplished through him, both during his earthly ministry and then through his messengers. Peter reminded his hearers on Pentecost about "Jesus the Nazarene, a man accredited by God to you by miracles, wonders and signs, which God did through him in your midst, as you yourselves know" (Acts 2:22). To Cornelius and his friends, Peter recalled Jesus' miracles of healing and exorcism as testimonies that "God was with him" (10:38). After Jesus ascended to heaven, the apostles' miraculous signs, done in his name, still testified to his authority. The declaration of God's wonders in diverse languages demonstrated that Jesus was the risen Christ, who pours out the Spirit (2:31–33). The healing of the lame man in Solomon's Colonnade signified that God had glorified his servant Jesus, by whose name God's saving power was at work (3:13, 16; 4:9–12).

The preeminent testimony to Jesus' messiahship was provided by his resurrection and exaltation to the right hand of God. In the light of Jesus' resurrection from the dead (Ps. 16) and his pouring out of the Spirit (Ps. 110 and Joel 2), Peter concluded, "Therefore let all the house of Israel know with certainty that God has made this Jesus, whom you crucified, both Lord and Christ" (Acts 2:36). After his resurrection, Jesus was seen by chosen witnesses, who then testified that he is the judge of the living and the dead (10:41–42).[7] The apostles' central mission was to bear witness to Jesus' resurrection (1:22; 13:30–31) because that was God's testimony on behalf of his anointed servant and Son.

The testimony of the Resurrection comes in concert with the testimony of the Scriptures. The Resurrection event needs to be interpreted in words, and such an interpretation was supplied by God in advance through ancient prophecies. Peter's first sermon (Acts 2:25–31) and Paul's first sermon (13:35–37) both argue that Psalm 16—especially verse 10: "You will not let your Holy One see decay"—has been fulfilled not in David's experience, but only in the experience of Jesus, the Messiah who descended from David and was foreseen by him. Jesus is the "stone" of Psalm 118:22, rejected by Israel's "builders," but exalted by God through Jesus' resurrection (Acts 4:10–11). Because his resurrection led to his enthronement at God's right hand (Ps. 110:1), his exaltation fulfilled God's promise to bring to David's throne an heir who would be God's Son (Ps. 2:7; Acts 2:30, 33–35; 13:32–33).

Equally important is the Scriptures' testimony to the Messiah's suffering and death. Jesus' crucifixion, after all, was the great stumbling block in the path of faith for the apostles' Jewish hearers (1 Cor. 1:23). Therefore, the apostles demonstrated that the suffering of the Messiah had been clearly predicted in the prophets: "What God had foretold through the mouth of all the prophets—that his Messiah would suffer—he fulfilled in this way" (Acts 3:18). "Those who live in Jerusalem and their rulers, not recognizing Jesus and the voices of the prophets that are read every Sabbath, by condemning him, fulfilled them" (13:27). "I stand testifying to small and great, saying nothing beyond what the prophets and Moses said would happen—that the Messiah would suffer and, as the first one of the resurrection of the dead, would proclaim light both to the people [of Israel] and to the Gentiles" (26:22–23).

Among the Scriptures that foretell the Messiah's suffering, according to the preaching in Acts, are Psalm 118 (rejection of the Messiah by Israel's leaders, Acts 3:11) and Isaiah 49–53, 61 (suffering of the anointed Servant, Acts 3:13–14; 8:32–35). Israel's historic pattern of repudiating divine messengers—Joseph, Moses, and the prophets—reached its climax in the murder of the Righteous One (cf. Isa. 53:11), of whom the prophets had spoken (Acts 7:9, 23–29, 35, 52). At prayer under pressure, the church discerned in Psalm 2 the international conspiracy against the Lord's Messiah that had been realized in history in the Jewish-Gentile collaboration to do away with Jesus (4:25–27).

Jesus' identity and authority as the Messiah are thus confirmed by the harmonious testimony of multiple witnesses provided by God himself: messianic miracle-signs, Jesus' resurrection, and the Scriptures, which predicted both the suffering and the resurrection of the Messiah.

The Messiah's Death. Jesus' shameful death on a cross made it unthinkable to many that he could be the promised Messiah. How did the apostles explain this scandal of the King's crucifixion?

On the one hand, they insisted that Jesus' death was a miscarriage of justice on the part of ignorant but guilty people. God's testimony to Jesus through the miracles he performed made the Jewish leaders culpable for seeking Jesus' death (Acts 2:22–23). God's righteous servant was disowned by his people (3:14) and hanged on a tree as one accursed (5:30; 10:39; 13:29). Gentiles joined in the conspiracy to overthrow the Lord's rule through his Christ (4:35–37). In this unholy alliance, the residents and leaders of Jerusalem and their leaders made use of "lawless men" (that is, Gentiles,[8] 2:23), specifically Pontius Pilate and the Roman soldiers he commanded (3:13; 13:28), in order to do away with the Author of life (3:15). Since Jesus' enemies found in him no ground for a death sentence (13:28), his death was the ultimate injustice, the product of their malice and ignorance (3:17; 13:27).

On the other hand, Jesus' death was not a tragedy that God was unable to avert. Rather, it had been *planned* by God. Peter speaks of Jesus to the Pentecost crowds as "this man, given over to you by God's determined purpose and foreknowledge" (2:23). For this reason, the Messiah's sufferings were predicted in the Old Testament Scriptures. Through the ignorant acts of the people of Jerusalem, God fulfilled his predictions that his Christ would suffer (3:18). The conspirators who sought to overthrow the Lord's rule in fact accomplished what his hand[9] and will had previously ordained to take place (4:28). Even Judas's treachery was part of the plan, for "it was necessary" (ἔδει) to fulfill the prediction in Scripture that the Messiah would be betrayed by a close friend (Ps. 109:4–5, 8; Acts 1:16, 20). Jesus himself had said that those who believed the prophets would recognize that "it was necessary" (ἔδει) for the Christ to suffer and then enter his glory (Luke 24:26).

Why was it necessary for the Messiah to inaugurate the kingdom through his suffering? What is the role of Christ's death in his work of salvation? Those accustomed to Paul's focus on the cross as the atoning sacrifice that reconciles us to God will notice a different emphasis in the preaching of Acts. These sermons stress the Resurrection, by which God reversed the unjust verdict of the human courts that condemned Jesus. By the Resurrection, God installed Jesus as Christ and Lord, the giver of repentance, forgiveness, the Spirit, peace, and cosmic restoration—in short, the blessing promised to Abraham for all peoples (Acts 2:36; 3:26; 10:43; 13:39). Yet the apostolic preaching in Acts also points us to the redemptive role of Jesus' death in three ways: (1) As God's righteous servant, Jesus was sent to suffer for others. (2) The cross on which he suffered was the "tree" of cursing. (3) His sacrificial blood was the price by which God purchased his church.

(1) *As God's righteous servant, Jesus was sent to suffer for others.* We have seen how the servant theme in Isaiah is applied to Jesus in Luke and Acts.[10] Here our focus is on the significance of the Servant's *suffering.* In only one sermon is Jesus explicitly called God's servant.[11] When explaining the healing of a lame man, Peter said, "The God of our fathers glorified [εδοξ-ασεν] his *servant* [παις] Jesus, whom you handed over [παραδιδωμι].[12] . . . You disowned the Holy and *Righteous One* [δικαιον] and asked that a murderer be given to you" (3:13–15). Peter's statements echo the song of the Servant's suffering and glorification (Isa. 52:13–53:12). The Servant would be "glorified" (δοξασθησεται) (52:13), despite having been shunned and disowned by the people (53:3). He was the Righteous One (δικαιον) who would justify many by bearing their iniquities (53:11). Thus, in calling Jesus the "Righteous One," Peter was declaring not only that Jesus did not deserve to suffer, but also that he suffered in the place of others. The Righteous One brings others into right standing before God by suffering for their iniquities, bearing their sin (v. 12), and being pierced for their transgressions (v. 5) as a lamb led to slaughter (v. 7).[13] When Peter said that the risen Servant had been sent to "turn [αποστρεφω] each of you from your wicked ways" (Acts 3:26), he was perhaps alluding to Isaiah 53:6, "We all, like sheep, have gone astray." In his first epistle, Peter would remind his readers, "You were like sheep going astray, but now you were caused to return [επιστρεφω] to the Shepherd and Overseer of your souls" (1 Peter 2:25). The Servant causes wandering sheep to return as he bears their sin through his suffering.[14]

(2) *Jesus' cross was the "tree" of cursing.* Twice in the preaching of Acts, Jesus is said to have been "hanged on a tree" (Acts 5:30; 10:39), and in another sermon he is said to have been taken down "from the tree" (13:29). The Greek word for "tree" (ξυλον) can refer to various objects made from wood, including the crosses used by Romans to execute dangerous and despicable criminals. But the normal word for *cross* is σταυρος, and the normal verb for *crucify* is σταυροω.[15] The unusual reference to the cross as a "tree," in combination with the verb "hang" (κρημαννυμι) in Acts 5:30 and 10:39, suggests that this formula has special significance for the interpretation of Jesus' death.[16] The third sermon confirms this suggestion, for it contains Paul's statements that the people and rulers of Jerusalem "fulfilled the voices of the prophets" when they condemned Jesus (13:27), and

that they took him down from "the tree" after they had completed "all that was written about him" (13:29). The meaning of being "hanged on a tree" is to be found in the Scriptures.

The Old Testament reflects the ancient Near Eastern custom of hanging the corpses of those slain as a token of public disgrace. Examples include Pharaoh's baker (Gen. 40:19), the king of Ai (Josh. 8:29), five Amorite kings defeated by Joshua (Josh. 10:26–27), and Haman, who was hanged on the gallows (LXX: ξυλον) that he had built for Mordecai (Est. 5:14; 6:4; 7:9–10; 8:7). This disgrace was invested with particular seriousness by the instructions in Deuteronomy 21:22–23: "If there occurs in anyone a sin warranting the judgment of death, and he dies and you hang him on a tree [ξυλον], his body shall not be left on the tree [ξυλον]; but you shall bury him in a tomb that day, because cursed by God is everyone who has been hanged [κρεμαννυμι] on a tree [ξυλον]." Public exposure by being hanged on a tree signified God's curse.

We speculated earlier whether Saul and other Jewish leaders might have seen this shameful circumstance of Jesus' death as proof of his blasphemy. But since the apostles insisted that Jesus did not deserve the death he died, why did Peter and Paul highlight the circumstances of Jesus' death in a way that associated it with God's curse? G. B. Caird comments: "Surely no Christian preacher would have chosen to describe the death of Jesus in terms which drew attention to the curse of God resting upon the executed criminal, *unless he had first faced the scandal of the Cross and had come to believe that Jesus had borne the curse on behalf of others.*"[17] This discovery—that Jesus bore the curse of the tree on behalf of others—is stated explicitly by Paul in Galatians 3:13, citing Deuteronomy 21:23. It also underlies Peter's comment in his first epistle that Christ "bore our sins in his body on the tree [ξυλον]" (1 Peter 2:24).[18] Caird correctly infers that the apostles' allusion to Deuteronomy 21:23 in their preaching presupposes the substitutionary character of Jesus' suffering.[19]

(3) *Jesus' sacrificial blood was the price by which God purchased his church.* Paul's farewell address to the elders of the Ephesian church (Acts 20:17–35) was occasioned by his departure, in the expectation of suffering awaiting him in Judea. This occasion dictated that his speech be a farewell and testament.[20] Paul spoke to Christian believers and church leaders, so of all the audiences in Acts, this one most closely resembled the recipients of Paul's epistles. When speaking to outsiders, the apostles emphasized the guilt of the human participants in Jesus' execution and God's reversal of Jesus' sufferings through resurrection. But here, speaking to the church's leaders, Paul focused on the intention of the divine participant in Jesus'

death. God was active through Jesus' death in a way that made an eternal difference to the Ephesian elders and the flock they shepherded. The redemptive activity of God was not a controversial doctrine that Paul needed to defend; rather, it was so foundational to their common faith that it could serve as the support for his summons to faithfulness in the elders' shepherding responsibilities.

Jesus' death was important to the elders' task in Ephesus because it established the immense value of the church—namely, the price God had paid to redeem it. God "bought" (περιποιεω) the church, his flock, with "the blood of his own [Son]" (20:28).[21] A psalmist had used this imagery to describe the Exodus—when the Lord "bought" (κταομαι) and "redeemed" (λυτροω) the sheep of his pasture—in his appeal to the Lord to overturn Israel's oppressors (Ps. 74:1–2). Having expended such effort to obtain his people, reasoned the psalmist, surely the Lord cannot remain indifferent to their present distress. In the same vein, Paul appealed to the Lord's costly acquisition of his flock to underscore his deep interest in its welfare, reinforcing the gravity of the elders' shepherding responsibility. They were called to exercise authority not over their own property, but over God's possession, obtained at great cost, the sacrificial blood of his Son.

Thus, the sermons of Acts, though they lack the theological reflection on the Cross that is found in the epistles of Paul and the epistle to the Hebrews, for example, bear witness to the redemptive and atoning significance of Jesus' death. Jesus, the suffering Servant, received the stripes that healed God's straying people. Jesus was hanged on a "tree," bearing the curse that others deserve. By the blood of his Son, God has made the church his own possession.

2. Jesus the Messiah Bestows the Blessings of the Kingdom

The "kingdom of God" is a formula that sums up the content of the apostles' gospel (Acts 19:8; 20:25), just as it encapsulates the heart of Jesus' message (Luke 4:43; 8:1; Acts 1:3). The good news of the kingdom is that the age promised by the prophets, in which the rule of God over his people breaks into history, reversing their rebellion and its results, has arrived.

The kingdom has not yet fully arrived, for believers must enter the kingdom by persisting in faith through afflictions (Acts 14:22). But the apostles also had good news of the kingdom for the present time, because they linked the name of Jesus to the kingdom of God (8:12; 28:23, 31). The connection between Jesus and the kingdom was his exaltation, encompassing his resurrection and his ascension to God's right hand. Raised from the dead and exalted to heaven, Jesus is Lord and Christ (2:36), Prince and Savior (5:31). At the beginning of his Pentecost sermon, Peter quoted the promise in Joel, "Everyone who calls on the *name* of the *Lord* will be saved" (2:21, quoting Joel 2:32). At the conclusion, Peter announced that the Resurrection was God's declaration that the "Lord" is Jesus, in whose "name" the repentant receive forgiveness and God's Spirit (Acts 2:36, 38).

As the risen and exalted Lord, Jesus bestows kingdom blessings in the present. From his throne at God's right hand, he pours out the promised Holy Spirit (v. 32). Since Jesus is the glorified servant of God, faith in his name brings complete healing (3:13, 16). In fact, his name is the only name through which salvation comes (4:10–12).

This salvation comes in the first place through the gift of a change of heart, repentance, which leads to the forgiveness of sins. God promised that blessing would flow through Abraham's seed to the nations, and through Jesus, the risen Servant, that blessing came "first" to Peter's audience in the temple courts, turning them from their evil ways (3:25–26). As the exalted Prince and Savior at God's right hand, Jesus gives repentance and forgiveness to Israel (5:31; cf. 2:38). The prophets testify that everyone who believes in Jesus receives forgiveness of sins in his name (10:43).[22] In the synagogue at Antioch of Pisidia, Paul announced that Jesus' resurrection had benefited his audience: "We tell you the good news that the promise that came to the fathers God fulfilled *for us, their children*, by raising up Jesus" (13:32–33). Again, the benefit he highlighted was the forgiveness of sins (v. 38). In the present, the exalted Lord dispenses kingdom blessings of repentance, forgiveness, and the Spirit—in a word, salvation.

3. Jesus the Messiah Will Return to Deliver and to Judge

Jesus' resurrection does not only testify concerning the past (overturning the shame and rejection of his death) and open the blessings of the kingdom in the present (repentance, forgiveness, and the Spirit). It also makes an announcement about the future. Human history has not seen the last of Jesus of Nazareth, and this fact gives reason both to hope and to fear.

There is reason to *hope*. Jesus' resurrection constitutes his appointment as Israel's Messiah (Acts 3:20).[23] Although he now dispenses kingdom blessing (here, healing that makes the lame to leap), there is better to come. He must (δεῖ, that is, ordained by God's invincible plan) remain in heaven until the times of the restoration of all things (3:21), the "seasons of refreshing" that will attend the sending of the Messiah from heaven to earth (3:20). The restoration of lame ankles and sin-stained hearts through the risen Christ's name and Spirit will climax in comprehensive restoration when he returns from heaven.

There is also reason to *fear*. Jesus' resurrection is God's declaration that this exalted Lord is invested with full authority to judge humanity. The witnesses of Jesus' resurrection were commanded "to testify that he is the one whom God appointed as judge of the living and the dead" (Acts 10:42 NIV). Athenian philosophers, amused by Paul's preaching about Jesus and the resurrection, needed to understand the warning message of Jesus' resurrection: Although God overlooked pagan idolatry in the past, a new age had dawned, in which he was calling all peoples to repent in light of the coming day of judgment (17:30–31). In raising Jesus, God certified that he is the man destined to judge the world in justice.

Intrinsic to the apostolic gospel is the return of Jesus the Christ, and particularly the reality of coming judgment. Before Felix, Paul insisted that his Christian faith was simply an extension of the confidence that he shared with his fellow Jews (at least the Pharisees, 23:6), namely, "that there will be a resurrection of both the righteous and the wicked" (24:15 NIV). Paul's later discourse on righteousness, self-control, and coming judgment evoked such fear in Felix that the governor interrupted Paul to bring the discussion suddenly to a close (24:25). Not every sermon in Acts explicitly points ahead to the climax of history, but it is evident that Jesus' resurrection entails the promise of his return. Jesus' authority as judge is established by his enthronement as Lord. The promise of comprehensive restoration is secured by the Spirit whom the exalted Lord has poured out from his seat at the Father's right hand.

4. Repent and Trust in the Name of Jesus

Divine Initiative. Luke emphasizes God's sovereign purpose not only in the events of Jesus' life, death, and resurrection, but also in the way in which people receive salvation through Jesus. Repentance is a gift bestowed by the exalted Jesus (Acts 5:31; cf. 11:18). God opened a door of faith for the Gentiles to enter (14:27). By God's "choice" (εκλεγομαι) the Gentiles heard the word of the gospel through Peter and believed it (15:7). The Lord opened Lydia's heart to receive Paul's message (16:14). Although the apostles faced jealous opposition from some, "all who were *appointed*[24] for eternal life believed" (13:48). Acts underscores the decision of God not only in Jesus' redemptive work, but also in people's reception of its benefits.

Yet this stress on the plan, power, and mercy of God, drawing people to faith in Jesus, does not slip over into impersonal determinism. The declaration that repentance and faith are gifts from God does not—and must not—lull those who hear the gospel into a complacent or hopeless passivity. Rather, the announcement of what God has done through Jesus' death and resurrection and of what Jesus is now doing as Lord must motivate people to repent and believe in Jesus.

Human Response. Repentance is a change of mind and attitude, a radical reassessment of Jesus and of one's own previous opinions and actions (μετανοεω). It can be pictured as a "turning" (επιστρεφω, αποστρεφω), an Old Testament metaphor that implies reversal of the direction of one's values, assumptions, and behavior.[25] Gentiles outside God's covenant must "turn" (επιστρεφω) to God from the emptiness of their idolatry (Acts 14:15; 15:19[26]), for this was God's summons to them through Isaiah: "Turn [LXX: επιστρεφω] to me and be saved, all you ends of the earth" (Isa. 45:22). Israelites also needed to (re)turn to the Lord, for they had brought their history of rebellion to a climax by opposing the Messiah promised through the prophets (Acts 7:51–53). Having repudiated the man whom God had exalted, they had to reverse their previous opinion of Jesus (3:14). Having killed the Prince of life, they had to repudiate their ignorant and evil verdict, bringing their allegiance and actions into conformity with the glory that God had bestowed on Jesus the Messiah (v. 15).

Repentance is therefore demanded of Jew and Gentile alike. It implies a profound realization that we have done wrong and are in the wrong in relation to God. When people realized that the Jesus whom *they* had crucified was the one whom *God* had made Lord and Christ, they were "pierced to the heart," asking how they should respond to this terrible news (Acts 2:37). The answer was repentance, manifesting itself in baptism in the name of Jesus the Messiah, a public transfer of allegiance to the One whom they had opposed (v. 38).

We might suppose that, although profound sorrow was appropriate for people directly involved in the lynching of Jesus, for other audiences (nice North American suburbia, for example) the theme of repentance can be minimized, if not eliminated. Not everyone, after all, has cried out for Jesus' execution. But this attempt to evade the apostles' impolite assault on human self-esteem fails to recognize that the call to repentance is a pervasive component of the preaching in Acts. It is not only certain types of people who need to be confronted with their rebellion against God. Paul summed up his ministry as one of calling both Jews and Gentiles to repentance (20:21; 26:20). The Gentiles' ignorance of God's revelation to Israel does not excuse their worship of images. Rather, having set a day of judgment and appointed Jesus as the eschatological judge through his resurrection from the dead, God now "commands all people everywhere to repent" (17:30–31).

The good news is a summons to live in the real world, in which God is Lord of all. All human beings, both the people of God's covenant and the nations who trust in phantoms, have failed to bring God the worship, gratitude, and trust that are due to him. The reality of the Messiah's future return as judge makes it imperative that people face honestly what they have done—and failed to do—in relation to this living God. If God's spokesmen withhold this painful and humbling truth, suppressing God's summons to change, they become liable for their listeners' death.[27] Paul could remind the Ephesian elders that he was innocent of such negligence because he had not hesitated to proclaim the whole will of God (20:26–27). He had not withheld anything helpful, but rather had announced to both Jews and Greeks their need for *repentance* toward God and faith in Jesus (vv. 20–21). Repentance is intrinsic to "the gospel of God's grace" (v. 24), for only those who see the ugliness of their sin can glimpse the beauty of God's grace.

Repentance is not only a turning *from* sin and misplaced worship, but also a turning *toward* God (Acts 14:15; 20:21; 26:20; see 1 Thess. 1:9). While repentance is appropriately shown in heartfelt grief for past evil, we should not overlook its positive dimension: turning in humble dependence to the living God who saves. Paul speaks of a "worldly sorrow" that leads to death (2 Cor. 7:10). Such was Judas's remorse when he saw his own treachery lead to Jesus' condemnation (Matt. 27:3). Whereas Judas turned away from God toward self-destruction, God's gift of repentance turns us back to him. Despite the folly and evil of past attitudes and actions, we turn to him in the hope that his mercy can overpower our guilt, and that his Spirit can overpower our proneness to rebellion. People who have repented in response to the gospel's call will "practice deeds worthy of repentance" (Acts 26:20).

Because repentance is a turning toward God, it is inextricably bound to faith. As the word of the Lord reached Antioch in Syria, "a great number believed and turned to the Lord" (11:21). Paul's message consisted of "repentance toward God and faith in our Lord Jesus" (20:21). Many whom Peter called to repentance (3:19, 26) believed the word (4:4). Jesus bestows the blessings of the age to come on people who believe in him: healing to a lame man at the temple (3:16), forgiveness of sins to the guilty (10:43), and justification from all that law could not remedy (13:39). By faith, not by circumcision and attempted observance of the law, God purifies the heart of Jew and Gentile alike (15:9, 11). Thus, Paul's calling was to turn

Gentiles from darkness to light, to take their place among the new people of God, set apart by faith in Jesus (26:18).

Faith includes the conviction that certain things are true, that certain events have happened and have redemptive power, and specifically that God has brought eschatological salvation in the death and resurrection of Jesus the Messiah. Therefore, faith is a positive response to the apostles' demonstration from the Scriptures that Jesus is the Christ (4:4; 14:1; 17:10–12; 18:4–5, 8). Yet the apostles did not merely call upon people to revise their intellectual opinions. The summons to faith is also a call to personal commitment to a living person. "Believe in the Lord Jesus, and you will be saved—you and your household" (16:31 NIV). Belief "in" or "upon"[28] Jesus is a transfer of trust and dependence to him, rooted in the reality of his resurrection life. Because Jesus is risen from the dead, the apostles "committed [Christians] to the Lord, in whom they had put their trust" (14:23 NIV).

This commitment of faith cannot leave people unchanged. People who believe in Jesus are drawn together by their trust in him: "All the believers were one in heart and mind" (4:32 NIV). This faith fills people with joy (8:39; 16:34). People of faith face the threats and dangers of life with calm confidence. Thus, Paul the prisoner comforted his fellow travelers in the midst of a storm that would sink their ship, reporting God's promise that no lives would be lost: "I believe God that it will happen just as he has spoken to me" (27:25).

This, then, is the structure of the gospel preached in Acts: God has kept his promises by sending Jesus the Messiah to suffer in others' behalf and to be raised to life and lordship. From his throne at God's right hand, Jesus bestows the blessings of the kingdom and awaits his return to bring final restoration and final judgment. In the light of these truths, God calls on all who hear his good news to repent of their sins and turn to him in faith. Such a radical change of allegiance will be shown in submission to baptism in Jesus' name and a lifestyle of joy, love, and holiness.

VARIETY OF AUDIENCE AND EMPHASIS IN THE APOSTLES' PREACHING

The great challenge of effective preaching is to adapt one's mode of communication to the hearers' experience and understanding without truncating or distorting the message itself, so that the message comes through clearly while remaining God's message and evoking the response he desires.

One example of this is provided by Paul's sermon in the synagogue at Antioch of Pisidia. He combines the central themes we have surveyed and adapts them to suit his audience (Acts 13:17–41).

This sermon is the first sample of Paul's preaching in Acts. Paul has preached in Damascus, Jerusalem, Antioch, and Cyprus (9:20, 28; 10:26; 13:5, 7), but not until Paul and Barnabas reach Pisidian Antioch does the reader find out what Paul preached.[29] Thus, in Luke's narrative this is Paul's inaugural sermon, like Jesus' sermon in the synagogue at Nazareth (Luke 4:16–21) and Peter's sermon on Pentecost (Acts 2). Paul's sermon is like Peter's also in its interpretation of Psalm 16 as fulfilled not in David's experience, but only in Jesus' resurrection, and its emphasis on the apostles' role as witnesses to Jesus' resurrection (2:24–32; 13:35–37, 31). It parallels Peter's sermon in Solomon's Colonnade in attributing Jesus' death both to human wickedness and ignorance and to the purpose of God announced through the prophets (3:17–18; 13:27). It also resembles Stephen's speech in rehearsing the history of Israel—although Paul's emphasis is on God's gracious provision, rather than on Israel's persistent rebellion (7:2–53; 13:17–22). These parallels emphasize Paul's continuity with the preachers who preceded him.

This sermon also has distinctive features, dictated by the speaker, setting, and audience. Only here (in Acts) do we encounter the important Pauline term "justify" (δικαιοω, 13:38–39), and it expresses the heart of Paul's doctrine of justification by faith, apart from the deeds demanded by the law, as that doctrine finds expression in the epistles to the Galatians and the Romans. In this synagogue sermon, Paul stresses that the justification and the forgiveness that the law could not confer[30] are received by those who believe in Jesus, the Son of David.[31] At Antioch, Paul distinguished the original apostles' sphere of witness from his own sphere of ministry: those who traveled with Jesus from Galilee "are now his witnesses to our people," whereas Paul and Barnabas were announcing the good news in the Dispersion (13:31–32). In fact, they were under divine mandate particularly to preach to the Gentiles (v. 47). Similarly, in Galatians 2:8–9 Paul speaks of a meeting with James, Peter, and John in Jerusalem, in which it was agreed that Paul and Barnabas should go to the Gentiles, while the original apostles testified to the Jews.[32]

Paul was preaching in a synagogue of the Dispersion. His audience was composed of Jews (Acts 13:16, 26, 43) and Gentiles, apparently both pious proselytes (v. 43) and uncircumcised God-fearers (vv. 16, 26). He could therefore presuppose that his audience had a thorough acquaintance with, and a reverent attitude toward, the Scriptures given to Israel. His "message of encouragement" followed the reading of the Law and the Prophets (v. 15). His sermon therefore took the form of a recital of God's covenantal dealings with Israel (Deut. 1:6–4:40; Pss. 78, 105, 106). This was not a history lesson for its own sake, but a selective chronicle of God's initiative in redeeming his people. Five elements stand out:

1. Focus on God's Action

With the exception of one statement in verse 21, God is the subject of every main clause in Paul's account of the history of Israel (Acts 13:17–22). God chose the fathers of Israel, exalted the people in Egypt, led them out, endured[33] them in the desert, caused them to inherit the land, gave them judges, then gave them Saul as king, removed Saul, and raised up David. This recital of God's deeds comes to its climax in God's recent action: from David's seed, God has led a Savior to Israel, Jesus (v. 24). God has raised him from the dead (vv. 30, 34, 37), thus fulfilling the promise made to the fathers (vv. 32–33). Now God has given (δίδωμι) to Paul's generation "the holy [οσιος] and sure blessings promised to David" by not giving (δίδωμι) his Holy One (οσιος) to see decay (vv. 34–35).[34]

On the other hand, the acts of the people of Israel have revealed their resistance to the Lord. In Samuel's day, they asked (αιτεω) for a king, and God gave them Saul, whom he would later remove from the throne (vv. 21–22). And recently the people and rulers of Jerusalem asked (αιτεω) Pilate to destroy Jesus, even though they could not find in him any offense deserving death (v. 28).

2. Focus on David

Paul traces God's actions from the election of Israel in the patriarchs, through the Egyptian sojourn and the Exodus, the period of the judges and the reign of Saul, to David. However, he passes over without mention the events of the millennium between David and Jesus, including the building of the temple, the division of the kingdom, and the Exile and return. David is the climax of this retelling of Israel's story because it is from the seed of David, the man after God's heart, the man who does all God's will, that the Messiah has now come. Jesus' suffering and resurrection are linked to God's faithfulness to David through the quotations from Isaiah 55 and Psalm 16 (Acts 13:34–37).

3. Focus on Prophetic Promise

Jesus came as Israel's Savior from the seed of David "according to promise" (Acts 13:23). Although the people of Jerusalem did not understand the words of the prophets as they were read each Sabbath, their condemnation of Jesus fulfilled these prophetic Scriptures (v. 27). The promise made long before to the fathers was then fulfilled for their children when God raised up Jesus (v. 33), as the apostles demonstrated with quotations from Psalm 2, Isaiah 55, and Psalm 16. This repeated appeal to the prophetic Scriptures was appropriate to the covenantal identity of Paul's hearers ("Israelite men," Acts 13:16; "sons of Abraham's race," v. 26) and to Paul's emphasis on God's gracious loyalty to "the people of Israel" (vv. 17, 24, 31). God had kept his word to his people.

Corresponding to the promises spoken through ancient prophets was "the word of this salvation" (v. 26) now spoken through Christ's messengers. John preached in advance (προκηρυσσω, v. 24). Now apostles who traveled with Jesus were his witnesses (μαρτυρες) to the people in Judea, while Paul and Barnabas proclaimed the good news (ευαγγελλιζομαι) among the Dispersion (vv. 31–32). The forgiveness of sins through Jesus was being announced (καταγγελλω, v. 38).

4. Focus on the Resurrection

The resurrection of Jesus, son of David and Son of God, displayed the faithfulness of God to Israel. This is the dominant theme of verses 30–37, a section that opens and closes with the affirmation that God raised (εγειρω) Jesus. In this section, Paul affirms twice more, using a different verb (ανιστημι, vv. 33, 34) that God raised Jesus from the dead. Paul's argument echoes that of Peter at Pentecost: not of David, but only of David's son Jesus could it be said, "You did not give your Holy One to see decay."

5. Promise and Warning

The sermon's conclusion is signaled in verse 38 by the clause, "Therefore let it be known to you."[35] The holy and faithful blessings promised to David, which God gave to this generation through Jesus' resurrection, include the blessing of the forgiveness of sins—that is, justification from those transgressions from which one cannot be justified by the law of Moses. This justification is granted to the one who believes (πιστευω, Acts 13:39). Although repentance is mentioned earlier (v. 24) and its necessity is implied in the promise of the forgiveness of sins, in this sermon the application focuses on faith. Paul warns his hearers to avoid the judgment announced in Habakkuk 1:5 against those who do not believe the message of God's amazing work: "Look, you scoffers, wonder and perish, for I am going to do something in your days that you would never believe [πιστευω], even if someone told you." As Paul and Barnabas were telling what God had done "in your days," their hearers—Jews, proselytes, and God-fearing Gentiles—were confronted with two alternatives: believe and be set right before God, or refuse and perish.

This sermon communicates forcefully in the context of a Dispersion synagogue. It stresses God's election of Israel and his provision of a land and leaders (judges and kings) for his people. Its central emphases—the Messiah's Davidic ancestry and his resurrection as the Son of God[36]—are reinforced by citations from the Scriptures that illustrate God's fulfillment of the promise spoken through the prophets. Finally, it announces that the Savior, Jesus (v. 23), has brought a salvation (v. 26) that transcends the power of the law: in him believers receive forgiveness of sins and a right relationship with God (vv. 38–39).

In the next chapter, we will survey a sermon of a different type in a different setting, Paul's speech to Athenian intellectuals (17:16–34). Among Greek philosophers, Paul's starting point would be creation, not the patriarchs. He would quote Greek poets, not Hebrew prophets. He would make no mention of Jesus' signs or his sufferings. Yet Luke reminds us that in this message, as well, Paul's theme was the good news of Jesus and the resurrection (v. 18).

Audiences with different backgrounds and worldviews must be approached with different starting points and methods if they are to recognize the gospel's challenge to their previous beliefs and lifestyles. Wherever the apostles start, however, their goal is to proclaim the risen Lord Jesus.

CONCLUSION: APOSTOLIC PROCLAMATION TODAY

How should the preaching in Acts influence preaching today? Since (with one exception, Acts 20:18–35) the preaching in Acts is evangelistic preaching to people who are not yet committed to Jesus as Lord, it is not the only New Testament model for regular preaching in a congregation, which must build up the committed as well as drawing in the curious. The epistles are apostolic messages delivered in absentia,[37] so they enrich our understanding of the range of topics and approaches in apostolic preaching. Nevertheless, the sermons of Acts were recorded to build up people like Theophilus, who have been taught the message of Jesus. They show how to preach to believers as well as how to witness to the watching world. The preaching in Acts is truth-centered, revelation-centered, God-centered, and Christ-centered.

Truth-Centered

The primary aim of the apostles' preaching was not to contribute to people's emotional health—not to train them how to cope with stress, to talk themselves out of despair, or to cultivate family relationships. The apostles' message was good news, eliciting "great joy" in those who believed it (Acts 8:8; 13:52), but their goal was not to make their hearers feel better. It was to tell the truth: about God and his plan, about humanity and our sin, about Christ and his victory, about the present opportunity for faith and the future certainty of judgment.

This truth caused intense grief (Acts 2:37) and hostile anger (7:54), as well as ecstatic joy (8:39). Whatever their hearers' response, apostolic preachers recognized their solemn obligation to tell the truth about Jesus. Since they were accountable to God for the eternal well-being of their hearers, they could not withhold anything that would be beneficial, but rather declared honestly "the whole will of God" (20:27). Their message was the testimony of witnesses who saw and heard God's mighty acts. Their mission was to call people to face the real world, created and ruled by God, the world into which God brought the Savior and coming judge, Jesus Christ.

Revelation-Centered

The apostolic proclamation of truth was derived not from human experimentation or speculation, but from God's self-disclosure. The apostles testified to the convergence of God's prophetic promise spoken in the Scriptures, on the one hand, and his eschatological fulfillment in Jesus the Messiah, on the other. The miracles that they had seen Jesus perform in person before his ascension and by the power of his name afterwards were God's signs, testifying on behalf of his Son and servant.

Paul reminded the Corinthians, "My message and my preaching were not with wise and persuasive words, but with a demonstration of the Spirit's power, so that your faith might not rest on men's wisdom, but on God's power" (1 Cor. 2:4–5 NIV). That contrast—human wisdom versus God's power—cautions modern preachers to reexamine the actual source and authority for the things they say in the pulpit. In Paul's day, traveling teachers could heighten their credibility and expand their audience by molding their message to fit the contours of current philosophical speculation or mystery cults from the East, or by following some other inventive strategy for penetrating and manipulating the secrets of the cosmos. In our "self-help" age, preachers can similarly select ingredients from pop psychology, sociology, politics, media and the arts, etc., to keep their hearers "tuned in."

Some of these tips for successful living, admittedly, may be compatible with God's truth. The God who sends his rain even on the unjust who refuse to thank him for it (Matt. 5:45) also grants insights to thinkers who do not acknowledge him for who he is (Acts 17:28; Titus 1:12–13). But the apostolic example in Acts calls Christ's heralds to handle with care and discernment the intellectual trends of our time. Every idea and piece of advice must be tested by the standard of God's revelation before it is broadcast from a pulpit. The message as a whole must announce what God has said in the Old and New Testaments; it must be a faithful declaration of the Father's testimony to the Son.

God-Centered

The preaching in Acts focuses on one relationship that has gone wrong and on what God has done to set it right. The interpersonal relationships that preoccupy so much discussion in late twentieth-century Western culture have little place in these early apostolic sermons, which call the curious to commitment. To be sure, the New Testament epistles show that human relationships can be transformed by the power of Christ's Spirit (e.g., Eph. 5:21–6:9; 1 Peter 2:11–3:17; James 4:1–12). Preachers certainly need to guide believers in all that it means to live together as a new creation in Christ.

But the preaching in Acts reminds us of the one relationship that must be set right first of all, if we are ever to hope for substantive healing of the wounds that deface our relationships with one another. We all, Jew and Gentile, have been implicated in a conspiracy against the Lord and his Anointed One (Acts 4:25–28). We are at odds with "the God who made the world and everything in it," who "is the Lord of heaven and earth" (17:24). He now calls us to account for the folly and arrogance of thinking that he is like an image made by man's skill, for he has set the day of judgment and appointed the judge—Jesus, the Risen One. It is the broken relationship between us and our Creator that lies at the heart of the matter, and this is the relationship that apostolic preaching addresses first of all. Its aim is not to enable people to function better at work and at home while they persist in their hatred toward God; rather, it is to bring us home to our Father, who will remake us in the Son's image by the Spirit's power, so that we reflect his love and holiness in all our relationships.

Christ-Centered

The pervasive, dominant theme in the sermons of Acts is Jesus—who he is and what he has done. This makes sense in view of the central relationship—our relationship to God—that apostolic preaching addresses. It also corresponds with key statements from the apostle Paul: "I decided to know nothing while among you except Jesus Christ and him crucified" (1 Cor. 2:2). "Christ in you, the hope of glory, whom we proclaim, admonishing everyone and teaching everyone in all wisdom, so that we may present everyone perfect in Christ" (Col. 1:27–28). How appropriate it is that Luke should leave his readers with the scene of Paul in custody at Rome, yet "preaching the kingdom of God and teaching the *things about the Lord Jesus Christ* with all boldness, unhindered" (Acts 28:31).

Modern preachers are under constant pressure to broaden their repertoires. Surely, we may think, the pastor who preaches fifty to one hundred sermons a year must soon exhaust all that can be said about Jesus! But the apostles took a different view. In Christ "are hidden *all* the treasures of wisdom and knowledge" (Col. 2:3). "In Christ *all* the fullness of the Deity lives in bodily form" (v. 9). The preaching that builds people toward spiritual maturity does not take them beyond Christ. Rather, it takes them more deeply into Christ, so that their thoughts, attitudes, values, desires, reactions, words, and behavior are transformed by their death with Christ to sin and their resurrection with Christ to life and righteousness. In this One who is God's mystery (now revealed), God's treasury of wisdom and knowledge, there is more than enough to keep the preacher occupied on a lifelong quest of new discovery, and more than enough to address the needs of the human heart and human society.

Notes

¹ The authenticity of the speeches in Acts has been challenged, e.g., by Martin Dibelius, on the grounds that the regular practice of ancient historians was to compose their own interpretations of events and then to place these interpretations into the mouths of the participants in the events themselves ("The Speeches of Acts and Ancient Historiography," in *Studies in the Acts of the Apostles* [London: SCM, 1956], 138–91), and/or on the grounds that the style and vocabulary of the speeches are consistent with Luke's own style and vocabulary. Other scholars, however, have challenged Dibelius's interpretation of the editorial philosophy of ancient historians in handling speeches and have noted features of both style (e.g., Aramaisms) and content in the speeches of Acts which, although not incompatible with the rest of Luke's writing, are not characteristic of it. See I. Howard Marshall, "The Resurrection in the Acts of the Apostles," in *Apostolic History and the Gospel*, ed. W. Ward Gasque and Ralph P. Martin (Grand Rapids: Eerdmans, 1970), 92–107; Michael Green, *Evangelism in the Early Church* (Grand Rapids: Eerdmans, 1970), 68–70; G. N. Stanton, *Jesus of Nazareth in New Testament Preaching* (Cambridge: University Press, 1974), 67–85; W. Ward Gasque, *A History of the Interpretation of the Acts of the Apostles* (Peabody, Mass.: Hendrickson, 1989), 224–33.

² Κατηχεω probably refers to initiatory instruction in the Christian faith (cf. Acts 18:25; Gal. 6:6). The verb can mean simply "report, inform" (cf. Acts 21:21, 24), so some have postulated that Theophilus was not a Christian but an interested observer, or a government official who could influence the outcome of Paul's trial in Rome. However, on the view that Luke's intended audience is non-Christian and his purpose strictly evangelistic or apologetic, it is difficult to account for the materials in Luke-Acts that are of particular relevance to the Christian community.

³ Some New Testament scholars have drawn a distinction between the κηρυγμα ("proclamation" of the gospel to unbelievers) and the διδαχη ("teaching" to Christian disciples about standards for daily behavior). But Luke's terminology does not support this distinction. He uses κηρυγμα only once (Luke 11:32) and ευαγγελιον ("gospel") twice (Acts 15:7; 20:24), whereas he applies διδαχη both to the instruction of disciples (Acts 2:42) and to the preaching to nondisciples (Luke 4:32; Acts 5:28; 13:12; 17:19). Of the corresponding verbs, Luke prefers *teach* (διδασκω, 33 times in Luke-Acts) over *proclaim* (κηρυσσω, 17 times) and *announce good news* (ευαγγελιζομαι, 25 times). Again, the "teaching" ministry of Jesus and the apostles is addressed both to disciples (7 times, e.g., in Luke 11:1; Acts 20:20) and to those outside (24 times, e.g., in Luke 4:15; Acts 4:2).

⁴ Παραδιδωμι is often a technical term for the transmission of sacred traditions. See, for example, 1 Cor. 15:3–5: "I passed on [παραδιδωμι] to you as of first importance what I had received: that Christ died for our sins according to the Scriptures, that he was buried, that he was raised on the third day according to the Scriptures, and that he appeared . . ."

⁵ Jesus' instruction in faithful living in the Gospel is not limited, of course, to his words to his disciples, but also includes his teaching to the crowds and his indictments of those who oppose the kingdom of God. The failures of the leaders and people of "old Israel" are sobering warnings to the leaders and people of the true Israel.

⁶ C. H. Dodd summarizes the *kerygma* of the early Jerusalem church, as reflected in Acts, in the following themes: "First, the age of fulfillment has dawned. . . . Secondly, this has taken place through the ministry, death and resurrection of Jesus. . . . Thirdly, by virtue of the resurrection, Jesus has been exalted at the right hand of God, as Messianic head of the new Israel. . . . Fourthly, the Holy Spirit in the Church is the sign of Christ's present power and glory. . . . Fifthly, the Messianic Age will shortly reach its consummation in the return of Christ. . . . Finally, the *kerygma* always closes with an appeal for repentance, the offer of forgiveness and of the Holy Spirit, and the promise of 'salvation.' " *The Apostolic Preaching and Its Developments* (London: Hodder & Stoughton, 1944), 21–23.

⁷ Paul tells Athenian philosophers that Jesus' resurrection is God's "proof" (πιστις) that he has appointed Jesus to be the judge of the world (Acts 17:31).

⁸ Ανομος, in a Jewish setting, means not merely "without law" (= "ungovernable") but "without *the law* (delivered to Moses)," as Paul's use of the term in 1 Cor. 9:21 illustrates.

⁹ God's "hand" is an anthropomorphic metaphor for his powerful control. In Ex. 3:20, the Lord announces that he will stretch out (LXX, εκτεινω) his hand and strike the Egyptians with all his wonders. Echoing this wording, the apostolic church prays that the Lord would stretch out (εκτεινω) his hand to perform wonders in the name of his servant Jesus (Acts 4:30). See also Acts 11:21: "The Lord's hand was with them."

¹⁰ See chapter 3 above, "The Spirit and the Servant."

¹¹ Also, in the prayer recorded in Acts 4:25–30, Jesus is called God's Servant (παις), whose sufferings were determined in advance by God's will (βουλη; cf. Isa. 53:10).

[12] Cf. Isa. 53:12: "His life *was handed over* to death . . . he *was handed over* on account of their sins." In both clauses the verb in the LXX is παραδιδωμι.

[13] Cf. Acts 7:52: Whereas previous generations killed prophets who spoke of the coming Righteous One (δικαιος), Stephen's hearers betrayed and murdered the Righteous One himself.

[14] We should also note Philip's exposition of the song of the Servant's suffering (Isa. 53:7–8), which the Ethiopian eunuch was reading when Philip came upon him (Acts 8:35). Philip, along with Stephen, was one of the Seven Servers, and Stephen had already declared that the prophets spoke of the Righteous One (Acts 7:52).

[15] Cross (σταυρος) appears 27 times in the New Testament, and crucify (σταυροω) appears 46 times.

[16] This suggestion is strengthened by the fact that "hanging [him] on a tree" in these verses is a participial phrase that amplifies another verb: "you had killed" (διαχειριζω) in 5:30, and "they killed him" (αναιρεω) in 10:39. Thus, the phrase supplements the bare statement of Jesus' death by calling attention to a circumstance that suggests theological commentary on his death.

[17] G. B. Caird, *The Apostolic Age* (London: Duckworth, 1955), 40 (emphasis added).

[18] These are the only New Testament passages outside of Acts that refer to the cross as a "tree."

[19] Leon Morris, *The Cross in the New Testament* (Grand Rapids: Eerdmans, 1965), 142–43.

[20] Compare the parting speeches by Moses (Deuteronomy, esp. chs. 29–31) and Samuel (1 Sam. 12), and such testamentary epistles as 2 Peter and 2 Timothy (cf. 4:1–8). Each contains vindication of the departing leader's past conduct, a charge to stay faithful, and dire predictions of future dangers.

[21] It is not immediately clear whether Paul here speaks of Jesus buying the church with "his own blood" or of God the Father buying the church with "the blood of his own [Son]" (δια του αιματος του ιδιου). Early manuscripts differ from one another, some reading "church of God," others "church of the Lord," others "church of the Lord and of God," and still others "church of the Lord God." Since "God" is the title typically applied to the Father in the New Testament (the deity of Christ and the Spirit is indicated in other ways), some early copyists apparently were troubled by a verse that seemed to say that the Father had shed his blood (a heresy referred to as Patripassianism). "Church of God" seems to be the original wording, but this leads us to another difficulty: "his own" (του ιδιου) could be an adjectival construction describing "blood" ("his own blood") or an independent (substantive) construction ("blood of his own [Son]"). Favoring the first option is the adjectival (attributive) use of "his own" in Acts 1:25 ("his own place," τον τοπον τον ιδιον) and Heb. 9:12 ("his own blood," δια του ιδιου αιματος). Favoring the second option is the similarity of thought between these words, which Luke attributes to Paul, and Rom. 8:32, "He who did not spare his own Son [του ιδιου υιου]."

[22] I. Howard Marshall ("Resurrection," in *Apostolic History and the Gospel*, ed. Gasque and Martin, 104) proposes that the prophetic Scriptures to which allusion is made are those that promise the Lord's readiness to forgive those who seek him (e.g., Isa. 55:6–7; Jer. 31:34).

[23] This is not to deny that Jesus was "Christ the Lord" even at his birth (Luke 2:11), or that Jesus was anointed (χριω) by the Spirit in his baptism for his preaching and healing mission (4:18–21; Acts 10:38). The pattern of David's career, in which royal anointing (1

Sam. 16:13) preceded enthronement (2 Sam. 5:1–10) by many years, is parallel to the phases of messianic authority through which David's greater Son was to pass, from his incarnation, through his baptism, ministry, and death, to his resurrection and exaltation.

24 Greek: τασσω. The verb appears twice in Matthew, twice in Paul (Rom. 13:1; 1 Cor. 16:15), once in Luke, and five times in Acts. It refers to a decision to appoint something or someone for a particular purpose—e.g., a meeting place (Matt. 28:16) or time (Acts 28:23). The passive voice here implies that God has appointed individuals to receive eternal life, as in Acts 22:10 Paul had been "assigned" (NIV) by God to accomplish certain tasks.

25 Cf. the Hebrew שוב, "turn" (= "repent") in 1 Kings 8:33–37; Ezek. 14:6; 18:30; etc.

26 See also "the turning [επιστροφη] of the Gentiles" (Acts 15:3).

27 Compare God's warning to Ezekiel concerning the responsibility of the watchman (prophet) to warn the wicked of coming judgment (Ezek. 33:1–9).

28 The Greek preposition here is επι, "in, on, for, toward of feelings, actions, etc. directed toward a pers[on] or thing" (BAG, 289). The same phrase ("believe upon") appears in Acts 9:42.

29 Jacques Dupont, "Je t'ai établi lumière des nations (Ac 13, 14.43–52)," in Nouvelles études sur les Actes des Apôtres (Paris: Les Editions du Cerf, 1984), 344.

30 The Pauline epistles also affirm the law's impotence to impart righteousness (e.g., Gal. 2:15–16; 3:21; Rom. 3:20–22; 8:1–3; Phil. 3:9).

31 In Acts 13:38–39, justification is virtually equated with forgiveness: "Through this man [Jesus] forgiveness of sins is announced to you, and from all [sins] from which you could not be justified in Moses' law, in [Jesus] everyone who believes is justified." Likewise, in Rom. 4:6–7 Paul speaks of justification both as the imputing (λογιζομαι) of righteousness to believers and as the nonimputing of our sins against us. Elsewhere Paul indicates that justification includes not only forgiveness of sins, but also the positive accounting of believers as "the righteousness of God" on the basis of Christ's righteousness (2 Cor. 5:21).

32 There are strong arguments for identifying this meeting not with the apostolic council of Acts 15, but with the "famine visit" of Barnabas and Paul recorded in Acts 11:30. See, e.g., F. F. Bruce, Commentary on the Book of the Acts (NICNT; Grand Rapids: Eerdmans, 1954), 244, 298–300; Bruce, Commentary on Galatians (NIGTC; Grand Rapids: Eerdmans, 1982), 108–9; D. Guthrie, New Testament Introduction, 4th rev. ed. (Downers Grove, Ill.: InterVarsity, 1990), 474–80; D. A. Carson, Douglas J. Moo, and Leon Morris, An Introduction to the New Testament (Grand Rapids: Zondervan, 1992), 293–94. If this identification is correct, Paul's words in Acts 13:31–32 can be seen as reflecting the agreement already reached.

33 Or "cared for." Some early and reliable manuscripts have τροποφορεω ("put up with"), while others have τροφοφορεω ("take care of, provide for"). Note Deut. 1:31 LXX: "The Lord your God carried [τροφοφορεω] you, as a father carries his son."

34 The quotation from Isa. 55:3 in v. 34 is addressed to a plural "you" (υμιν), namely, the "children" mentioned in v. 32. The repetition of the verb give (διδωμι) and the adjective holy (οσιος) links this quotation with the one that follows from Ps. 16:10.

35 Compare the conclusion to Peter's Pentecost sermon: "Therefore let all the house of Israel know certainly . . ." (Acts 2:36).

36 See the Christological confession with which Paul opens his epistle to the Romans (1:3–4), in which Davidic descent and resurrection are placed in parallelism as messianic credentials of the Son of God—although the emphasis falls on the Son's resurrection by

the Spirit of holiness. See Martin Hengel, *The Son of God: The Origin of Christology and the History of Jewish-Hellenistic Religion* (Philadelphia: Fortress, 1976), 59–63; R. B. Gaffin, Jr., *The Centrality of the Resurrection: A Study in Paul's Soteriology* (Grand Rapids: Baker, 1978), 98–113.

[37] The author of Hebrews, in fact, refers to his epistle with the same term, "message of encouragement" (λογος παρακλησεως), that describes Paul's sermon in the synagogue at Antioch (Acts 13:15; Heb. 13:22).

T E N

THE MASTER VERSUS THE MAGICIANS

Religious Pluralism Then and Now

We live, it is often observed, in a "post-Christian age." No longer is the intellectual life of Western civilization controlled by the biblical view of reality, which is centered in God the Creator, supremely wise, pure, and kind, ruling and redeeming human beings created in his image, and directing history toward a consummation of justice and joy. Quickly following the Bible's worldview into the Museum of Archaic Ideas are such concepts as culture-transcending truth and absolute moral values, as well as the societal structures that have been based on the belief that truth can be distinguished from error, and good from evil.

Christianity's cultural dominance in the West has been eroded by successive waves of secularism, humanism, and self-centered individualism. In *Habits of the Heart*, Robert Bellah and his associates conclude that most Americans simply lack a conceptual framework to think of the Good as a value transcending personal preference. Concepts such as self-sacrifice, obligation, and lasting commitment are foreign to these Americans' idea of love and marriage.[1] Rising rates of divorce, drug abuse, and violent crime are symptomatic of a societal shift toward everyone doing what is right in his or her own eyes.

Combined with this shift in the West's cultural mainstream is the infusion of new religious alternatives, flowing from the far reaches of the earth. The global village is shrinking through transportation, relocation, and technological interconnectedness. This contraction of the world community brings Europeans and North Americans into close contact with

166

people from other cultures and religions. Towns whose main religious options a generation ago ranged from Episcopalian, Roman Catholic, and Lutheran to Presbyterian, Pentecostal, and Baptist now observe the construction of Muslim mosques and Buddhist temples in their midst. Eastern thought, in various permutations and hybrid forms, some labeled "New Age" and some not, permeates such areas as education, counseling, the media, and business—and even Christian churches.[2] Alarm over the ecological crisis and a sense of corporate guilt for past injustices stir in many European-Americans a new respect for Native American religion and its reverence toward the natural world. A revival of ancient paganism, with its worship of Mother Earth (*Gaia*), seems to provide the perfect religious matrix for combining feminism and environmentalism. Far from its origins in the Middle East, Islam portrays itself among African-Americans and Hispanics as a faith to bring hope and unity to people dispossessed and oppressed by the power structures of the West.

From other perspectives, however, it is not at all correct to call ours a "post-Christian age." In the theology of the New Testament, the late twentieth century still falls within that era about which Jesus proclaimed, "All authority in heaven and on earth has been given to me. . . . Disciple all nations. . . . I am with you all the days to the end of the age" (Matt. 28:18–20). Jesus has not been dethroned from his position at God's right hand. The Spirit has not been withdrawn from the world. God has not "pulled the plug" on his project of bringing "salvation to the ends of the earth," uniting the world's peoples under the gracious kingship of his Messiah, Jesus.

When we lift our eyes from the discouraging trends in Europe and North America to view the rest of the world, the evidence of Christianity's vitality is undeniable. Sub-Saharan Africa is rapidly becoming predominantly Christian. Conversion rates in Latin America lead some researchers to project that evangelical Protestants will be a majority there early in the twenty-first century.[3] The church in Korea not only continues to grow, but also sends increasing numbers of missionaries to other countries and peoples. Despite governmental oppression, the church in China gains strength. The dissolution of the Soviet Union has disclosed a spiritual hunger and openness to the gospel that would have been inconceivable a few years ago. In the light of this evidence of the church's growth in Asia, Africa, and Latin America, to label our generation a "post-Christian age" is to display an embarrassingly provincial perspective on God's work in the world, as though the trends in our "neighborhood" were the only ones that count.

As Christian influence declines in the West, even while it grows in the rest of the world, these phenomena call for certain responses. First, we should recognize our solidarity with the church in the rest of the world, humbly learning from the vibrant church in Africa, Latin America, and Asia. Then we need to discover afresh the parallels between our mission in a culture of religious pluralism and the strategy of the early church in a similar setting. Finally, we should shake off both complacency and discouragement, and so reenter the battle for the minds and hearts of people and for the direction of our culture.

In a way unparalleled for centuries, Christian witness in the West today confronts a context of religious pluralism like the Hellenistic world in which the apostles proclaimed Jesus, "who is Lord of all" (Acts 10:36). The Hellenistic period into which the gospel of Christ came has been called "a materialistic and fatalistic age."[4] Belief in the old gods of traditional Roman and Greek religion was in decline. Because of increasing individual mobility and relocation (some voluntary, some not), individualistic approaches to religion were replacing the earlier corporate religious expressions of communities and nations. Mystery religions, promising insight and life for the initiated individual, were gaining adherents, while the civil religion of city-states and clans was losing its appeal. Interaction between different religious and ethical traditions from East and West produced eclectic evolution in some people's conceptions of deity, while others became suspicious of any claim that truth can be known, embracing an ancient version of cultural relativism. In a fragmenting and diverse society, people hungered for connection, so clubs and associations for a variety of purposes (religious, philosophical, vocational, recreational, artistic) multiplied.[5]

The goals of human religions and philosophies are knowledge and power. Particularly in the first-century world, the spectrum of religious options, from popular superstition to sophisticated philosophy, promised adherents the ability to understand and control the forces that impinged on their lives (forces that often seem mysterious, capricious, and even malevolent), or at least to insulate their sense of well-being from the "slings and arrows of outrageous fortune." Thus, the Stoics' concept of a world-pervading Logos provided an intellectual rationale for preoccupation with astrological signs and omens.

Into this mix came the message of the kingdom of God and of Jesus the anointed King and Savior. This good news addressed the deepest hunger of the individual, but it also drew the individual into a holy community of mutual compassion. It made sense of suffering and gave hope. Although it did not empower its adherents to manipulate cosmic forces for their own comfort and prosperity, it did put them in contact with the Lord of all, who overrules hostile humans and forces to do good for and through his servants.

Luke provides a sampling of the gospel's confrontation with the religious and philosophical options of the Hellenistic world: magic and the occult, institutional polytheism, and the worship of rulers as divine.[6] As the word of Jesus confronts the Greco-Roman world's religions, a theme from the prophecy of Isaiah finds fulfillment: The Lord is filing a lawsuit against the hollow gods in which the Gentiles trust, proving the idols guilty of false advertising for having claimed that they can rescue their worshipers. The idols can present no witnesses to attest their claims, but the Lord subpoenas his servant Israel to testify to his power to save: " 'I have announced and saved . . . and no foreign god was among you. You are my witnesses and I am witness,' says the Lord your God" (Isa. 43:12). God's truth confronts humanity's religions. His redemptive acts in history refute the myths invented by human imagination and speculation. Through the words of his witness-bearing church, Christ the risen Lord extends his arms to fugitives who have sought refuge from life's assaults in idols of wood or images of the mind: "Turn to me and you will be saved, you from the ends of the earth; for I am God, and there is no other. . . . To me every knee will bend; and every tongue will confess to God, saying, 'Righteousness and glory will come to him' " (Isa. 45:22–23).

MAGIC AND THE OCCULT

The Greek term μαγος, *magus*, from which we get *magic*, originally referred to a member of the priestly caste in Persia, and then, by extension, to possessors of supernatural knowledge and power.[7] In the Hellenistic-Roman world, "magic" (μαγεια) focused on the manipulation of supernatural forces for the benefit of individuals or for harm to their enemies. While the institutional religions of Greece and Rome concerned themselves with experiences important to the community, magic promised control over the uncontrollable in private experience: romance, birth, illness, death, business, and travel.[8]

By invoking the names of one or more gods or demigods, sometimes using as many divine names as he could muster (from any and every religious background), together with appropriate rituals, the magus assured his clients that he could expel demons, heal diseases, warm the heart of a reluctant lover, bring misfortune on a political rival, ward off storms and pirates at sea, enable a wife to conceive a son, and so on.[9] Closely related to astrology, magic sometimes claimed to offer insight into the future as well. To people crushed by oppressive, immutable fate, magic promised the possibility of gaining control of the unseen forces that impinged on one's life. But syncretistic magic was no match for the word of the Lord.

SIMON OF SAMARIA (ACTS 8:9–24)

The Great Power Meets a Greater Power

When Philip arrived in Samaria with the proclamation of the Christ, he was entering a city that had been dominated by another religious teacher: Simon, whom the people praised as "the Great Power of God." Simon practiced sorcery or magic (μαγευω, Acts 8:9) and through his magical arts (μαγεια, v. 11) had amazed the Samaritans. The title that they gave him, "the divine power known as the Great Power," suggests that they regarded him as an incarnation of deity.[10] The Gnostic library discovered at Nag Hammadi in Egypt has yielded a fourth-century discourse, *The Concept of Our Great Power*, in which "Great Power" is a divine title.[11]

Simon's "power" could not compete with the might of the message of Jesus, announced by Philip. Parallel themes in the descriptions of Simon's previous influence and Philip's ministry invite us to compare and contrast them. Whereas previously the Samaritans had "paid attention to" Simon (προσειχον, twice in Acts 8:10, 11), now they "all paid attention to" what Philip was saying (προσειχον, v. 6). Whereas they had been "amazed" (εξιστημι) by Simon's magical arts (vv. 9, 11), now Simon himself was "amazed" (εξιστημι) as he saw the miracles performed through Philip (v. 13). Whereas Simon "had boasted that he was someone great [μεγας]" (v. 9) and had been acclaimed as "the *Power* called *Great*" (η δυναμις . . . η καλουμενη Μεγαλη, v. 10), he now stood astonished at the "signs and *great acts of power* [δυναμεις μεγαλας, lit., *great powers*]" taking place through the gospel (v. 13). Whereas Simon had spoken of himself (v. 9), Philip spoke "the good news of God's kingdom and the name of Jesus Christ" (v. 12; cf. v. 5).

Healings and exorcisms were among the routine wonders that μαγοι such as Simon claimed to perform. Yet when Philip arrived in the city, there were still many Samaritans afflicted by unclean spirits and many "paralytics and cripples" in need of healing (v. 7). Why had Simon not delivered them from their afflictions? Either he lacked the power he claimed to have, or the Samaritans lacked the funds to pay for his services. In either case, his previous career in Samaria had failed to bring to his neighbors the well-being that promptly resulted from Philip's ministry in Jesus' name. It is no wonder that, when the Messiah's ambassador arrived, "there was great joy in that city" (v. 8).

Yet Luke's emphasis rests, finally, not on the powerful miracles that impressed Simon, but on the message that Philip proclaimed in Samaria. Philip's ministry illustrates Luke's summary of the dispersion caused by Saul's persecuting zeal: "Those scattered were passing through [Judea and Samaria, cf. v. 1], announcing the good news [ευαγγελλιζομαι] of the word" (v. 4). Accordingly, when Philip arrived in Samaria, he *"preached* [κηρυσσω] the Christ." And the Samaritan crowds "were giving attention to *the things being said* [τοις λεγομενοις] by Philip as they heard [his words] and saw the signs that he was doing" (v. 6). They came to faith as Philip *"preached the good news* [ευαγγελλιζομαι] of the kingdom of God and the name of Jesus Christ" (v. 12). In the concluding summary on Samaria and Simon, we read that the apostles, having *"testified* [διαμαρτυρεομαι] and *proclaimed* [λαλεω] *the word of the Lord,"* returned to Jerusalem, *"preaching the gospel* [ευαγγελλιζομαι] in many Samaritan villages"* along their way (8:25).[12] Miracles attested Philip's message, but it was the word of the Lord that drew people into the kingdom through faith in Jesus Christ.

Not for Sale

When Simon observed the marvelous phenomena that demonstrated that the Holy Spirit was given through the apostles' hands, he recognized a power that was worth procuring, even at a high price. His reasoning was consistent with that of the religious professionals of his day. Only one hundred years after Philip's visit to Samaria, Pakebkis, son of Marsisouchus, offered 2200 drachmae to purchase the office of prophet in the temple of Soknebtunis (Cronus) in Egypt. His written application also specified, of course, that he expected to receive 20 percent of the temple's revenues.[13] Even in the early church, Paul found it necessary to warn against teachers who "regard religion as a source of profit" (1 Tim. 6:5).

Peter pronounced God's curse on the attempt to mingle silver and the Spirit (Acts 8:20–23). Because the Spirit is a free gift from God, his coming cannot be manipulated through buying and selling. Judas Iscariot had a share (κληρος) in the apostles' ministry (1:17, 25), but he forfeited that share in his pursuit of silver (αργυριον, Luke 22:5). Now Simon's offer of silver (αργυριον) to purchase the power to dispense the Spirit revealed that he had no share (κληρος) in the word[14] of salvation that the apostles and Philip were proclaiming (Acts 8:20–21). In treating God's grace as a business commodity, Simon showed himself to be not a divine power, as he was acclaimed, but an enemy of the omnipotent Lord. Peter's words of indictment echo Old Testament language, linking Simon's sin to the infidelity that threatened Israel's relationship to God. Simon's heart was "not straight before God"[15] (v. 21), just as the psalmist described the Israelite generation that died in the wilderness: "Their heart was not straight with him,[16] nor were they faithful in his covenant" (Ps. 78:37). Simon was "in the gall of bitterness" (εις χολην πικριας, Acts 8:23), the sort of person against whom Moses warned Israel, describing those who turn from the Lord to worship idols as "a root growing up in gall [χολη] and bitterness [πικριας]" (Deut. 29:18). For centuries the Samaritans had practiced the syncretism that Moses had condemned (2 Kings 17:25–41), and Simon was continuing to promote that poisonous mixture. Despite his claim to divine power, Simon was chained to unrighteousness as its slave.[17]

The account of Simon is tantalizingly open-ended. Peter summoned Simon to repentance and prayer for forgiveness, but Simon seemed too terrified to pray directly to God, asking Peter instead to intercede for him. Luke says nothing of Peter's response to this appeal, or of Simon's subsequent relationship to the church. For Luke's purposes we have heard all that we need to know when we have heard Simon, the once so-called Great Power, humbly appealing to Peter and John[18]—who attributed healing not to their own power (δυναμις), but to the name of Jesus (Acts 3:12)—to be his intercessors (8:24). Was Simon's repentance genuine and deep? Or were his words only a display of superficial terror at the harm that could be inflicted by a wonder-worker as powerful as Peter? Such questions, which pique our curiosity, are evidently beside the point. Whatever his motives, Simon, the spokesman for ancient magic, confessed the superiority of the word of Jesus after his attempts to enfold its power into his own syncretistic system were rebuffed.

ELYMAS OF CYPRUS (ACTS 13:6–12)

A second confrontation between the word of the Lord and ancient magic occurred at the start of the gospel's spread to the Gentiles beyond Palestine. Barnabas and Saul, sent out by the Spirit from Antioch (Acts 13:2, 4), traveled across the island of Cyprus, Barnabas's birthplace (4:36), preaching God's word from the eastern port of Salamis to the provincial capital, Paphos, on the southwestern coast. There they found a Jewish magus and false prophet by the name of Bar-Jesus. Whereas Simon had impressed the Samaritans as an incarnation of divine *power*, Bar-Jesus' access to the proconsul of Cyprus rested on his claims of divine *knowledge*.

In narrating the apostles' confrontation with Bar-Jesus, Luke focuses more on the defeat of the magician than on the conversion of the proconsul. Bar-Jesus is introduced before Sergius Paulus and in greater detail. He is the more prominent actor in the narrative as the opponent of Christ's messengers, and he is the subject of the climactic apostolic word (a word of judgment) uttered by Paul. Luke's emphasis on the judgment of this Jewish opponent of the gospel suggests that God judged such unbelieving obstructions in order to open the door of faith to the Gentiles, for when Sergius Paulus saw Bar-Jesus' blindness, he believed, amazed at the teaching of the Lord. The encounter on Cyprus provides a preview of the pattern that would develop in the apostles' witness at Antioch in Pisidia (13:13–52) and throughout Paul's ministry (28:25–28): the unbelief and blindness of many (but not all) Jews is accompanied by the spread of salvation to the Gentiles through faith in Jesus.

Bar-Jesus' names and titles indicate his significance. *Bar-Jesus* is a transliteration of an Aramaic name meaning "son of Yehoshua [Joshua]," that is, "son of salvation." Perhaps his father was named Joshua. Or, since the expression "son of . . ." is a Semitic way of describing an individual's character (e.g., *Barnabas* means "son of encouragement," that is, "encourager," 4:36), this sorcerer may have called himself Bar-Jesus in order to claim to bring salvation to those who heeded his words. In any case, Paul declared in the most forceful of terms that Bar-Jesus was misnamed: he was not a "son of salvation," but a "son of the devil" (13:10)!

Bar-Jesus, like Simon in Samaria, was a μαγος ("magician, sorcerer," vv. 6, 8). His practice as a magus, in contrast to Simon's, seems to have emphasized prophetic words more than powerful acts. He was a "false prophet" (v. 6), and his name, Elymas, which (Luke tells us) is equivalent to the Greek word μαγος, is probably related to a Semitic word meaning "the wise one."[19] If Elymas, "the sage," claimed to have supernatural insight into matters yet future as a prophet of the Lord, the God of the Hebrews, this could explain his role in the retinue of Sergius Paulus. The existence of established synagogues (v. 5) indicates a prominent Jewish presence on Cyprus. What government official would not welcome access to insights about tomorrow as he faced today's decisions?

Bar-Jesus' "insights," however, did not come from the Lord, the God of Israel, for he was a false prophet (ψευδοπροφητης, v. 6). Whether Elymas's previous actions had shown him to be a false prophet before the arrival of Barnabas and Saul, we do not know; but his reaction to the word of God preached by Paul and Barnabas to the proconsul revealed that he was no prophet of the Lord. Jesus was the eschatological prophet promised by Moses, and "all the prophets from Samuel on" had testified about him

(3:21–24; cf. 10:43; 13:27–29). No true prophet of God could oppose the message about Jesus, as Elymas was doing.

The emphasis in the account falls on Paul's word of judgment and its results.[20] Contrasts underscore the differences between Christ's truth and Elymas's lies. Bar-Jesus was not, after all, a "son of salvation," but a "son of the devil" (v. 10). Paul was *"filled* [πιμπλημι] with the Holy Spirit" (v. 9) —Luke's signal for prophetic inspiration (Luke 1:15, 42, 67; Acts 2:4, 17; 4:8, 31). By contrast, Elymas was *"full* [πληρης] of all deceit and fraud" (v. 10).[21] In trying to "turn" (διαστρεφω) the proconsul from the faith (v. 8), Elymas was trying to "twist [διαστρεφω] the straight ways of the Lord" (v. 10).[22] Consequently, Elymas brought upon himself the Lord's judgment: "Now the hand of the Lord is against you" (v. 11 NIV), just as it was against Israel in its times of infidelity under the judges (Judg. 2:15) and the kings (1 Sam. 12:15).

Specifically, the Lord's hand of judgment came against the false prophet in the form of blindness, a misty darkness appropriate to one who is "full of all deceit." We noticed in chapter 3 the significance of blindness as a covenant curse (Deut. 28:28–29) and the parallel between the blindness of Elymas and the blindness of Paul, who here pronounces judgment on him in the Lord's name. Paul himself had been the blind servant of Isaiah 42:19–20, refusing to see what God had done in handing over his Messiah as the sacrificial lamb and raising him from the dead. Paul had once needed people to lead him by the hand (χειραγωγεω, Acts 9:8), just as Elymas now sought someone to lead him by the hand (χειραγωγος, 13:11). But Paul's blindness had come to an end. Could his promise that Elymas's blindness would be only "for a time" imply a healing to come that is more than physical? Another intriguingly "inconclusive" conclusion leaves the reader wondering.

The apostles left Elymas in darkness (v. 11), but they proceeded to announce in a synagogue of the Dispersion that the Lord had called them to be "a *light* to the Gentiles" (v. 47). The confrontation with Elymas prefigured the amazing exchange of unbelief and faith, judgment and mercy, which Paul would later describe: "For just as you [Gentiles] once disobeyed God but now have been shown mercy by means of their [unbelieving Jews'] disobedience, so they too have now disobeyed for the sake of the mercy that has become yours, in order that they too may now receive mercy" (Rom. 11:30–31). Although the Jewish sorcerer could not see (μη βλεπων) the sun, the Gentile proconsul saw (ιδων) what happened—and he believed (Acts 13:11–12). Luke describes Sergius Paulus as "intelligent" (συνετος, "insightful, having understanding")—not, as some commentators suppose,[23] because the proconsul had "seen through" Bar-Jesus all along, but because he was eager to hear the word of the Lord when Barnabas and Paul brought it.[24] Ironically, in Luke-Acts people close to God's revelation typically fail to understand it: Jesus' parents (Luke 2:50), Jewish crowds (8:10), the disciples (18:34),[25] Joseph's brothers (Acts 7:25), and the people of Israel (Acts 28:26–27, the climactic quotation from Isa. 6 in Acts).[26] In the surprising movement of God's grace, a Gentile belonging to "a nation lacking understanding" (ασυνετος, Rom. 10:19, quoting Deut. 32:21), becomes the one who shows true understanding, "amazed at the teaching of the Lord" (Acts 13:12).

This concluding comment reinforces the primacy of the word in the Lord's conquest of the nations. Barnabas and Saul "proclaimed the word of God" in the synagogues of Salamis (v. 5), and so when the proconsul summoned them, his desire was "to hear the word of God" (v. 7). Even after his "court seer" was struck blind, what amazed the proconsul was not the raw power of a curse that imposed physical blindness, but rather "the teaching about the Lord" (v. 12; cf. Luke 4:32). The magician uses words to manipulate forces surrounding an individual, bending them to the magician's will, but the words of God's messengers address the conscience of their hearers, bending their will to the lordship of Jesus.

THE FORTUNE-TELLER OF PHILIPPI
(ACTS 16:16–24)

Who Can Tell the Future?

Related to the magi's claims to have supernatural knowledge is the incident involving a spirit-possessed slave girl in Philippi. Here again the Lord's lawsuit against the idols in Isaiah is important as background. To demonstrate his claim to be the true and living God, the Lord declared: "I am the Lord; this is my name! I will not give my glory to another or my praises to idols. Look, things [spoken] from the beginning have come! And new things that I will declare—even before they arise I have shown them to you" (Isa. 42:8–9). "I am God, and there is none except me, announcing from the first the last things before they come into being. . . . I have said: My purpose will stand, and as many things as I will, I do" (Isa. 46:9–10). The Lord's ability to announce the future proves his power to control the future.

The idols' impotence, on the other hand, is shown by their muteness in the face of the future's uncertainties: "Let them draw near and announce to you things that will happen, or say what the former things were. . . . Announce to us the things that are coming at the last time, and we will know that you are gods" (Isa. 41:22–24). This is not to say that the idols have no spokespersons who *claim* to divine the future in the idols' names. The ancient Near East of Isaiah's day, no less than the Hellenistic world of Paul's, abounded with prophets and oracles, diviners and fortune-tellers. About these the Lord said, "I am the Lord. . . . Who else scatters the signs of 'oracles'[27] and divinations,[28] who frustrates the sages and makes their purpose foolishness, who causes the words of his servant to stand and proves true the purpose of [i.e., announced by] his messengers?" (Isa. 44:24–26). As the sovereign who rules the future, the Lord not only fulfills what he foretells, but also thwarts predictions made on behalf of his empty competitors. As the spirit-possessed girl herself confessed, the highest God was bringing salvation to Macedonia through the witness of his servants (δοῦλοι) (Acts 16:17, cf. v. 9).

The Philippian slave girl was trapped in the system of pagan divination.[29] She was controlled by "a python spirit" (v. 16)—a title derived from the serpent oracle Python, which (according to myth) the god Apollo slew to establish his own oracle at Delphi, southeast of Philippi in Achaia.[30] Daemons (spirits of less dignity and power than the gods) were thought to reveal the future through oracles.[31] The Hellenistic world also honored the Sibyls, prophetic women who uttered ecstatic predictions.[32] Thus, the slave girl, who spoke involuntarily due to demonic possession, was used to give oracles regarding the future (μαντεύομαι[33]). This word is used consistently in the LXX to identify "diviners," who sought to pierce the veil of the future in ways forbidden by God, including recourse to mediums (Lev. 19:31; 1 Sam. 28:8), idolatry (2 Kings 17:16–17; Zech. 10:2), and astrology (2 Kings 21:3–6). The appropriate alternative to divination is listening to the word of the Lord, as the Moses reminded the people of Israel:

> When you enter into the land that the Lord your God is giving you, you shall not learn to act according to the abominable practices of those nations. There shall not be found among you . . . one who practices divination [μαντεύομαι μαντείαν], who gives omens and interprets them, a sorcerer, one who sings incantations, who delivers oracles, a diviner, or one who inquires of the dead. . . . These nations you will dispossess listen to omens and divinations [μαντείαν]. But . . . a prophet from among your own brothers like me the Lord your God will raise up for you. To him you must listen. (Deut. 18:9–15)[34]

The girl's oppression had its profitable side—not for herself, but for her owners. Their profit motive is emphasized by the repetition of εργασια, "profit," in Acts 16:16, 19. As the Samaritan Simon's silver contrasted with God's free gift of the Spirit, so the knowledge-for-a-price business of these profiteers differed radically from the priceless message that God's servants proclaimed without price (vv. 13–14, 30–31). Whereas the girl's owners promised "inside information" that was worth paying for, her liberators, Paul and Silas, divulged a secret far beyond human purchasing power, pointing out a "road to salvation" (οδος σωτηριας) for which admission and tolls had been paid by Another. The operative motive for the practitioners of divination is neither the quest for truth nor the pursuit of holiness. Rather, profit is their bottom line, however politically correct the owners' later appeals to Roman citizenship and propriety may have sounded (16:21). At a later point, Ephesian silversmiths who found their profit (εργασια, 19:24–25) threatened would similarly mask their greed by declaring that it was their civic duty as loyal citizens to defend the honor of the city's patron goddess (vv. 27–28).

Christ's Way Is Supreme over the Spirits

The superiority of the gospel of Christ over pagan divination was shown first in the girl's announcement of the apostles' mission: "These men are servants of the highest God, who announce to you the road to salvation" (16:17). Demons confronted by Jesus during his earthly ministry confessed truly that he was "the holy one of God" (Luke 4:34), "the Son of God" (4:41), or—in the Gentile setting of Decapolis (as here in Philippi)—"the Son of *the highest God*" (8:28). This spirit also spoke truthfully about the relationship of Paul and Silas to God and about the saving power of their message.

Nevertheless, this testimony, true as it was, came from a source that the representatives of the living God could not condone. Just as Jesus silenced the unclean spirits, refusing to imply their legitimacy as a source of knowledge about the transcendent (Luke 4:35, 41), so also Paul found the slave girl's incessant testimonial aggravating (Acts 16:18). If Paul and Silas had been mere religious entrepreneurs, they would have welcomed such an endorsement from a recognized local authority on matters mysterious. But, consistent with the Lord's exclusive claims, from the first of the Ten Commandments through the lawsuit sections of Isaiah, the servants of Jesus rejected convenient alliances with religious systems that are, at the heart, lies.

The gospel's supremacy is seen also in the exorcism of the spirit from the girl. Paul's words are brief, and Luke's description is matter-of-fact: " 'I command you in the name of Jesus Christ to come out of her!' And it came out that very moment" (16:18). There were no rituals, no concatenation of secret syllables, no manipulation of talismans, and no examination of omens. Only one thing explains the instantaneous result: "the name of Jesus Christ." The "salvation" to which the python spirit had given its twisted testimony is found, Luke has told us, only in the name of Jesus (4:12). By invoking Jesus' name, Paul, like Peter before him, pointed away from his own power and piety to the authority of his Lord (cf. 3:6, 12, 16). Unlike the sons of Sceva at Ephesus, who would attempt to forge a parasitic connection with the name of "Jesus, whom Paul preaches," in order to empower their own exploits in exorcism (19:13–17), Paul himself was authorized to use Jesus' name because he was Jesus' servant. "For we do not preach ourselves, but Jesus Christ as Lord, and ourselves as your servants for Jesus' sake" (2 Cor. 4:5 NIV).

The climactic demonstration of the gospel's victory over pagan divination was the vindication of the apostles through their imprisonment, the midnight earthquake, the conversion of the jailor, and the apology of the city magistrates at daybreak. Luke makes clear the cynical hypocrisy of the slave girl's owners in provoking the arrest of Paul and Silas. In a play on words, Luke notes that when the spirit "went out" (εξηλθεν) of the girl (Acts 16:18), her owners saw that their hope of profit "went out" (εξηλθεν). To the girl's owners, the spirit that controlled their slave's speech was a business asset, not an object of faith. Their cynicism is obvious when we compare the girl's confession regarding Paul and Silas with her owners' accusation. She said that "these men" (ουτοι οι ανθρωποι) were servants of the highest God, who "announce" (καταγγελλουσιν) the road of salvation (v. 17). Her owners, on the other hand, told the magistrates that "these men" (ουτοι οι ανθρωποι) were Jews, who "announce" (καταγγελλουσιν) customs unlawful for Romans (vv. 20–21). They had made others pay for the knowledge ostensibly revealed through their slave, but they themselves did not believe her words, even when she spoke the truth.

Philippi was a Roman colony, a rank of distinction shared by selected cities (mainly military centers) throughout the empire. Together with such perks as exemption from taxation and the privilege of local self-government, this status bestowed on the citizens of a colony the citizenship privileges of Rome itself.[35] Thus, the owners were appealing to Philippi's civic pride when they charged that the customs proclaimed by the apostles were not lawful for "us Romans"[36] to receive or practice (vv. 20–21). The irony is that the only violation of Roman law in this incident was the beating and imprisonment of Paul and Silas, "men who are Romans,"[37] without a trial. Not the apostles but their persecutors were the real opponents of civil order.

The triumph of God over the practitioners of divination entailed the suffering of his servants. Nevertheless, the vindication of their Lord's reputation was clear as the Philippian magistrates escorted Paul and Silas from the prison, a public symbol of their innocence, as Paul had demanded (vv. 37, 39).[38]

Exorcists and Occultists at Ephesus (Acts 19:11–20)

With his account of Paul's Ephesian ministry, Luke draws to a close his narrative of the apostle's uninhibited spread of the gospel. Although Acts speaks briefly of a subsequent journey of Paul into Macedonia and Greece (20:1–6), after the events of Acts 19 the reader's attention is focused on Paul's determination to return to Jerusalem, and on the bonds and suffering that await him there.[39] Thus, the gospel's confrontation with Hellenistic religions reaches a climax in Paul's ministry at Ephesus. The final summary statement in Acts, tracing the growth of the word, is found in the midst of Paul's Ephesian ministry (19:20).

Ephesus provided a suitable setting for this series of showdowns between Jesus' servant and the proponents of other religions. Ephesus was not only the site of the famous temple of Artemis, but also a renowned center for the magical and occult arts—so much so, that papyri containing magical formulae and incantations were commonly called "Ephesian letters" (Εφεσια γραμματα).[40] The growing word of God thus confronted both the popular, personal religious practices (magic, vv. 11–19) and the institutional religion (temple of Artemis, vv. 23–41) for which Ephesus was well known.

Sceva's Sons: Abuse of the Lord's Name Frustrated
The accounts of the shaming of the sons of Sceva and the incineration of magical manuscripts are surrounded by Luke's recurring theme of the effectiveness of the word of the Lord. Paul's two-year preaching ministry, first in the synagogue and then in a lecture hall, had the result that "all those dwelling in Asia, both Jews and Greeks, heard the word of the Lord" (v. 10). The readiness of believers to break with their occult practices by burning their precious magical books illustrates how "the word of the Lord spread widely and grew in power" (v. 20 NIV). The miraculous signs

recorded between these two statements are subordinate to, and supportive of, the Lord's word.

Power is a prominent theme in Acts 19:11–20. In the Greek text, the first word of verse 11 is δυναμεις ("miracles, acts of power"), and the last word of verse 20 is ισχυεν ("became strong"). Moreover, earlier in the same summary, Luke speaks of the word growing "mightily" (κατα κρατος, v. 20).[41] Those who attempted to use Jesus' name without a commitment to his authority found themselves "overpowered" (ισχυσεν) by a demoniac (v. 16). Invincible power resided in the name of the Lord Jesus, but its benefits could not be received apart from faith in him.

The healings and exorcisms that God was doing through Paul set the context for the attempt by the sons of Sceva to tap into the power of Jesus' name, just as the generosity of Barnabas earlier provided the positive counterpoint to the deception of Ananias and Sapphira (4:36–5:11), and as the miraculous ministries of Philip, Peter, and John evoked Simon's desire to acquire their powers (8:13, 18). The sons of Sceva were representative of a larger group of itinerant Jewish exorcists, all of whom were attempting to exorcise demons with the formula, "In the name of Jesus, whom Paul preaches, I command you to come out" (19:13 NIV). The reputation of Jews as magicians and exorcists can be documented from Hellenistic writings.[42] Magical incantations, particularly those dealing with spirits, sometimes were thought to amass additional power through the inclusion of mysterious Hebrew words and names of God. A magical papyrus written in Egypt about A.D. 300 instructs exorcists to heap up various divine names, apparently including the name of Jesus, "the god of the Hebrews," in order to expel a demon.[43]

For the sons of Sceva, however, the name of Jesus did not "work." The formula they used implied that they had no direct connection with Jesus: "Jesus, whom Paul preaches." These exorcists were trying to exploit a name without regard for the person to whom the name belongs, as the evil spirit's response shows: "Jesus I know, and I know about Paul, but you—who are you?" (v. 15) Demons knew Jesus (Luke 4:34, 41; 8:28) and recognized Paul as a servant of God Most High (Acts 16:17). But the sons of Sceva had no relationship with the Lord Jesus that would authorize them to use his name. Only the faithful servant can act in the Master's name.[44]

The outcome brings two surprising reversals. First, the would-be exorcists were pounced upon by the demoniac, beaten, and sent fleeing naked and bleeding.[45] The shame of their nakedness and their bleeding wounds made them resemble the noteworthy demoniac Legion, who rushed to meet Jesus in the region of the Gadarenes. This man had wandered naked among the tombs (Luke 8:27) and slashed himself with sharp stones in anguish of heart (Mark 5:5). Now, in Ephesus, sons of a Jewish "high priest"[46] had been stripped and bloodied by Satan's power.

Magnification of the Lord's Name

The second reversal is even more striking: "And this became known . . . and fear fell upon them all, and the name of the Lord Jesus was magnified" (Acts 19:17). The "name of the Lord Jesus" had not accomplished what these exorcists had hoped to achieve through it (v. 13), but as a result of this incident the "name of the Lord Jesus" received even greater reverence![47] How can this be? The incident instilled in the people of Ephesus an awe-filled recognition of the terrifying holiness of Jesus' name. Just as the deaths of Ananias and Sapphira produced fear in all who heard of them (5:5, 11), so also in Ephesus the shameful defeat suffered by Sceva's sons at the hands of the demoniac moved Jews and Gentiles to fear Jesus' name. Who but "Jesus whom Paul preaches" had the power to use even hostile spirits to punish people who tried to manipulate and exploit his name in a magical incantation?

This sobering demonstration of the realities at work in the warfare between Christ and Satan prompted Christian believers to make a clean break with their pagan past in the occult arts. They confessed their evil practices, and those who had practiced sorcery proved their repentance by bringing their scrolls of forbidden knowledge and charms to be destroyed by fire (19:18–19). The Greek word translated "sorcery" (περιεργα) elsewhere refers to illegitimate curiosity or meddling in the affairs of others (1 Tim. 5:13; cf. 2 Thess. 3:11). Here, the forbidden intervention is through spells, curses, and other rituals by which these Ephesians had thought to enlist the aid of gods or demons in order to defeat enemies, thwart competitors in business or love, protect themselves and their families from harm, and accomplish other ends. The saving power of the gospel in the hands of Paul, Jesus' faithful servant, in combination with the failure of Sceva's sons to tap Jesus' power without allegiance to his authority, convinced Ephesian believers that they could not maintain dual loyalties (see 1 Kings 18:21; Luke 16:13).

Many Ephesians publicly repudiated their past efforts to use magical formulas to manipulate the mysterious forces that impinged on their lives. Scrolls once purchased at great personal expense, once thought to contain secret word weapons to fight Fate and foes, were now destroyed as useless, spiritually toxic waste. The accumulated value of these treasured manuscripts was 50,000 drachmas. The readiness of these Ephesians to pledge their allegiance to Jesus at such personal cost shows the real power of the gospel in its conflict against sorcery. Although the Lord can defeat the idols' wonder-workers in a contest of raw power (as when Aaron's staff swallowed those of Pharaoh's magicians, Ex. 7:10–12), Luke mentions Paul's miracles in Ephesus only briefly (Acts 19:11–12), emphasizing rather that it was "the word of the Lord" that transformed hearts and liberated minds from the lies of spiritual counterfeits (v. 20).

RESPONDING TO THE MODERN MERCHANTS OF MAGIC

"Magic" is alive and well in the late twentieth century, not only in isolated jungle villages, but also in the storefronts and apartments of Los Angeles, New York, and the other great cities of the world. A *Los Angeles Times Magazine* article describes the spread of Santeria, an ancient West African religion carried to the U.S. through Cuban immigrants and others, among college-educated residents of Los Angeles. One adherent, now a *santero* (priest) of Oshun, the goddess of love, described his first contact with Santeria: "[A santero] did a reading, which consists of throwing 16 cowrie shells on a tray and interpreting the numerical patterns of how many land face up or face down. The patterns . . . reveal the *orisha's* [spirit's] divine answers to specific human questions."[48] More recently, a single edition of the *Times* featured stories on the growing market for American New Age gurus in Japan and on a San Diego shop that markets how-to-hex books, spell candles (to break up a romance, get a job, control enemies), good luck sprays, and voodoo dolls, along with crucifixes and Last Supper paintings.[49] Televangelists distribute "prayer cloths" for health and wealth, to be returned with a donation for their ministries. A recent U.S. president consulted a personal astrologer, while countless people check out the horoscope column in their daily newspaper. Prominent entertainers advocate reincarnation and channeling, while others find personal peace in an ideology that promises the mental power to manipulate the circumstances of life. As we face these and other manifestations of modern magic, what lessons can we learn from the gospel's encounter with ancient magic in Acts?

The Uniqueness of the Living God
The logic behind magic is that a variety of competing spiritual forces operate behind the scenes in people's daily lives. Since none of these forces

is almighty, yet all have some influence on whether things go well or ill, it becomes a prudent strategy to enlist as many as possible into one's personal coalition for prosperity and happiness. If reality is like this, syncretism makes sense: invoke the God of the Hebrews to expel demons, pray to Asclepius for healing, consult the oracle at Delphi for a glimpse into the future, meditate with crystals or mantras, and contact a spirit guide from a bygone age. Such diversification of faith is safer than putting all your eggs in one basket.

But reality is not as the devotees of magic, ancient or modern, suppose it to be. While God's word reveals that unseen spiritual creatures, both good and evil, influence human life, it also makes clear that God alone is the creator and ultimate controller of all that happens. For that reason, the servants of Jesus Christ resisted the syncretistic overtures of Hellenistic magic. In Samaria, Peter rebuffed Simon's offer to purchase the Spirit; in Philippi, Paul silenced a slave oracle's "endorsement" of the gospel; in Ephesus, Jewish exorcists learned that Jesus' name brings no benefit to those who do not serve him. What would the apostles say about an eclectic California shop that markets Bibles and hex candles side by side? Advocates of religious pluralism, who view different faiths as alternative avenues to the divine or as complementary components to be combined at will, are living in a world fabricated by human imagination. The reality is that Jesus is Lord of all, and salvation is found in no name other than his.

The Gift of Grace

The gospel's encounter with magic has to do with money. Simon offered money for the power to bestow the Spirit, and the owners of the Philippian slave girl used her preternatural powers to turn a profit. As we will see in the next chapter, the silversmiths connected with the worship of Artemis at Ephesus worried over declining income because of Paul's preaching. Contemporary Americans are no strangers to the spectacle of religion as a moneymaking racket.

The relationship between money and divine favor exposes the central conflict between the Master and the magicians: Is there something we can do—some price to pay, some formula to recite, some work to accomplish —that will place God in our debt and obligate him to do our will? Peter's rebuke to Simon of Samaria goes to the heart of the issue: "You thought you could buy the gift of God with money!" (Acts 8:20 NIV). The theme recurs throughout the book of Acts: The Spirit is God's *gift*, not a product to be purchased, a service to be contracted for, or a wage to be earned (2:38; 3:6, 16; 5:31–32; 10:45; 11:17; 15:8; 20:32).

Magical manipulation is a manifestation of the common human quest for a "salvation by works," our hunger to control our own destinies, to break free from our need for, and dependence on, divine grace. But the message of Jesus is a message of God's gift, unearned, undeserved, unmanipulated, and uncoerced. It is the good news of rescue for the penniless, the helpless, the hopeless, who can neither pay their Benefactor in advance nor repay his kindness in their gratitude. God's gift unmasks our pretensions to independence, our delusion that we can bargain or barter with the Lord of the universe. God's gift also destroys despair over our impotence in the face of the forces that threaten us. Over all these forces stands the God who gave his Son over to the cross's cursed death in behalf of those who trust in his Word.

The Power of the Word

As Christianity confronted the magical and occult practices of the Hellenistic world, conflicting convictions were locked in a contest of power. Simon of Samaria, once acclaimed as the "Great Power of God," was astonished at the acts of power accomplished in Jesus' name by Philip, Peter, and John. Paul's powerful exorcisms evoked the imitation of Sceva's sons, and their disgrace at the demoniac's hands only served to increase the powerful growth of Jesus' name and word.

Nevertheless, although Jesus' witnesses overpowered representatives of rival religions in wonder-working strength, Luke turns our attention to the word of Jesus and its impact on people's minds and hearts (Acts 8:5, 12, 25; 13:5, 7, 12; 10:10, 20). Signs and wonders are God's testimony to the truth of the apostles' witness about Jesus (Heb. 2:3–4), and for this reason they are subordinate to that message. Apostolic preachers turn their listeners from wonder-evoking miracles toward Jesus, the content of God's good message (Acts 2:15–22; 3:12–13).

As Christ's people interact with adherents to other religions today, the temptation arises to go "one-on-one" in a duel of marvels and miracles: prayers answered, astonishing coincidences, inexplicable healings, unforeseen riches. But if we listen to Luke, we realize that such surface events are not the point. Of course the Lord alone is the living God who hears and answers prayer, who choreographs the details of our lives, who can and sometimes does give to his followers physical healing or even material prosperity. What really matters, though, is not whether God makes our daily life more pleasant or less painful. The heart of the matter is the power of the word of Jesus Christ to give eternal life.

Notes

¹ Robert N. Bellah, Richard Madsen, William M. Sullivan, Ann Swidler, and Steven M. Tipton, *Habits of the Heart: Individualism and Commitment in American Life* (New York: Harper and Row, 1985). Among their comments: "This egalitarian love between therapeutically self-actualized persons is also incompatible with self-sacrifice" (p. 100). "In its pure form, the therapeutic attitude denies all forms of obligation and commitment in relationships, replacing them only with the ideal of full, open, and honest communication among self-actualized individuals" (p. 101). Bellah and his colleagues found what they call "an older idea of marriage" still operative in a congregation of evangelical Christians whom they interviewed: "Only by having an obligation to something higher than one's own preferences or one's own fulfillment, [the evangelicals] insist, can one achieve a permanent love relationship" (p. 97).

² Peter R. Jones, *The Gnostic Empire Strikes Back: An Old Heresy for the New Age* (Phillipsburg, N.J.: Presbyterian and Reformed, 1992), 1–18, 43–112.

³ Andrés Tapia, "Why Is Latin America Turning Protestant?" *Christianity Today* 36, no. 4 (April 6, 1992): 28–29.

⁴ Ralph P. Martin, *New Testament Foundations: A Guide for Christian Students*, 2 vols. (Grand Rapids: Eerdmans, 1975–78), 2:29.

⁵ Everett Ferguson, *Backgrounds of Early Christianity* (Grand Rapids: Eerdmans, 1987), 105–10; Helmut Koester, *Introduction to the New Testament*, vol. 1: *History, Culture, and Religion of the Hellenistic Age* (New York: Walter de Gruyter, 1982), 65–67.

⁶ See D. W. J. Gill and B. W. Winter, "Acts and Roman Religion," in *Acts in Its Graeco-Roman Setting*, ed. Gill and Gempf, 79–104.

⁷ G. Delling, "μαγος," *TDNT*, 4:356. It is probably in one of these senses that Matthew uses μαγος to refer to the astrologers from the East who sought out the Christ child (Matt. 2:1).

⁸ Koester, *History, Culture, and Religion*, 379.

⁹ Ramsay MacMullen, *Paganism in the Roman Empire* (New Haven: Yale University Press, 1981), 50–51.

¹⁰ Ernst Haenchen, *The Acts of the Apostles: A Commentary* (Philadelphia: Westminster Press, 1971), 303.

¹¹ James M. Robinson, ed., *The Nag Hammadi Library*, rev. ed. (San Francisco: Harper, 1990), 311–17.

¹² The verb "to preach good news/the gospel" (ευαγγελλιζομαι) is prominent in connection with Philip's ministry. It appears five times in this chapter, three times in connection with Samaria, once in Philip's witness to the Ethiopian, and once in his ministry in the coastal towns. Ευαγγελλιζομαι appears ten times elsewhere in Acts, and ten times in Luke's gospel. Philip's role as a herald of glad tidings is later emphasized by the title "the evangelist" (Acts 21:8).

¹³ A translation of this application is found in C. K. Barrett, *The New Testament Background: Selected Documents*, rev. ed. (San Francisco: Harper & Row, 1989), 32–33.

¹⁴ Λογος, which sometimes means "subject matter under discussion" (hence the NIV's rendering, "You have no part or share in *this ministry*"). Typically in Luke-Acts, however, λογος refers to a spoken or written message, as it does elsewhere in this passage (vv. 4, 14, 25).

¹⁵ Greek: η γαρ καρδια σου ουκ εστιν ευθεια εναντι του θεου.

¹⁶ Greek: η δε καρδια αυτων ουκ ευθεια μετ' αυτου.

¹⁷ Greek: εις . . . συνδεσμος αδικιας, "in . . . a chain of unrighteousness."

¹⁸ The verb "pray" in Simon's request is plural (δεηθετε υμεις).

¹⁹ Most commentators believe that *Elymas* is related to the Arabic word *'alim*, "wise," or an Aramaic cognate of it. See, e.g., Haenchen, *Acts*, 398–99; I. Howard Marshall, *The Acts of the Apostles* (Grand Rapids: Eerdmans, 1980), 219; F. F. Bruce, *Commentary on the Book of the Acts* (NICNT; Grand Rapids: Eerdmans, 1954), 264.

²⁰ Luke subtly indicates a twofold transition in Paul's ministry at this point: (1) For the first time we learn that Saul "was also called Paul," and from this point on the name Paul becomes overwhelmingly predominant, while the name Saul is used only in the accounts of the apostle's conversion (22:7, 13; 26:14). (2) Paul here takes the lead in speaking, and hereafter will be named first when paired with Barnabas (e.g., 13:13, 42, 46, 50; 14:1, 3), in contrast to the earlier order, "Barnabas and Saul" (11:30; 13:1–2, 7). As the Apostle to the Gentiles moves into Gentile territory, his Hebrew name "Saul" recedes and is replaced with the cognomen *Paulus*, which was his as a Roman citizen.

²¹ The "filling" theme continues in Acts 13:13–52, showing that the confrontation with Elymas is a preview of the Jewish opposition to the gospel in Pisidian Antioch. When crowds of Gentiles gathered at the synagogue to hear the Lord's word, unbelieving Jews were "filled [πιμπλημι] with jealousy" (v. 45). But as the word spread throughout the region, "the disciples were filled [πληροω] with joy and with the Holy Spirit" (v. 52).

²² Paul's indictment here combines two Old Testament texts: Prov. 10:9 speaks of the one "who takes crooked paths" (rendered in the LXX, "the one who perverts his ways" [ο διαστρεφων τας οδους αυτου]); Hos. 14:9 declares, "The ways of the Lord are right" (14:10 LXX: ευθειαι αι οδοι του κυριου).

²³ David J. Williams, *Acts* (Good News Commentary; San Francisco: Harper and Row, 1985), 214; Marshall, *Acts*, 219.

²⁴ So Haenchen, *Acts*, 398.

²⁵ Cf. Jesus' comment that the disciples are "lacking understanding" (ασυνετος, Matt. 15:16; Mark 7:18).

²⁶ In all these texts the verb is συνιημι ("to understand"), a cognate of the adjective συνετος. The only instance in Luke-Acts in which this verb occurs in a statement describing people who understand (rather than failing to understand) God's truth is Luke 24:45: the disciples *understood* the Scriptures announcing Jesus' death and resurrection only because Jesus had opened their minds.

²⁷ LXX: εγγαστριμυθων, "ventriloquists" who claim to deliver messages from gods (LS).

²⁸ LXX: μαντεια, "divination," a cognate of the verb μαντευομαι in Acts 16:16.

²⁹ "The mantic arts, ranging from technical divination to inspired divination, were an integral feature of the social and religious life of the Greeks during the entire Greco-Roman period." David Aune, *Prophecy in Early Christianity and the Ancient Mediterranean World* (Grand Rapids: Eerdmans, 1983), 47.

³⁰ Pierre Grimal, *The Dictionary of Classical Mythology*, trans. A. R. Maxwell-Hyslop (Oxford: Blackwell, 1986), 400, s.v. "Python."

³¹ MacMullen, *Paganism*, 82, citing Apuleias, *De deo Socr.* 4.128 and 6.132, and Plutarch, *Moral.* 418Df.

³² Koester, *History, Culture, and Religion*, 171–72.

³³ Although this verb seems sometimes to refer to ventriloquism as a manifestation of ecstatic speech, Luke clearly emphasizes the preternatural knowledge that the python spirit imparted to the girl, for she declared truly that Paul and Silas were servants of the Most High God (Acts 16:17).

³⁴ In Acts 3:22–23 Peter identifies Jesus as this promised prophet.

³⁵ D. W. J. Gill, "Macedonia," in *Acts in Its Graeco-Roman Setting*, ed. Gill and Gempf, 405: "The most privileged cities in the province were the four Augustan colonies of Philippi, Kassandreia, Dion and Pella; all but Pella came under the *ius italicum*, which placed them on an equal footing to communities in Italy itself."

³⁶ The Greek text places even more emphasis on the Philippians' Roman citizenship: "These men are upsetting our city, *being Jews* [Ιουδαιοι υπαρχοντες], and announcing customs which are not lawful for us to receive or practice, *being Romans* [Ρωμαιοις ουσιν]."

³⁷ Paul's statement in v. 37 corresponds to and answers the accusation of the slave owners in vv. 20–21: Whereas the owners appealed to anti-Jewish prejudice (Ιουδαιοι υπαρχοντες) and boasted in their own Roman citizenship (Ρωμαιοις ουσιν), Paul announced that he and Silas (although ethnically Jewish) were Roman citizens (Ρωμαιοις υπαρχοντας). The magistrates reacted in fear because they had violated the rights of Romans (Ρωμαιοι εισιν, v. 38).

³⁸ The Greek verb in Paul's ultimatum (Acts 16:37) and the description of the magistrates' response (v. 39) is the same: εξαγω (at both points in the aorist tense).

³⁹ Haenchen, *Acts*, 558: "[Acts 19] is the last chapter in which Paul can freely pursue his missionary efforts. Over Chapter 20 already lie the shadows of departure, not merely from missionary work but also from life."

⁴⁰ Philo, *Symposiaca* 7.5; Clement of Alexandria, *Stromateis* 5.8.46.

⁴¹ Whereas the theme of the word's "growing" (αυξανω) is common to several summaries in Acts (6:7; 12:24; 19:20), the word's "being strong" (ισχυω) appears only in 19:20.

⁴² The Roman historian Pliny lists among various types of magic one branch associated with Moses, Jannes, Lopates, and the Jews (*Natural History* 30.2.11). Josephus boasted on behalf of Solomon's vast wisdom that "God allowed him to learn even the skill of dealing with demons, leading to the benefit and healing of people. And he composed incantations by which illnesses are cured and left behind forms for exorcisms" (*Antiquities* 8.45).

⁴³ "I adjure [ορκιζω, as in Acts 19:13] thee by the god of the Hebrews *Jesu* [!], Jaba, Jae, Abraoth, Aia, Thoth, Ele, Elo, Aeo, Eu, Jiibaech, Abarmas, Jaba-rau, Abelbel, Lona, Abra, Maroia, Bracion, thou that appearest in fire, thou that art in the midst of earth and snow and vapour, Tannetis: let thy angel descend, the implacable one, and let him draw into captivity the daemon as he flieth around this creature which God formed in his holy paradise." Paris Magical Papyrus, lines 3019–27, Greek text and English translation in Deissmann, *Light from the Ancient East*, 252, 256, emphasis added.

⁴⁴ Clearly this situation differs from that described in Luke 9:49–50. The exorcist whom John had rebuked as outside the disciples' company apparently used Jesus' name in genuine faith.

⁴⁵ Or "wounded" (τραυματιζω).

⁴⁶ If extrabiblical sources are correct, as they seem to be, no person named Sceva served as *the* high priest in the second temple. Probably Sceva was of the high priestly family, or (less likely, since Luke does not challenge the authenticity of the title) he falsely claimed

to be a high priest. On the sons (disciples) of the Pharisees expelling demons, see Luke 11:19; Matt. 12:24, 27.

[47] Greek: μεγαλυνω. See Luke 1:46; Acts 10:46.

[48] Rick Mitchell, "Power of the Orishas," Los Angeles Times Magazine (February 7, 1988), 16–21, 30, 32.

[49] Theresa Watanabe, "Cars? No, Japan Buys Our Gurus," Los Angeles Times (March 6, 1992), sec. A, pp. 1, 12–13. John M. Glionna, "A Shop That Casts a Spell," Los Angeles Times (March 6, 1992), sec. B, pp. 1–2.

ELEVEN

THE GREAT KING ABOVE ALL GODS

CIVIL RELIGION

Citizens of the United States are accustomed to debates over the "wall of separation" between church and state. Whether the topic is abortion, prayer in public schools, instruction about origins, or discrimination based on "sexual orientation," it is self-evident to many Americans that religious convictions belong to a "private" sphere of life and must not be allowed to influence public, governmental decisions.

Yet this viewpoint—that religion is a private matter and will threaten others' rights and communal justice if permitted to invade public life—is itself a religious conviction, and one that contradicts the beliefs and practices of people of faith belonging to various religions (and thus, in the language of the U.S. Constitution, interferes with their "free exercise" of religion). Sociologist Robert Bellah and his colleagues observe:

> Religion, at least biblical religion, which in a variety of forms constitutes the major religious tradition in America, cannot be private. Firstly, both Christians and Jews recognize a God who created heaven and earth, all that is, seen and unseen, whose dominion clearly transcends not only private life but the nations themselves. There is nothing in the private or public realm that cannot concern such a religious tradition.[1]

Throughout the world and throughout history, religious faith has come to expression in public life, both in governmental and legal structures and in nongovernmental patterns of community and culture. Islamic countries certainly make no pretense of maintaining a "wall of separation" between religion and government. Republics of the Commonwealth of Independent States are abandoning the separation of church and state that had been written into the defunct Soviet Union's constitution, and are now seeking the church's help in reforming public education to fill the vacuum of values left by the failed Marxist-secularist experiment.[2]

The ancient world of the New Testament never tried to pretend that religious conviction and public life could be kept separate. The gods of the Roman and Greek pantheons were simply the ruling classes, with both their virtues and their vices, magnified to mythic proportions. Temples stood at city gates or overshadowed the agora (the marketplace), which were the centers of public life. Each city revered its patron deity or deities, seeking divine help for campaigns to be launched and returning due honor for victories achieved. Contacts with the East introduced the idea of divine rulers, linking political subservience to religious worship. Roman emperors were hardly inclined to discourage such devotion, recognizing the power of religious commitment either to unify or to fragment their far-flung and diverse empire.

In the previous chapter, we observed how the word of Christ opposed Hellenistic magic and individualistic religious experience; now we focus on the gospel's challenge to public religion. Just as magic in its various forms addressed the individual's hunger for control over life's threatening forces, so institutional polytheism and the worship of rulers as deities served the community and the social order. Even philosophers who critiqued traditional mythology recognized the political expedience of institutional polytheism. Panaetius, a second-century B.C. Stoic philosopher, "suggested that there were three kinds of gods: those of the philosophers (the natural gods), which are true; those of the poets (the mythical gods), which are false; and those of the state (the political gods), which are . . . to be worshipped for their value to society."[3]

The message of Christ inevitably posed a threat to the institutionalized religious pluralism of the Hellenistic-Roman world. When the apostles proclaimed a message from the living God, who *alone* "created heaven and earth and all that fills them," they challenged not merely the marble images in a city's temples, but also the very concept of divine patrons governing different regions or spheres of life. Such a message—that the Lord alone is God and Savior, and that Jesus is Lord and judge of all—could be seen as dangerous, insulting to civic dignity, and disruptive of the fabric of social order, as Christianity's opponents were quick to point out: "These men who incited disturbances throughout the empire have come here" (Acts 17:6).[4]

INSTITUTIONAL POLYTHEISM

By the first century, the classical conception of the gods, as expressed in Greek mythology, was undergoing criticism and modification. Philosophers found implausible the pettiness, immorality, deceit, and deceivability that the old myths attributed to Zeus and his pantheon. Increasing mobility diminished people's connection to the patron deities of their home cities. Cosmopolitan contacts with Egypt and Persia introduced new gods and goddesses into the religious menu of the Greco-Roman world. Sometimes the new arrivals replaced or became fused with traditional deities.[5] Nevertheless, the worship of divine patrons and patronesses provided public expression of a city's unity. Luke portrays three encounters of Paul with institutional polytheism, at Lystra, Athens, and Ephesus.

ZEUS AND HERMES AT LYSTRA
(ACTS 14:8–18)

The healing of the lame man at Lystra and the Lystrans' subsequent confusion, mistaking Paul and Barnabas for gods, led to Paul's first sermon to Gentiles who were pagan polytheists. Since his audience was ignorant of the Scriptures, Paul's starting point and method of persuasion were different from the argument from Israel's covenantal history that he used in synagogues (Acts 13:16–41).

The opening for Paul's preaching at Lystra was provided by the healing of a man who had been "lame from his mother's womb."[6] This description, together with the statements that the apostle "fixed his gaze on him"[7] and that the man "leaped up and was walking,"[8] link this healing with that of the lame man in the Jerusalem temple through Peter and John (Acts 3). As through Peter in Jerusalem, so through Paul among the pagans, healing was taking place, not through the apostles' own power or piety, but through faith in the name of Jesus (3:12, 16; 14:9, 15–16).[9]

Mistaken for Gods
The lame man's healing was the prelude to the central crisis at Lystra. This instantaneous healing, enabling a man who had never walked suddenly to leap, led the Lystrans to believe that Paul and Barnabas were two gods, Zeus and Hermes, walking the earth in human guise. The Roman poet Ovid recounted a story from Phrygia-Lycaonia (in which Lystra was located, Acts 14:6) in which Jupiter and Mercury (Latin equivalents of the Greek Zeus

and Hermes), traveling in human form through the region, received hospitality only from a poor, elderly couple. The two gods rewarded the couple by transforming their humble hut into a glorious temple and appointing them its caretakers, while their inhospitable neighbors were drowned in a flood.[10] With such a legend circulating through the region, it is hardly surprising that the Lystrans, awestruck over the astonishing healing, hastened to show their "divine" visitors warm hospitality!

Since the Lystrans were speaking in their native Lycaonian dialect rather than Greek, Paul and Barnabas did not realize what was afoot until the priest of the temple of Zeus at the city gates showed up with sacrificial bulls draped with ceremonial garlands of flowers. As Luke summarizes it, the apostles' response was not a complete presentation of the message of Jesus, but it shows Paul's sensitivity to express God's truth in a way that was appropriate to his listeners' background and understanding. The Lystrans could not be expected to acknowledge the authority of the Scriptures given to Israel. Therefore, although the apostles' concepts were derived from the Old Testament, they did not explicitly appeal to the Scriptures. Instead, Paul and Barnabas pointed to God's self-disclosure through the world he created and sustains, which the Lystrans observed every day.

The Distance Between Creator and Creatures

The apostles insisted that they must not be worshiped, because they were mere men, subject to pain and pleasure just as the Lystrans themselves were (Acts 14:15). Echoes in the Greek text show that Paul's and Barnabas's objection answered and refuted the Lystrans' exclamation. It was not that "the gods, having been made like [ομοιωθεντες] humans [ανθρωποις], have come down to us" (v. 11), but rather that the apostles were humans (ανθρωποι) who had passions like (ομοιοπαθεις[11]) the Lystrans (v. 15). This statement signaled the difference between the true God proclaimed by the apostles and the mythical gods worshiped by the Lystrans. In mistaking the apostles for Zeus and Hermes, the Lystrans took them to be father-and-son deities, for the myth recounted that Hermes was conceived by Maia, one of the Pleiades, through relations with Zeus.[12] This was only one of many liaisons attributed to Zeus in ancient mythology. One scholar indicates that Zeus was said to have fathered children by eight goddesses and fifteen human women[13]—truly a god "of like passions" with men! Zeus was a magnified replica of human nature (perhaps particularly of the ruling class), with human instabilities, foibles, and passions writ large. But Paul and Barnabas were servants of the living God. Compared to the true Creator, "the great King above all gods" (Ps. 95:3), Zeus and his entourage were nothing but "empty things" (ματαιων, Acts 14:15). The apostles stood in continuity with the Old Testament prophets as they dismissed the gods of the nations, images crafted from mutable materials and figments of human imagination, as hollow, empty, and useless (1 Sam. 12:21; 1 Kings 16:13, 26; Jer. 2:5; 8:19).[14]

Paul and Barnabas were the messengers of the God who "made the heaven and earth and sea and everything in them" (Acts 14:15 NIV). This wording comes from the Sabbath commandment in the Decalogue (Ex. 20:11; cf. Ps. 146:6), but the truth is revealed in Genesis. This claim distinguishes the living God from Zeus, the king of the Greek pantheon. According to the ancient myths, Zeus came to preeminence not by creating all things, but by rebelling against his father Cronus, and the outcome of this war was that the allied insurgents of Zeus's generation divided the great spheres by lot, Zeus receiving heaven, Poseidon the sea, and Hades the underworld.[15] In contrast to this system of "checks and balances" between the gods of paganism, the God preached by the apostles is the Lord over every sphere of the created order and human life.

The apostles drew a contrast between two great eras of God's relationship to the Gentile nations. "In the past," God "allowed all the Gentiles to follow their own ways" (Acts 14:16), which implies that in the present this terrible divine abandonment of the nations has come to an end. No longer will the Creator exclude the Gentiles from his redemptive correction, consigning them to the dreadful pseudofreedom that brings self-destruction.[16] Yet even during the earlier epoch, the living God still spoke to the nations. "He has not left himself without testimony [αμαρτυρον]" (14:17 NIV). This adjective evokes the motif of the Lord's witness (μαρτυρια) before the nations. Even in the past, while the Lord left the nations to the folly of their own ways, a witness testified to them that the living God alone is worthy of worship. That witness was the abundant generosity of his providence, giving them rain, harvests, food, and joy. Several Old Testament passages speak of the heavenly gift of rain, bringing harvests (Lev. 26:4; Deut. 11:14; Ps. 147:8–9; Jer. 5:24), but Paul and Barnabas were perhaps thinking particularly of the Lord's provision portrayed in Psalm 104.[17] Zeus does not give rain; nor is Cybele, the Great Mother, the giver of fruitfulness to the earth or the womb. Through these good gifts, the one true God, the Creator and King over all, has borne his own witness to the nations.

But now the time of the Lord's wordless witness through rainfalls and harvests has given way to a new age: "We are announcing good news [ευαγγελλιζομαι] to you. Turn [επιστρεφω] from these empty things to the living God" (Acts 14:15). Paul's and Barnabas's joyful message was indeed that God had come down among humans (Isa. 40:9), bringing peace and salvation (52:7)—but not in the persons of Barnabas and Paul. Their message was good news not only for Israel, to whom it had been promised long ago, but also for the Gentiles, who formerly fixed their hopes on vanities (44:9), but whom the Lord now summoned: "Turn [επιστρεφω] to me and be saved, all you ends of the earth; for I am God, and there is no other" (45:22).

This announcement of God's good news, so briefly sketched in the sample that Luke records, was apparently explained by the apostles in subsequent days, until life-threatening persecution cut short their ministry in Lystra. The fruit of their evangelizing is shown in the circle of disciples who gathered around the body of the stricken Paul (Acts 14:20). Although the majority of the Lystrans, it seems, moved quickly from a readiness to worship Paul to a readiness to kill him (at the instigation of outsiders from Antioch), some turned from the emptiness of Zeus and Hermes to the God who created all, and who gives every good and perfect gift.

THE UNKNOWN GOD AT ATHENS
(ACTS 17:16–34)

By the middle of the first century, Athens was in decline from its earlier glory, eclipsed by the growing commercial and political strength of nearby Corinth. Nevertheless, Athens retained its renown in religious, cultural, and intellectual matters—as well as its reputation, mentioned by Luke (Acts 17:21), for a certain dilettantism, an idle curiosity more interested in intellectual novelty than in truth.[18] The Athenians' religious devotion to the gods, attested by the abundance of images and shrines that Paul observed in the city (v. 16), was also well known.[19] The Parthenon and some of the other temples on the brow of the Acropolis were visible from the marketplace (αγορα), where Paul reasoned daily with anyone who would enter into dialogue (v. 17). The people of Athens were indeed "very religious."[20]

While popular piety kept Athens's reputation for devotion to the gods alive, the leading philosophical schools of the time, Epicureanism and Stoicism, were subtly undercutting or modifying traditional religion and its mythology. By noting that Epicurean and Stoic philosophers were among Paul's disputants at Athens, Luke invites his readers to listen to Paul's message from the perspective of its interplay with the worldviews of these two schools.

Epicureans

Epicurus (341–270 B.C.) was hailed by his intensely loyal disciples as the one who had saved them from religious delusion and its resultant obligations. Lucretius (ca. 99–55 B.C.), for example, praised the courage and insight of Epicurus's materialistic philosophy, by which "underfoot is tamed religion trod, and, by his victory, Man ascends to God."[21] According to Epicurus, the gods, although they probably exist, are serenely aloof from, and indifferent to, human affairs. The world was not created and has no comprehensive purpose. There is no future life, since at death the refined matter that makes up the "soul" evaporates into the atmosphere. Therefore, people who understand reality will not be motivated by fear of future judgment, by the promise of future reward, or by the threat of divine intervention in the present life. Consequently, the wise contemplate the gods not with fear or gratitude, but with admiration for their life of undisturbed pleasure, a way of life that the philosopher himself can choose. Rather than seeking to placate the gods, Epicureans concentrated on avoiding pain and pursuing personal peace through the pleasures of the mind and of friendship.[22]

Stoics

While Epicureanism repudiated traditional Greek mythology, Stoicism reinterpreted it. Although they were materialists like the Epicureans, the Stoics affirmed that a mind permeates all reality, a fiery breath that they called Reason, or Logos (λογος), since they conceived of it as the rational principle that permeates and connects all beings and events. This Logos is divine (θεος). Stoic poets could personify this principle as Zeus. The "Hymn to Zeus" written by Cleanthes (331–232 B.C.), for example, is a song of praise to the Logos, the universal law that ties reality together: "Thus hast thou fitted all things in one, the good with the evil, that thy word should be one in all things abiding forever."[23] This concept of cosmic rational unity enabled the Stoics to offer an intellectual defense of such popular practices as divination, omens, and magic.[24] Since all human beings contain a spark of the Logos, Stoic authors such as Cleanthes and Aratus of Soli (ca. 314–240 B.C.) could say of this Logos/God, "We are all his offspring," a confession that Paul would quote and reinterpret (Acts 17:28).[25] The goal for the Stoic was to conduct one's life in harmony with the Logos, for such an approach brings self-sufficiency (αυταρκεια), a contentment impervious to external events or fluctuating emotions.

Paul's Message to Greece's Intellectuals

Paul's remarks before the Areopagus[26] concurred with the philosophers' critique of popular polytheism and idolatry, but Christ's apostle also challenged cherished Epicurean and Stoic convictions. This intermingling of concurrence and contradiction illustrates the paradoxical theme that pervades this text: the Athenians *know of* the God whose message Paul is preaching, but they do not *know* this God. Because they knew something of the true God, Paul was not an advocate of "foreign" gods, as they supposed (Acts 17:18). Rather, he brought a word from the God to whom they themselves had erected a shrine (v. 23). Their own poets displayed enough knowledge of God to show the folly of the idolatry that filled the city (vv. 28–29).

On the other hand, the true God was "unknown" to them (v. 23), as though they were groping in the dark to find him (v. 27). Luke's repeated reference to knowledge signals the importance of this theme: "May we *know* [γνωναι, aorist infinitive of γινωσκω] this new teaching?" (v. 19). "We wish to *know* [γνωναι] what these things want to be" (v. 20). "To an *unknown* [αγνωστος] god" (v. 23). "What you are worshiping *without knowing* [αγνοουντες] ..." (v. 23). "God, having overlooked the times of *ignorance* [αγνοια], now commands all people everywhere to repent" (v. 30). The Athenians, in their religious and philosophical traditions, had admitted that they knew that they did not know what they needed to know about the One who controlled their lives.[27] Their admission was Paul's starting point.

Paul's hearers could not be expected to admit their ignorance readily. Their intellectual pride tipped its hand as they called him "this scavenger" (σπερμολογος, v. 18). This word was applied to birds that scavenge for seeds, to rag pickers who scavenge through discarded clothing, and to academic parasites who pick up others' juicy ideas without understanding them. In the philosophers' eyes,[28] Paul was patching together his bizarre message from the odds and ends of other people's ideas. How else could he have linked a god with a Jewish name, Jesus, with a new goddess bearing the Greek name Resurrection (Αναστασις)?[29]

The speculation that Paul was preaching "foreign gods" (ξενων δαιμονιων) (v. 18) and the comment that he was "bringing foreign ideas [ξενιζοντα] to our ears" (v. 20) echoed the charges that led to Socrates' suicide 450 years before.[30] In the time between Socrates' day and Paul's, Alexander's empire building had brought Greece into increasing contact with the religions of Egypt, Persia, and other regions. Thus, the Athenians addressed by Paul were more tolerant of alien opinions than were Socrates' contemporaries. Paul's listeners were intrigued by religious novelties from afar, but their cosmopolitan curiosity should not be confused with a real openness to Paul's message. Epicureans disapproved of undue attention to any gods, foreign or domestic. Stoics, recognizing that traditional Greek religion had a certain political usefulness, would hardly welcome exotic, sub-Athenian conceptions of deity.[31] Paul faced an attentive but resistant audience.

Paul began with the Athenians' own confession of their ignorance in erecting a shrine to an "unknown God" (v. 23). Whatever origin and interpretation the Athenians attached to this shrine, Paul knew the God whom the residents of Athens, despite their wisdom, did not (1 Cor. 1:21). As at Lystra, Paul described this God as the Creator of all and the Lord of providence (Acts 17:24). At Lystra, the apostles pointed to the phenomena of nature and agriculture as God's testimony to his dominion (14:17); in Athens, the emphasis fell on God's control of human affairs (17:26). He created humanity from one ancestor and determined the temporal[32] and geographical[33] limits that delineate the diverse ethnic groups in the human family.

Points of Contact

At several points, Paul's message corresponded formally to tenets held by his Epicurean and Stoic listeners. His affirmation of the unity of humanity and the divine order in human affairs would strike a responsive chord in Stoic minds. Epicureans, picturing the gods as aloof in their self-sufficiency and uninterested in mere humanity, would have mentally applauded Paul's insistence that God has no need of man-made shrines and sacrifices (v. 25). Both schools could have agreed that the insight of the Stoics Cleanthes and Aratus, "We are all [God's] offspring," shows the folly of equating a gold, silver, or stone image with the divine being (vv. 28–29) —the Stoics, because they equated "God" with the fiery Reason that permeates the universe; the Epicureans, because their gods were far removed from the grosser forms of matter from which the statues on the Acropolis had been sculpted.

The God They Knew They Didn't Know

On the other hand, the "unknown God" proclaimed by Paul was profoundly unlike the deity imagined by the philosophers. While Epicureans believed correctly that God is not dependent on human help, they were wrong to think that he is uninvolved with humanity. The true God is intimately related to his creatures, giving them "life and breath [πνοή] and everything" (v. 25). Paul's thought reflects not only the biblical account of Creation (Gen. 2:7), but also the prophetic comment that God provides the breath of life to every generation:

> Thus says the Lord God, who made the heaven and stretched it out, who made firm the earth and the things in it and gives breath [πνοη] to the people on it and life [πνευμα, translating Heb. רוח] to those who walk on it. (Isa. 42:5)

Paul's critique of idolatry goes beyond exposing the foolishness of equating carved marble with the Creator of the universe. The problem with the idols on the Acropolis was not that they were composed of the wrong grade of matter, as the Epicureans held. Rather, their conceptions of God were fatally flawed because they were the product of human cleverness. These Athenian intellectuals should have known better than to suppose that God is like "an image made by man's skill and thought [ενθυμησις]" (Acts 17:29). Paul suggested that all ideas about the nature of the divine that arise from human speculation are inadequate. The philosophers' mental constructs, no less than the sculptors' marble statues, are produced by a blind groping for the God whose existence is undeniable, but whose character is unknowable through human wisdom alone.

The decisive point of Paul's presentation came when he surveyed the history of God's self-revelation to humanity (v. 30). Previously, God had "overlooked" the ignorance of people who failed to recognize him as the Creator and the ruler of human affairs, but a new stage of his self-revelation had arrived, in which he called upon all people to repent. But even in those earlier times of ignorance, people should have known better than to identify the Deity with idols made out of inanimate minerals, since people are God's "offspring" and image (v. 29).

Now, Paul declared, God is speaking to all people everywhere in a form that is clear, bringing a message that is inescapable. And what marked the transition from the "times of ignorance" (τους χρονους της αγνοιας) to the present time of God's universal call to repentance? God designated the man who would carry out final judgment, demonstrating that man's authority by raising him from the dead. With this one sentence (vv. 30–31), Paul moved the discussion into areas that directly challenged the Epicurean and Stoic philosophies: the significance and eschatological goal of history, the accountability of individuals before the justice of God, and the unique authority of the man appointed by God through resurrection to administer divine justice.

Whereas Epicureans' gods had no interest in human affairs, Paul was proclaiming a God who would call all to account in future judgment and who was calling all to present repentance. They held that personal identity ceases at death, which conveniently excludes the prospect of future judgment.[34] Paul, on the other hand, proclaimed a God who had raised a man from the dead to become the judge of all.

Stoics took comfort in a cyclical conception of history, in which three phases were rehearsed over and over again in successive "regenerations": (1) the creative fire of the Logos produces (2) a period of stability in the universe, but that stability eventually gives way to (3) dissolution and conflagration. When this destruction has run its course, the cycle begins again.[35] Paul, on the other hand, proclaimed a God who directs history linearly toward his intended goal: times of ignorance in the past, a time of opportunity to repent in the present, and a time of judgment in the future.

Just as God's control over human affairs was all-inclusive during the "times of ignorance," so his summons to repentance in the present time includes all. Whereas in times past he "made *every* [πας] nation of men, that they should inhabit the *whole* [πας] earth" (v. 26 NIV), "now he commands *all* [πας] people *everywhere* [πανταχου] to repent" (v. 30 NIV). Formerly he *"appointed* [οριζω] their designated times and the boundaries they inhabit [κατοικια]" (v. 26), but now he has *appointed* (οριζω) the man through whom he will judge the whole inhabited world (οικουμενη) (v. 31). This is no "foreign god" smuggled into sophisticated Athens in a ragpicker's pack. This is the Creator and Master of all that is, who now commands all people to turn to him for refuge from his coming judgment. The religious pluralism of the past was not a beautiful manifestation of cultural diversity to be celebrated, but a pitiful expression of human folly and ignorance.[36] From Paul's perspective, the age of religious pluralism is over, for now God is calling those who have worshiped idols of stone or wood (or images of the mind) out of their darkness and into his light. His message of salvation reaches as far as his worldwide authority in creation and providence.[37]

Although God "overlooked" the Gentiles' ignorance in the past (v. 30), this did not excuse their idolatry. When God "overlooked" past ignorance, he was not forgiving guilt, but only postponing judgment.[38] Peter had said that the people and leaders of Jerusalem had "acted in ignorance [κατα αγνοιαν]" in repudiating God's holy servant (3:15, 17). Their ignorance, however, did not obviate their need to repent (μετανοεω) in order for their sins to be forgiven (v. 19). Similarly, Paul insists that the Athenians' ignorance (αγνοια) in the past, far from excusing them, made it necessary for them to repent (μετανοεω), in light of the coming judgment (17:30).

Paul's address ended by dealing with the matters that had caused him to be brought before the Areopagus: Jesus and the resurrection (v. 31; see v. 18). In contrast to other sermons in Acts, he made no mention here of the miracles that attested Jesus' authority, of his death as the way to forgiveness, or of the testimony of the Scriptures.[39] Instead, Paul focused on two events: Jesus' resurrection and the coming day of judgment.

Jesus' resurrection from the dead was God's "proof" (πιστις) that he had designated him to be his agent of righteous judgment (v. 31). This connection between Jesus' resurrection and his authority as eschatological judge developed the implications of earlier apostolic preaching. At Pentecost, Peter had declared that Jesus, who could not be held by death, was now enthroned at God's right hand (2:24, 34–36). To Cornelius, Peter had declared that the risen Jesus was the one appointed (οριζω, as in 17:31) by God as judge of the living and the dead (10:40–42). By his resurrection, Jesus was appointed "Lord and Christ" (2:36), and as "Lord of all" he had authority to execute divine justice (10:36).

Without explicitly citing the prophetic Scriptures (since he was speaking to pagans), Paul described Jesus' future coming in terms that recall the eschatological hope of Psalms 96 and 98:

> Sing to the Lord, all the earth. . . . Declare among the Gentiles [εθνη] his glory. . . . For all the gods of the Gentiles are idols [LXX, δαιμονια], but the Lord made the heavens. . . . Bring to the Lord, O families of the Gentiles, bring to the Lord glory and honor. . . . He will judge the inhabited world [οικουμενη] in justice,[40] and peoples in his truth. (Ps. 96:1, 3, 5, 7, 13; cf. Ps. 98:9)

Because Jesus was the coming Lord who would judge the world in righteousness, Paul was proclaiming him among the nations, calling upon them to abandon the futile gods they had worshiped and to bring glory to the God who created heaven and earth. Paul moved the discussion from a critique of popular idolatry, with which his cultured listeners could concur, to a declaration of their accountability before a sovereign God who is both transcendent (contrary to Stoicism) and immanent (contrary to Epicureanism). Paul advanced from the generalities of God's creation and governance to the specifics of a judgment day and a judge already appointed to administer justice on that day: Jesus, the One raised from the dead.

Paul's message received a mixed response (Acts 17:32–34). Some scoffed at the thought of resurrection. These would have included Epicureans,[41] although the thought of an individual's return to physical life after death would be no more palatable to Stoics. Others, their interest piqued, wanted Paul to explain his message more fully on another occasion. Still others became Paul's associates and disciples, having believed his gospel.[42] These new believers had begun the day as those who, not knowing the true God, mocked his messenger as a "ragpicker" and found his message of "Jesus" and "Resurrection" confusing or silly. Although not previously exposed to the preparatory promises of the Scriptures, they came so far so quickly only through the power of the apostolic word applied by the Spirit, drawing Gentiles to give glory to the coming Lord.

ARTEMIS AT EPHESUS
(ACTS 19:23–20:1)

Unlike many of the accounts in Acts, the report of the riot instigated by the silversmiths associated with the temple of Artemis at Ephesus contains no sample of apostolic preaching. Paul's desire to address the tumultuous mob was thwarted by his fellow Christians, whose wisdom was confirmed by the counsel of Paul's friends among the Asiarchs (Acts 19:30–31). In the design of Acts, therefore, this narrative fulfills a different role than the accounts that set the context for apostolic speeches. The story is, admittedly, dramatic and entertaining.[43] But through the thrilling turmoil, Luke does not want us to forget the central issue: the message that Paul carries.

Although the time reference in Acts 19:23 is vague ("about that time"), Luke's order suggests that the disturbance took place after Paul had announced his intention to leave Ephesus to travel to Jerusalem and then to Rome (v. 21), and after he had sent Timothy and Erastus to Macedonia to prepare the churches for his visit on his way to Jerusalem.[44] Since Paul had announced and initiated plans for his departure from Ephesus even before the disturbance instigated by the silversmiths, it is clear that Paul's decision to leave was not motivated by threats or fear. Luke includes an account of the riot at Ephesus, not to explain why he left, but rather as a preview of the sufferings that lay ahead for him in Palestine, and of the confusion of crowds and councils stirred up by his opponents there (21:30–36; 23:9–10).

This incident was the capstone of Paul's ministry in Ephesus. There the word of the Lord had been resisted and slandered by Jewish people affiliated with the synagogue (19:9), unsuccessfully imitated by Jewish exorcists (vv. 13–16), honored by both Jews and Greeks (v. 17), and embraced by people formerly enmeshed in the occult (vv. 18–19). Climactically, the gospel confronted the religious center of Ephesian self-identity, the temple of Artemis.

In Greek mythology, Artemis was a virgin and a huntress. Modern scholars, attempting to interpret extant statues of the Ephesian Artemis, have theorized that in traveling across the Aegean to Asia, Artemis was transformed into a many-breasted fertility goddess, identified with Cybele, Great Mother (*Magna Mater*), who was worshiped in central Asia Minor.[45] This theory is contradicted, however, by other evidence regarding the worship in the Ephesian temple. It now appears more likely that the Ephesians worshiped Artemis essentially as Greek mythology portrayed her.[46] Acclaimed as one of the seven wonders of the ancient world, the temple attracted devotees from throughout the Mediterranean. It wielded significant economic influence, both as a banking institution and as the owner of vast farmlands.[47] Artemis's worldwide fame and financial importance explain the dynamics of the riot generated by Demetrius.

In his speech to a meeting of the silversmiths' guild, Demetrius wasted no time in getting to the bottom line: "This fellow Paul," with his declaration that idolatry is empty, was threatening their profitable business (19:26).[48] Miniature models of the shrine of Artemis, made from terra cotta, have been found at Ephesus and elsewhere. Demetrius and his colleagues apparently cast similar replicas in silver, to be sold to the pilgrims who came from throughout the Roman Empire to worship and to wonder. Particularly during the month-long celebration in honor of the goddess each spring, crowds would flood into the city for athletic games, plays, concerts, banquets, and other festivities. It would hardly enhance the silversmiths' profits (εργασια[49]) to have an influential itinerant preacher persuading pilgrims and local residents "that gods that are handmade [οι δια χειρων γινομενοι] are not gods" (19:26).

Demetrius understood Paul correctly. At Lystra, Paul and Barnabas had called idols "worthless things" (ματαια), echoing the terminology of the Old Testament prophets (14:15). At Athens, Paul had not only stated that the God who created all things does not live in temples built by hands (χειροποιητης,[50] 17:24), but had also announced, "We should not think that the divine being is like gold or silver or stone—an image made by man's skill and thought" (v. 29). It is ironic, then, that the Ephesian city clerk tried to quell the disturbance with the assurance, "These men have neither robbed temples nor slandered our goddess" (19:37). It is hard to imagine how this Ephesian official could extol the great Artemis and her image that had fallen from heaven, and yet fail to see that Paul's critique of idolatry "slandered" (from an idolater's perspective) the goddess.

Both Demetrius's accusation and the city clerk's defense of Paul linked dishonor of the goddess with financial loss. One affirmed that Paul was dishonoring the goddess, bringing financial ruin on those who supplied silver idols to worshipers; the other denied that Paul and his team were temple robbers or deity slanderers. One asserted that Paul posed a danger (κιν-δυνεύω) both to the silversmiths' trade and to the honor of the goddess (19:27); the other asserted that the silversmiths had placed the city in danger (κινδυνεύω) of being accused of insurrection against Roman authority (v. 40). Who was right?

As narrator, Luke endorses the city clerk's contention that Demetrius and his guild placed the city in danger by provoking an illegal assembly that bordered on insurrection (v. 40). We might assume, therefore, that Luke also affirms the clerk's statement that Paul and his companions had not slandered the goddess. Was the clerk speaking only of Gaius and Aristarchus, Paul's companions who had been brought to the theater, and not of Paul, who had been prevented from joining them?[51] Or was he denying that Paul and his colleagues had gone out of their way to launch an offensive smear campaign against the goddess or to vandalize pagan shrines for personal profit, as the Jews were accused of doing?[52] Was he resting his defense of Paul on the technicality that Paul's critique of "handmade" gods did not apply to the image in the temple of Artemis, which had fallen directly from heaven?[53] None of these explanations is satisfying. Most likely, Demetrius understood the implications of Paul's message more clearly than the clerk, whose defense of Paul was motivated by a concern to restore public order. The city clerk may not have foreseen where Paul's radical critique of idolatry could lead (as Demetrius had), but at least he knew that the Christians were not responsible for instigating the chaotic demonstration that had the appearance of open rebellion (στάσις). It was not the messengers of Christ, but rather their opponents, who were responsible for the civil turmoil that followed the spread of the gospel.

Demetrius frankly placed concern for financial gain first and foremost in portraying the crisis to his colleagues in the guild, but when they took their cause to the streets, the rhetoric of piety and patriotism eclipsed talk of profit and loss. When Paul had sent the divining spirit out of the Philippian oracle, her owners masked their resentment over their loss of revenue behind a façade of political correctness: "These men, who are Jews, are creating a disturbance in our city and are proclaiming customs which are unlawful for us to accept or practice, since we are Romans" (16:19–21). Likewise, the Ephesian silversmiths' financial concern was transformed into devotion to the patron goddess of the city: "Great is Artemis of the Ephesians!" (19:28). The city clerk, placating the mob, responded that neither their city's reputation nor its patroness's glory was threatened by Paul's team and his message (v. 35). The danger to the city, said the clerk (and our narrator agrees), came from the gospel's opponents, whose lawlessness had opened Ephesus to the threat of disgrace and intervention at the hands of imperial authorities.

Paul, on the other hand, could count among his friends the Asiarchs, who demonstrated concern for his safety (v. 31). Political and religious responsibilities were combined in the office of the Asiarchs, who were elected annually to serve in the provincial league of Asia. During his term of office, each Asiarch served as chief priest of a provincial temple, promoting the cult of the emperor and the goddess Roma. Consistent with this religious role, Asiarchs also wielded significant political influence as representatives of Roman authority in their respective cities.[54] Their support of Paul, whatever their personal religious convictions may have been, demonstrated that Paul was not an instigator of civil unrest.[55]

Thus, at the close of Paul's Ephesian ministry, we see institutional idolatry in disarray. Luke's description of the crowd that gathered in the theater is apropos: "Some were shouting one thing, some another, for the assembly was bewildered and the majority did not know why they had come together" (v. 32). Demetrius's fears were, in part, justified. Paul's message did threaten the livelihood of those who trafficked in idols, because it exposed the emptiness of worshiping Artemis. On the other hand, Paul could not be charged with fomenting rebellion against Rome or the provincial authorities. On the contrary, as Luke emphasizes, Paul was a law-abiding Roman citizen, while his opponents violated Roman law and disrupted civil order. The social stability that Romans prized so highly was upheld not by the partisans of the idols, but by the messengers of Jesus.

THE CULT OF THE DIVINE RULER

Acts does not record a direct confrontation between the gospel and the imperial cult, although the worship of the genius of the Roman emperors, past and present, was already flourishing in Asia Minor when Paul was planting churches there. Luke does record, however, one incident in which the issues raised by the worship of the ruler as god—the closest identification of religion and state—are addressed.

The account of the sudden death of Herod Agrippa I while he reveled in praises of his divinity (Acts 12:20–23) is a brief postlude to the narrative of Peter's deliverance by an angel after he was imprisoned by that same Herod. Herod's frustrated attempt to wound the church and silence the word contrasts sharply with the praises he later received from the people of Tyre and Sidon, and this contrast invites us to note the appropriateness of his miserable demise. Three contrasts between the two incidents are worth noting:

1. The people of Tyre and Sidon were dependent upon the favor of Herod for their food (v. 20). Therefore, they flattered him in divine style in gratitude for the reconciliation of past tensions. In relation to his Jewish subjects, however, Herod was in a dependent role, so he arrested Peter when he saw that his execution of James had pleased them (v. 3).

2. Whereas the Tyrians and Sidonians flattered Herod as a god (v. 22), the church addressed its prayer to God (v. 5), with the result that Herod's attempts to find Peter were utterly frustrated (v. 19).

3. In a verbal pun, Luke invites us to compare the opposite results when the angel of the Lord "struck" Peter, awakening him to lead him from a dungeon of death (v. 7), and when the angel of the Lord "struck" Herod, dooming him to a worm-eaten death (v. 23).[56] Clearly, the people of Tyre and Sidon were sadly mistaken to flatter Herod as a divine ruler, and Herod erred fatally in accepting their praises.[57]

Luke implies that the crowd's shout, "The voice of a god, not of a man" (v. 22) was nothing more than political flattery. The coastal cities of Tyre and Sidon were dependent on Galilean farmlands in Herod's domain for grain and oil, as they had been during the time of Solomon (1 Kings 5:9, 11) and the divided kingdom (Ezek. 27:17). For that reason, Herod's disaffection threatened severe economic hardship, and the conciliation achieved through the mediation of Blastus, the king's trusted attendant, occasioned both relief and gratitude on the part of the Phoenicians. Apparently they sent a delegation south to Caesarea to solidify the alliance and communicate their loyalty to Agrippa.[58] The mingling of political and economic motivations with religious veneration was typical of ancient ruler cults. Kings of Egypt, Babylon, and Medo-Persia had been worshiped as divine prior to Alexander's conquests, and the great Macedonian conqueror was most willing to incorporate these ideas into his own conception of himself and his dominion. After the fragmenting of Alexander's empire, his Seleucid successors in Syria sought to seal their subjects' allegiance by fostering the ruler cult. Religious loyalty is a powerful motivater, and political leaders, ancient and modern, have not been reluctant to harness this power for their own purposes.

There is, however, a perilous self-deception involved when a human

leader tries to attach himself too closely to that honor and loyalty that belongs only to God. Herod stands in a long line of rulers brought low for
their arrogance and pretensions. Nebuchadnezzar, though warned in advance by a dream, boasted in the glory of his own power and majesty; as a
result, he was humbled by insanity and driven away from human society
to live as a beast until he acknowledged the sovereign dominion of God
(Dan. 4; 5:20–21). Through Isaiah, the Lord promised that one day his oppressed people would taunt the king of Babylon, "Your glory has gone
down to the grave, and your great celebration; maggots will be spread out
beneath you and the worm [σκωληψ] is your covering" (Isa. 14:11). The
humiliation of Herod took God's judgment on human pride one step further. Whereas Isaiah contrasted the Babylonian king's splendor in life with
his worm-eaten corpse after death, in the case of Herod, God initiated the
wormy decomposition (σκωληκοβρωτος) even before the king had ex-
pired (Acts 12:23)! The word of the Lord through Ezekiel pronounced judgment on the king of Tyre (the city of Herod's flatterers!) because he had
said in the pride of his heart, "I am a god" (Ezek. 28:2, 9). Instead of his
former splendor and beautiful adornments (vv. 13–14), this arrogant king
would be brought down to the pit, like ashes on the ground (vv. 8, 18).[59]
Psalm 146, alluded to in Acts 4:24, contrasts solid hope in the Lord with
the futility of trusting in princes, who, when their spirit departs, "return to
the ground; on that very day their strategies are destroyed" (Ps. 146:3–4).
Herod is one more illustration of this truth.

CONCLUSION: THE GOSPEL'S SUBMISSIVE SUBVERSION OF THE STATUS QUO

Civil religion—the conjunction of religious devotion, political power, and
economic pressure—is a potent and appealing rival to genuine faith. Its
devotees are so admirably loyal to the status quo, such good citizens, so prudently supportive of the prevailing social order. Who could argue with such
a stable and comfortable state of affairs?

But civil religion has its intolerant side as well. The interconnections
between pagan, human-centered religion (whatever its form) and political-
military might make Christianity a dangerous threat to the established cultural consensus. The apostles summon Christ's people to live quiet lives (1
Thess. 4:11), at peace with all (Rom. 12:18), with due respect for governing authorities (1 Peter 2:13–17). Nevertheless, those who confess Jesus as
"Lord of all" cannot acknowledge the legitimacy of any rival lords or sav-

iors (1 Cor. 8:5–6). Their allegiance to "another king, Jesus" (Acts 17:7) so threatens entrenched powers that it cannot be tolerated. Jesus' messengers travel the empire with words, not weapons, lacking political clout and shunning revolutionary violence, yet they are slandered as the provocateurs of social turmoil and the advocates of illegal acts (16:20; 17:7).

Politically powerless, Jesus' people represent a power transcending politics. For that reason, despite the nervous and sometimes violent opposition brought against the gospel by the rulers of this age, Luke shows us the invincible power of Jesus to bring salvation to the ends of the earth through the "foolish" and "weak" proclamation of his cross (1 Cor. 1:18–25). Christians in the late twentieth century will do well to reflect on this paradox. We are too easily seduced by the manipulation of religious affections in the service of political agendas, too easily tempted to promote the kingdom of God through alliance with the power brokers of our culture. God calls us, of course, to be good citizens and good neighbors, not withdrawn from society and its problems, but rather engaged in the pursuit of mercy and justice. But Luke's portrait of the gospel's confrontation with "institutional religion" in the Greco-Roman world reminds us that our combat weapons are not the feeble weapons of the flesh. Rather, we are empowered by God to overthrow fortresses, "reasonings and every high thing that sets itself up against the knowledge of God," and to "take captive every thought to make it obedient to Christ" (2 Cor. 10:4–5).

Notes

[1] Robert H. Bellah, Richard Madsen, William M. Sullivan, Ann Swidler, and Steven M. Tipton, *The Good Society* (New York: Alfred A. Knopf, 1991), 179.

[2] Does the nervousness in the U.S. about the public advocacy of religious commitments and values reflect a similar vacuum in American society? Bellah and his colleagues quote a student orator at a recent Harvard University graduation: "They tell us that it is heresy to suggest the superiority of some value, fantasy to believe in moral argument, slavery to submit to a judgment sounder than your own. The freedom of our day is the freedom to devote ourselves to any values we please, on the mere condition that we do not believe them to be true." *The Good Society*, 44.

[3] Everett Ferguson, *Backgrounds of Early Christianity* (Grand Rapids: Eerdmans, 1987), 287–88.

[4] The KJV translation of the verb αναστατοω as "turn upside down" has sometimes been given a positive "spin" by later Christians. Unquestionably, on the lips of the gospel's opponents in Thessalonica, no compliment was intended. Rather, they charged Paul and Silas with disrupting law and order in society, "defying Caesar's decrees," and "saying that there is another king, Jesus" (Acts 17:7).

[5] Luther Martin, *Hellenistic Religions: An Introduction* (New York: Oxford University

Press, 1987), 84, concludes his chapter on "the sovereignty of the feminine": "As the once localized goddesses, originating from Greece, Egypt, Syria, and Phrygia, emerged from their regional origins to become international deities in the Hellenistic world, they became sympathetically associated with one another through their common antithesis to the rule of Tyche/Fortuna."

[6] Greek: χωλος εκ κοιλιας μητρος αυτου. The same expression appears in Acts 3:2.

[7] Greek: ατενισας, translated "looked straight" in Acts 3:4 NIV.

[8] Greek: ηλατο και περιεπατει. Compare Acts 3:8, "Jumping up, he stood and began to walk [εξαλλομενος εστη (stood) και περιεπατει] . . . walking and jumping [περιπατων και αλλομενος]."

[9] This pair of salvation stories fits the apostles' role as witnesses of the Lord. Through two signs, through different apostles in different settings, God fulfills his own requirement through his servant-witnesses. "A matter must be established by the testimony of two or three witnesses" (Deut. 19:15 NIV). See Allison A. Trites, The New Testament Concept of Witness (SNTS Monograph 31; Cambridge: Cambridge University Press, 1977), 133–35, 153.

[10] Ovid, Metamorphoses 8.611–724. Several ancient inscriptions linking Zeus and Hermes have been found in this region. See W. M. Calder, "Acts 14, 12," ExpTim 37 (1925–26): 528.

[11] Ομοιοπαθης means "of similar feelings, circumstances, experiences" with someone else (BAG, 569). Its only other New Testament use is in James 5:17, which stresses Elijah's vulnerability to common human weaknesses.

[12] Pierre Grimal, The Dictionary of Classical Mythology, trans. A. R. Maxwell-Hyslop (Oxford: Blackwell, 1986), 209.

[13] Grimal, Dictionary, 467–68, 559.

[14] The LXX translators found an excellent match when they translated the Hebrew הבל ("breeze, nothingness, vanity"), which the Old Testament applies to idols, using the Greek word ματαιος ("empty, useless, futile").

[15] Grimal, Dictionary, 467.

[16] On occasion, God's judgment even on Israel manifested itself this way. "Israel would not submit to me. So I gave them over to their stubborn hearts to follow their own devices" (Ps. 81:11–12 NIV; cf. Rom. 1:28).

[17] Ps. 104 speaks of the gift of rain (v. 13) and the fruit (καρπος) it brings (cf. καρποφορους in Acts 14:17). In the psalm, the food that the Lord provides through his rain is described in terms of the three great crops of Palestine: "wine that gladdens [ευφραινω] the heart [καρδια] of man, oil to make his face shine, and bread [αρτος] that sustains his heart [καρδια]" (v. 15). In Acts 14:17, the apostles seem to be echoing a portion of this description when they remind the Lystrans that the Lord "filled your hearts [καρδιας] with food [τροφη, roughly synonymous with "bread"] and joy [ευφροσυνη, a cognate of the verb ευφραινω, "gladdens," in the LXX of the psalm]."

[18] Demosthenes, First Philippic 10, chides the Athenians for constantly asking one another, "Is anything new [καινα] being said?" Thucydides, History of Peloponnesian War 3.38, includes a speech delivered by Cleon son of Cleanetus to the city assembly, in which he depicts his fellow citizens as "deceived by novel proposals . . . slaves of each new paradox and scorners of what is familiar."

[19] Pausanias, Description of Greece 1.17.1, describes altars to Mercy, Effort, Shame, and other deities in Athens.

[20] Greek: δεισιδαιμονεστερους, the comparative form of δεισιδαιμων, which can be used

in a negative sense ("superstitious," as in KJV; cf. the use of the related noun in Acts 25:19), but probably here is used positively, "religious, devoted to deity."

[21] Lucretius, *On the Nature of Things* 1.62–79, cited in C. K. Barrett, *The New Testament Background: Selected Documents*, rev. ed. (San Francisco: Harper & Row, 1989), 78–79.

[22] Epicurus, *Epistle to Menoeceus* 127ff. "The right understanding of these facts enables us to refer all choice and avoidance to the health of the body and [the soul's] freedom from disturbance, since this is the aim of the life of blessedness." Barrett, *New Testament Background*, 80.

[23] Cleanthes, *Fragment*, quoted in Barrett, *New Testament Background*, 67.

[24] Chrysippus (280–207 B.C.), who stimulated a revival of Stoicism in the late third century B.C., proved (to his satisfaction) the legitimacy of divination on the basis of the benevolent character of the gods and the advantages that human beings receive from knowing the future. *Fragment 1192*, cited in Barrett, *New Testament Background*, 69.

[25] Cleanthes, *Fragment* l.5, cited in Barrett, *New Testament Background*, 67; Aratus, *Phaenomena* 5.

[26] The word *Areopagus* ("hills of Ares") originally designated a small hill that rose between the agora (marketplace) and the Acropolis. By extension it was applied to the council of philosophers and civic leaders that at this time apparently oversaw educational and religious affairs. It was "before" (επι) this council that Paul was brought (Acts 17:22)—although it is likely that the council no longer met on the hill, but rather in a large covered colonnade (στοα) adjoining the marketplace.

[27] For a theological analysis of this tension between the pagans' knowledge of the true God and their ignorance of him, see Ned B. Stonehouse, "The Areopagus Address," in *Paul Before the Areopagus and Other New Testament Studies* (Grand Rapids: Eerdmans, 1957), 25–30.

[28] Ernst Haenchen (*The Acts of the Apostles: A Commentary* [Philadelphia: Westminster Press, 1971], 517–18) suggests that the Epicureans dismissed Paul as a babbler, while the Stoics suggested that he was preaching foreign gods.

[29] In Greek religion, it was not unusual for the concept expressed by an abstract noun to be personified or personalized as a deity. For example, there was the goddess Τυχη, "the deified personification of Chance or Fortune" (Grimal, *Dictionary*, 460). The idea that the philosophers were mistaking Paul's proclamation about the resurrection (αναστασις) for the name of a goddess goes back to Chrysostom (*Hom. in Act.* 38.1).

[30] Xenophon *Memorabilia* 1.1 cites the indictment against Socrates, including the charge of "rejecting the gods acknowledged by the state and bringing in strange deities [ετερα καινα δαιμονια]." See also Plato, *Euthyphro* 3B (Socrates responds to the charge that he is the maker of new gods) and *Apology* 24B–C (Socrates introduces strange new gods [ετερα δαιμονια καινα]).

[31] The Stoic philosopher Posidonius (ca. 135–ca. 50 B.C.) developed a "geographical sociology" in which he argued that, because certain races and ethnic groups were intended to live in different regions, peoples or nationalities harm and eventually destroy themselves when they migrate to regions not their own. Ferguson, *Backgrounds*, 288.

[32] It is unclear whether the "times" (καιροι) are the annual cycle of seasons that regulate human activity, as a parallel reference in the Lystra speech would suggest ("fruitful seasons [καιροι]," 14:17). See Gen. 1:14 and especially Ps. 74:17, which affirm the Lord's control over the temporal variation of seasons. On the other hand, Paul may be affirming the Lord's control over longer periods, the times of the ascendancy and decline of particular nations or kingdoms.

[33] Deut. 32:8 NIV says, "When the Most High gave the nations their inheritance, when he divided all mankind, he set up boundaries for the peoples according to the number of the sons of Israel." While this concept is derived from the Old Testament, no doubt it would have been warmly received by any disciples of Posidonius (see n. 31 above) who might have been present.

[34] Ferguson, Backgrounds, 298.

[35] Ibid., 284.

[36] There is a beauty to the cultural diversity of the human race, and Scripture promises a coming day when "a great multitude . . . from every nation, tribe, people, and language" will stand before the throne of God and before the Lamb with songs of praise (Rev. 7:9). This scene, however, is the very antithesis of religious pluralism, for it portrays the nations united in worship of the one true and living God, rather than divided by the deities of their own imaginations.

[37] In a similar way in Rom. 10, Paul draws a connection between the universality of God's revelation in creation and the universal spread of the gospel. Observing that not all Israelites have accepted the good news of Christ (v. 16), Paul hastens to make clear that, although faith comes by hearing the message of Christ (v. 17), the unbelief of Jews cannot be excused on the grounds that they have had no access to the message, no opportunity to hear. On the contrary, "their voice has gone out into all the earth, their words to the ends of the world" (v. 18 NIV)—quoting the description in Ps. 19:4 of the heavens' ceaseless and universal declaration of God's glory. The gospel is now being spread as far and as wide as the skies' testimony to their Creator.

[38] Paul expresses a related, but different, idea in Rom. 3:25–26. The death of Christ "now" (v. 21) demonstrates God's justice in leaving previously committed sins unpunished, so that God is shown to be just, even as he justifies the sinner who trusts in Jesus. Paul's reasoning implies that Christ's sufferings were the punishment warranted by the "previously committed sins" of believers who lived in the age of promise—such as Abraham, who trusted "God who justifies the wicked" (Rom. 4:3, 5). In the case of Abraham, the archetypal believer, God's forbearance not only delayed judgment (to the cross of Christ), but also transferred judgment to the Messiah Jesus, the object of Abraham's hope and faith. In Acts 17:30, God's "overlooking" of the idolatries of past generations refers only to his delay of final judgment, postponing sin's disastrous consequences, which in perfect justice he could have imposed instantly.

[39] Paul would not have appealed explicitly to the Scriptures in addressing this skeptical and biblically illiterate audience, but we may reasonably suppose that at some point he would have elaborated on the saving (as well as the judging) work of Jesus. Perhaps his discourse was interrupted by the derisive laughter of those who scoffed at the resurrection of the dead (17:32). Another, more likely possibility is that the speech itself contained more than is recorded in Acts, since "Luke has here concentrated on what was distinctive in Paul's address to the philosophers of Athens" (I. Howard Marshall, The Acts of the Apostles [Grand Rapids: Eerdmans, 1980], 291; see Stonehouse, "Areopagus Address," Paul Before the Areopagus, 36–38).

[40] Note the similarity of wording between Ps. 96:13 and Acts 17:31. Ps. 96:13 (95:13 LXX): "He will judge the world in justice" (κρινει την οικουμενην εν δικαιοσυνη). Acts 17:31: "He will judge the world in justice" (μελλει κρινειν την οικουμενην εν δικαιοσυνη).

[41] Haenchen, Acts, 526.

[42] When the NIV says that "a few men" became Paul's followers (v. 34), it is translating

a pronoun (τις in a plural form) that normally means "some," without specifying whether the group contains many or few. Within this chapter, for example, the same Greek word appears in vv. 4 (*"some* of the Jews"), 5 (*"some* bad characters"), 6 (*"some* other brothers"), 18 (*"a group* of Epicurean and Stoic philosophers"), and 28 (*"some* of your own poets"). Moreover, "few" in v. 4 ("not a few"—Luke's understatement for "many") corresponds to a different Greek word (ολιγαι). Although Luke does not emphasize that Paul's ministry bore the abundant fruit in Athens that it did in other places (e.g., Thessalonica, 17:4), neither does he emphasize the meagerness of the response at Athens—in contrast to some later scholars, who have seized on Paul's alleged failure in Athens as a pretext for avoiding the intellectually challenging bridge-building approach to evangelism that Paul models here. In *St. Paul the Traveller and the Roman Citizen*, 3d ed. (London: Hodder and Stoughton, 1897), 252, W. M. Ramsay argues that Paul, disappointed with the results of his "philosophical" argumentation in Athens, adopted a simpler, kerygmatic approach in Corinth; Stonehouse effectively answers this view ("The Areopagus Address," *Paul Before the Areopagus*, 31–36).

⁴³ Richard I. Pervo, *Profit with Delight: The Literary Genre of the Acts of the Apostles* (Philadelphia: Fortress, 1987), 37–39, 63–64.

⁴⁴ Paul's correspondence (1 Cor. 16:1–4; 2 Cor. 8–9; Rom. 15:25–28) shows the importance that Paul attached to the offering for the Christians of Judea, which he intended to carry to Jerusalem. This gift, a tangible sign of the unity of Gentiles and Jews in the church of Christ, was the rationale for his plan to travel to Jerusalem before Rome. Luke alludes to this purpose only in Acts 24:17.

⁴⁵ Ferguson, *Backgrounds*, 133; F. F. Bruce, *Commentary on the Book of the Acts* (NICNT; Grand Rapids: Eerdmans, 1954), 398, n. 53; W. S. LaSor, "Artemis," in *The International Standard Bible Encyclopedia*, ed. Geoffrey W. Bromiley (Grand Rapids: Eerdmans, 1979), 1:306–8.

⁴⁶ Richard Oster, "Ephesian Artemis as an Opponent of Early Christianity," in *Jahrbuch für Antike und Christentum* (Münster: Aschendorff, 1976), 28, cites this evidence contradicting the view that Artemis of the Ephesians was a fertility goddess: an inscription in which the Ephesian Artemis is called the virgin, the sexual purity of the priests of Artemis, and the exclusion of prostitutes from the Ephesian temple. I am indebted to my colleague, S. M. Baugh, for bringing Oster's study to my attention.

⁴⁷ Steven M. Baugh, "Paul and Ephesus: The Apostle Among His Contemporaries" (Ph.D. diss., University of California at Irvine, 1990), 39–42.

⁴⁸ From Luke's comment that Demetrius "brought in no little business for the craftsmen," we may infer that Demetrius was president of the guild, and thus felt himself responsible to protect not merely his own interests, but also the interests of all who worked in silver.

⁴⁹ Εργασια appears twice in this text. The NIV translates it "business" in v. 24, and "income" in v. 25.

⁵⁰ In Acts 19:26 Paul speaks of "gods made through hands [δια χειρων]."

⁵¹ Haenchen, *Acts*, 575.

⁵² Josephus, *Antiquities* 4.8.10, attributes to Moses the following warning: "Let no one blaspheme those gods which other cities esteem such; nor may any one steal what belongs to strange temples; nor take away the gifts that are dedicated to any god."

⁵³ Scholars speculate that the clerk was referring to a meteorite, such as the one that had been enshrined in the temple of Cybele at Pessinus in Phrygia until 204 B.C., when it was moved to Rome. Haenchen, *Acts*, 575; David J. Williams, *Acts* (Good News Com-

mentary; San Francisco: Harper and Row, 1985), 335; J. B. Polhill, *Acts* (NAC; Nashville: Broadman, 1992), 413.

[54] Baugh, "Paul and Ephesus," 134–52.

[55] Baugh (ibid., 161) concludes: "It is probable that the religious beliefs of the Asiarchs were not threatened by Paul the Roman citizen. If he had taught rebellion against Roman authority, then their friendship with him would be more difficult to explain. But Paul believed in and taught obedience to civil authorities (Rom. 13:1–7)."

[56] The verb is πατασσω, which appears in Luke-Acts also in Luke 22:49–50 (Peter's striking of the high priest's servant with the sword in Gethsemane) and Acts 7:24 (Stephen's account of Moses striking down the Egyptian taskmaster). Also noteworthy is the use of πατασσω in the LXX translation of 1 Sam. 25:38, "The Lord *struck* Nabal and he died." The parallel between Acts 12:7 and Acts 12:23 is strengthened by the repetition of "angel of the Lord" (αγγελος κυριου).

[57] Josephus, *Antiquities* 19.347, similarly states that Herod Agrippa was struck with intense abdominal pain while his subjects praised him as a god during a great festival at Caesarea. Josephus claims that Herod immediately recognized the error of accepting such praise and confessed his mortality to the crowds.

[58] Josephus (ibid., 19.343) states that the occasion was a festival in honor of Caesar, which Herod had instituted.

[59] Second Maccabees 9 describes the death of Antiochus IV (Epiphanes), who had not only defiled the temple and waged war against the faithful Jewish remnant, but had also claimed divine glory and power (vv. 7–8, 12). According to 2 Maccabees, Antiochus died in intense abdominal pain, being eaten by worms even as he lingered on in agonizing pain (vv. 5, 9). In 1 Maccabees 6, on the other hand, Antiochus's death is attributed to severe melancholy.

TWELVE

SUFFERING AND VINDICATION

"Security, Comfort, and Pleasure"

In *The Children of Men*, novelist P. D. James envisions England and the world in the year 2021. Sterility has fallen on the human race for the last twenty-six years. Not since 1995 has a baby been conceived or born. Young adults who were born in the early 1990s now enjoy special privileges as the Omega generation—the end. Healthy men and women of childbearing age submit to regular fertility testing by government decree—but no child is conceived. In this world without a future, people willingly exchange personal liberty for immediate comfort. They turn a blind eye to the Quietus (government-coerced suicide of the aged) and ignore the exploitation of Sojourners (immigrant laborers). Prudent people willingly silence conscience in exchange for the blessings promised by the State: "security, comfort, and pleasure," that is, "freedom from fear, freedom from want, freedom from boredom."[1]

There is, however, a tiny, helpless pocket of resistance—five misfits who call themselves the Five Fishes, including two Christians: a priest subject to seizures and a young woman with a withered hand. These rebels against hopelessness argue that there is more to life than security, comfort, and pleasure. There is compassion, justice, and love.[2] In their quest to keep hope and conscience alive, this little flock of outcasts attracts the hostility of settled society's wielders of power.

James's tale weaves together the strands of hope, conscience, and suffering. At the start, the story's fictional narrator, an Oxford historian, is enmeshed in the hopeless, amoral pragmatism of Omega. Reflecting on the heroic folly of the Five Fishes, he observes: "It was reasonable to struggle,

213

to suffer, perhaps even to die, for a more just, a more compassionate society, but not in a world with no future where, all too soon, the very words 'justice,' 'compassion,' 'society,' 'struggle,' 'evil,' would be unheard echoes on an empty air."[3] When there is no future, he sees no point to risking present personal peace in order to pursue a quixotic crusade to right wrongs.

A similar linkage between hope and a willingness to suffer for the sake of conscience is drawn by Charles Colson and Ellen Santilli Vaughn in *The Body*.[4] They narrate the quiet courage of real-life Christians throughout Eastern Europe and the Soviet Union before the spontaneous combustion of the Communist system—Christians such as Joseph Tson in Romania, Hanani Mikhalovich in the Soviet Union, Joseph Cardinal Mindszenty in Hungary, Bishop Karol Woytyla (now Pope John Paul II) in Poland, a young Lithuanian woman named Nijole Sadunaite, Warsaw priests such as Father Jan Sikorski and Father Jerzy Popieluszko, East German pastors such as Jürgen Weidel and Johannes Richter, and Lazlo Tokes, pastor of the Hungarian Reformed Church in Timisoara. These Christians endured imprisonment, police harassment, beatings, the sabotage of their vehicles, the bombing of their homes, and even death itself because of their confidence of the presence of Christ's Spirit and the power of his promise.

By contrast, Colson and Vaughn profile the American church's willing servitude to the consumer mentality of the surrounding society. Pressured to compete with a plethora of self-serving recreations, many churches—conservative, mainline, New Age—are preoccupied with what will market well to the unchurched.[5] A conservative church in Denver has changed its name to the Happy Church because, as the pastor explained, "It draws people."[6] *Time* religion editor Richard Ostling reports that America's baby boomers, who "forgot God" in the counterculture movement three decades ago, are now rediscovering an appetite for the spiritual: "Increasing numbers of baby boomers who left the fold years ago are turning religious again, but many are traveling from church to church or faith to faith, sampling creeds, shopping for a custom-made God."[7] Surveying churches' attempts to satiate the baby boomers' taste for self-help therapy and entertainment, Ostling observes that efforts to connect with them run the risk of shifting the focus of faith "from the glorification of God to the gratification of man."[8] Can churches preoccupied with preparing a menu palatable to self-absorbed baby boomers afford to tell seekers the hard truth that Paul and Barnabas laid on the young Christians in Asia Minor, "It is through many afflictions that we must enter God's kingdom" (Acts 14:22)?

Suffering might seem to be a disheartening theme with which to end a study of the book of Acts. It is, admittedly, one that requires sober cost-counting, as Jesus reminded his disciples: "Whoever does not carry his cross and come after me cannot be my disciple" (Luke 14:27). But to people who are alive to the hope of God's kingdom, the realistic expectation of suffering in the footsteps of the King is not, in the final analysis, discouraging. The apostolic call to endure hardship is a call to embrace hope, the hope of the kingdom of God. It is people who have lost sight of hope who will pay any price to shun suffering—whether in a despair-filled, fear-gripped world of a fictional 2021 or in the self-absorbed, pleasure-driven world of the 1990s.

THE NECESSITY OF SUFFERING

Although suffering often takes Western Christians today by surprise, it is no surprise that Luke and the leaders whose ministries he profiles place suffering at the center of Christian experience. They knew the Scriptures—Isaiah's Servant Songs, the psalms of innocent sufferers, accounts of the prophets' afflictions, and especially the teaching and example of Jesus Christ himself. Therefore, they could hardly paint a portrait of the life of faith as a life of "security, comfort, and pleasure," of health and wealth. They knew better.

When the apostles told new disciples in Asia Minor that "it is necessary" (δει) that we enter God's kingdom through many afflictions, their word choice suggests that suffering is ordained by God. Throughout Luke-Acts, the expression "it is necessary" (δει) describes events planned by God and announced by him in the Old Testament Scriptures. It was necessary for Jesus to be in his Father's house (Luke 2:49), to preach the good news throughout the towns of Israel (4:43), to liberate a woman from crippling bondage on the Sabbath (13:16), to continue his work until his destined death in Jerusalem (13:33), and to bring salvation to the house of Zacchaeus (19:5).

The Messiah Must Suffer

In particular, the Messiah's suffering and subsequent glory were necessary because they were central to God's plan and announced in his word. Unrecognized by his downcast disciples as they trudged toward Emmaus, the risen Jesus rebuked their faithlessness: "Was it not necessary [εδει] that the Christ suffer these things and enter his glory?" He then showed them this necessity from the writings of Moses and the prophets (Luke 24:26–27). Later he enabled other disciples to see that "it is necessary [δει] that all

things written about me in Moses and the prophets and the psalms be fulfilled" (vv. 44–45). Jesus had told these disciples in advance that he would
have to suffer (9:22, 44; 17:25; 18:31–33; 22:37; 24:7). He had warned Judas,
"The Son of Man will go as it has been decreed [ορίζω], but woe to that
man through whom he is handed over" (22:22). But his faithful followers
could not grasp the comforting assurance that the trauma that lay in store
for their Master was the centerpiece of God's redemptive strategy.

Only after Jesus' resurrection do we hear his disciples picking up his language of divine necessity with reference to his sufferings. Waiting for Pentecost, Peter commented to the expectant church that it was *necessary* for
the Messiah to be betrayed by an intimate friend, as foreshadowed in Scripture (εδει, Acts 1:16; δει, v. 21; see Pss. 69:25; 109:8, cited in Acts 1:20).
On Pentecost, Peter proclaimed that Jesus' sufferings were ordered by God's
determined (ορίζω) purpose (Acts 2:23; see 4:25–28). Later in Thessalonica, Paul would prove from the Scriptures that it was necessary (εδει)
for the Christ to suffer and rise from the dead (17:3).

The People of the Messiah Must Suffer

It is likewise necessary for Jesus' disciples to enter the kingdom's fullness
through suffering. In God's plan, suffering is the path to glory not only for
Jesus, but also for those who follow him. The paradigm was sketched in the
experience of the prophets. Thus, as Jesus ministered in Galilee, he had no
fear that Herod's machinations would cut short his work, for "no prophet
can die outside Jerusalem" (Luke 13:33–34). He anticipated cynical unbelief from Galileans, since "no prophet is accepted in his hometown"
(4:24). He said that in building tombs for the prophets, the people of his
generation had not honored the prophets as they thought, but rather had
symbolized their agreement with their ancestors' murder of them (11:47–
49). In fact, the generation to whom Jesus came would be liable for the
prophets' blood shed in all previous generations (vv. 50–51). The basis for
this shocking declaration is shown in Jesus' parable of the wicked tenants,
which dramatized how Israel's history of mistreating God's servants would
reach its climax in the murder of his Son (20:9–19). As Stephen charged,
previous generations had persecuted and killed prophets, but his generation had murdered the Righteous One, whose coming the prophets had
foretold (Acts 7:51–53).

The prophets were not only previews of the Messiah, but also forerun-
ners of his followers. Israel's shameful history of resisting God's messengers
reached its climax in the rejection and killing of Jesus the Messiah, but the
pattern did not end there. Jesus' disciples would be brought as defendants

before synagogues, rulers, and authorities, who would pressure them to re-
nounce their allegiance to him (Luke 12:8–10). Therefore, Jesus drew together the triad of hope, conscience, and suffering to reassure his followers of the Father's blessing: "Blessed are you when men hate you, when they
segregate you and insult you and expel your name as evil, for the sake of
the Son of Man. Rejoice in that day and jump for joy, because, look, your
reward in heaven is great. For their fathers used to do the same things to
the prophets" (Luke 6:22–23). Disciples of Jesus will suffer hatred, exclusion, and insult—for the sake of conscience—"because of the Son of Man"
and their loyalty to him. Therefore, they must be fortified by joyful hope
as their Lord pronounces over them the blessings of covenant faithfulness,
"your reward in heaven."[9] Jesus sealed their hope of heavenly reward by
pointing to the pattern laid down long ago in the experience of the
prophets: as surely as God's ancient messengers suffered hatred, isolation,
and insult, but have now entered into the joy of God's presence, so also
those who now suffer in allegiance to the Son of Man can anticipate that
same divine welcome.[10]

The necessity of suffering is built into the call to be the Lord's witness.
Because Paul was a vessel chosen to carry Jesus' name before Gentiles, kings,
and Israelites, the Lord announced concerning Paul, "I will show him how
much he must [δεῖ] suffer for my name" (Acts 9:16 NIV). This opening announcement prepares us to recognize the hand of God in the conspiracies,
rejection, false accusation, beatings, imprisonment, stoning, shipwreck, and
other indignities that Paul suffers in the narrative that follows. But Paul
and his fellow messengers were not a unique class of Christians. Rather,
their words to the new believers of Pisidia make it clear that God's plan is
for "many afflictions" to mark the path of all who enter God's kingdom
(14:22). As Paul would write, "All who want to live piously in Christ Jesus
will be persecuted" (2 Tim. 3:12).

THE SOURCES OF SUFFERING

Consider this paradox: The message of Jesus is good news, announcing salvation, liberation, and hope—news of the joyful life of the age to come,
invading this sin-sick world in the power of God's Spirit. Why should the
spreading of such good news inevitably involve suffering? Should we not
expect the Messiah's messengers to be greeted with open arms in every village and city they enter? Should those who come under the protection of
Jesus, the risen Prince of Life, not be set free from sin-caused miseries

rather than encountering increased difficulties, pains, opposition, and hostility?

The reason for this is that the coming of God's kingdom upsets human structures of power and control, threatening the status quo and provoking the opposition of the status quo's custodians and beneficiaries. Mary had anticipated a great inversion of power that God would bring about through her son, the coming King: "He brought down rulers from thrones, and lifted high the lowly. The hungry he filled with good things, and the rich he sent away empty" (Luke 1:52–53). Simeon had foreseen it as he held the infant Messiah in his arms: "This child is destined to cause the falling and rising of many in Israel, and to be a sign that will be spoken against [αντιλεγω]" (2:34 NIV).[11]

So in Acts, as Luke traces the proclamation of God's kingdom through the authority of the risen Messiah, messengers meet a mixed reaction. On the one hand, many people outside the church are attracted to the healing, reconciling power of the Spirit and to the message of Jesus. In the weeks following Pentecost, believers were "having favor with all the people" (Acts 2:47).[12] Although the judgment that befell Ananias and Sapphira evoked an awe-filled fear that made the uncommitted keep their distance, the people were extolling Jesus' followers (5:13). Luke stresses that when Christians have been accused of causing social disruption (see 16:20; 17:6; 24:5), these charges have been dismissed as baseless.[13] At Corinth, the proconsul Gallio dismissed the objections of Paul's opponents as an internal dispute within Judaism (18:12–17). At Ephesus, the city clerk exonerated Christians of temple robbery and blasphemy against the goddess (19:37).[14] In his hearing before Festus, Paul asserted his innocence of any crimes against the Torah, the temple, or Caesar (25:8–11). Festus found Paul innocent of capital crime (v. 25), and King Agrippa, called in by Festus as a special consultant, confirmed Paul's claim of innocence: "This man could have been released if he had not appealed to Caesar" (26:32). Jesus' people do not bring sufferings on themselves through illegal or antisocial behavior.

Rather, the sufferings of Jesus' disciples spring from the unworthy motives of their opponents. Luke indicates that when Jewish leaders opposed Christ's witnesses, the persecution was typically motivated by jealousy. As increasing numbers of men and women were coming to faith in Jesus, "the high priest and all those with him, the party of the Sadducees, were filled with jealousy [επλησθησαν ζηλου]" and arrested the apostles (Acts 5:17–18). In Pisidian Antioch "almost the whole city" gathered in the synagogue to hear the word of the Lord from Paul and Barnabas, but "the Jews, seeing the crowds, were filled with jealousy (επλησθησαν ζηλου) and were contradicting, slandering" Paul's message (13:44–45). In Thessalonica, some Jews were persuaded of the gospel, as were God-fearing Greeks and prominent women; other Jews, however, "were jealous [ζηλοω¹⁵]" and incited thugs in the marketplace to riot against the apostles (17:4–5). Elsewhere the Scriptures speak of an appropriate "jealousy" or "zeal," an ardent commitment to the honor of God (for example, John 2:17; 2 Cor. 11:2). Such a zeal for God may be sincere yet deluded, as in the persecuting zeal of Saul of Tarsus (Acts 22:3; Gal. 1:14; Phil. 3:6; see Rom. 10:2). The "jealousy" of the Sanhedrin and synagogue leaders, however, was not a noble, but a misguided, zeal for God. It was an envious resentment of God's blessing on the good news of his Messiah Jesus. This was a zeal not for truth, holiness, or God's reputation, but for power, influence, and one's own reputation. The unsettling grace of God's kingdom threatened the balance of power in the religious establishment, marginalizing men accustomed to standing in the center of the system. Although the apostles were far from advocating armed resistance or even avoidance of the temple ceremonies (see Acts 21:20–26), their message shook the foundations of first-century Judaism, which, given its instinct for self-preservation, reacted with violence.

When Jesus' servants were the objects of hostility from Gentile quarters, their opponents' motive was typically greed. We have seen this self-serving profit motive in the owners of the Philippian slave girl "oracle" (16:19) and the silversmiths associated with the Ephesian temple of Artemis (19:24–27). In both cases, the materialistic motive was veiled by a politically correct veneer of civic pride and concern for social order. The oracle's owners charged Christ's apostles not with ruining their business, but with teaching customs illegal for Roman citizens and with causing civil unrest (16:20). Likewise, the silversmiths' economic insecurities subtly receded behind their zeal for the honor of their city's divine patroness (19:27–28, 34). The gospel's opponents, not its proponents, were the provocateurs of riot (συγχυσις, v. 29) and uproar (θορυβος, 20:1; see 17:5; 21:34; 24:18), bordering on rebellion (στασις, 19:40). When God's kingdom spreads through the Spirit and the word, it shakes to its roots the system of power and profit in which the pillars of society have sought their security. Threatened with the loss of what (in the end) they cannot keep, they retaliate against messengers who offer a priceless gift that cannot be lost.

Faithful servants of King Jesus recognize that suffering is intrinsic to their pilgrimage. Suffering is not inevitable because Christians go out of their way to alienate those around them. On the contrary, their behavior attracts the respect and admiration of "the people."¹⁶ Suffering is intrinsic to faithful service because the word of God's kingdom initiates the overturning of the patterns of pride and exploitation that permeate sinful human society. Those with a vested interest in maintaining the injustices of the status quo cannot be expected to welcome God's good news to the poor, his release of the oppressed (Luke 4:18).

VARIETIES OF SUFFERING

Since we modern Western Christians are unaccustomed to suffering, we may assume that enduring persecution for one's faith is the stuff of heroic romance, set in distant climes or far-off ages and peopled by champions of stellar courage. But we need to realize that we live in the same world that the early Christians inhabited, and we are engaged in the same struggle for faith and faithfulness against an opposition that, despite external metamorphosis, remains essentially unchanged in its objectives and its methods. The varieties of sufferings, miseries, setbacks, and irritations portrayed in Acts disclose the spiritual dimension of our own daily struggles, and so steel us to face the minor, mundane costs of discipleship with faith-filled hope.

Our survey begins with the words of Jesus in Luke's gospel, for the Lord himself prepared his witnesses to anticipate opposition in many forms. For the sake of the Son of Man, they would experience hatred, exclusion, insult, and rejection (Luke 6:22; 10:16). Instead of the warm welcome their message merits, they would encounter closed doors (9:5; 10:10). The Son of Man's homelessness must be shared by his followers (9:57–58). They would be arrested and brought to trial before synagogues, rulers, and authorities (12:11). Becoming Jesus' disciple means being willing to give up one's family, and even life itself, to follow him (14:26–33). His disciples must shoulder the cross—the instrument of scandalous execution—in the confidence that "whoever loses his life for my sake will save it" (9:23–24).

In Acts we see the full breadth of suffering predicted by Jesus. There were the martyrs who gave "the last full measure of devotion": Stephen (Acts 7:54–60), James, the son of Zebedee (12:2), and probably some of those seized by Saul as he "breathed out threat and murder" against the disciples of Jesus (9:1). Others confronted the danger of death close at hand. Peter was arrested by Herod when the king saw that James's death had pleased the Jews (12:3). Paul was threatened on numerous occasions by conspiracies against his life (in Damascus, 9:23; Jerusalem, 9:29; 21:31, 36; 22:22; 23:12–22; Lystra, 14:19; Greece, 20:3; Ephesus, 20:19; and Caesarea, 25:3). As Jesus had foretold, his disciples suffered arrest, imprisonment, and trials before the Jewish councils (4:2; 5:17–42; 6:12; 8:3; 9:1–2; 22:23–23:10), before rulers (12:3–19), and before Roman officials (18:12–17; 24:1–26; 25:1–12; 25:23–26:32). Some imprisonments entailed floggings (5:40; 16:23; 22:24–25—almost!). Trials were tainted by false testimony (6:13; 16:20; 17:6–7; 21:27–29; 24:5–8, 12–21). When their witness could not be silenced by legal means, the followers of Jesus were threatened by mob violence and civil disorder, instigated by their opponents.

More pervasive than the varieties of physical threat was the constant undercurrent of hostile words that assaulted Jesus' witnesses: ridicule, rejection, false accusation, and slanderous criticism. This, too, fulfilled the pattern established by the sufferings of the prophets. The author of Chronicles summarized Judah's contemptuous treatment of the prophets sent to them by God: "They were mocking [LXX: μυκτηρίζω] his messengers and scorning [εξουδενεω] his words, and ridiculing [εμπαιζω] his prophets until the wrath of the Lord arose against his people and there was no cure" (2 Chron. 36:16).[17] Jesus himself endured derisive laughter[18] from those who doubted his power (Luke 8:53). He was subjected to mocking ridicule (εμπαιζω: 18:32; 22:63; 23:11, 32) and sneering contempt (εκμυκτηρίζω: 16:14; 23:35[19]) from those who rejected his claims. He was rejected (εξουθενεω, a variant spelling of εξουδενεω) by Israel's leaders, but exalted by God (Acts 4:11, citing Ps. 118:22). When the risen Lord poured out his Spirit on his church, some observers dismissed the heavenly gift with scornful laughter[20] (Acts 2:13). And when Paul proclaimed Christ's resurrection, his message was met with sneering contempt[21] by the intellectual elite (17:32). Jesus experienced insults (υβρίζω: Luke 18:32) and slanderous attacks (βλασφημεω: 23:39). Likewise, his witnesses were met with insults (υβρίζω: Acts 14:5) as well as stones at Iconium, and with slander in Antioch and Corinth (βλασφημεω: 13:45; 18:6).[22]

Western nations today pride themselves on having outgrown the "immaturity" of religious intolerance and conflict that have characterized other ages and cultures. Nevertheless, among the sophisticates of postmodern Europe and America, antipathy toward the message of Christ remains both alive and eloquent. An open acknowledgment of allegiance to Jesus may not (yet) lead to employment discrimination, imprisonment, beating, or death in North America or Europe. However, the virulent intellectual revolt on those continents against the Christian worldview that once formed their cultures expresses itself in increasingly intolerant expressions of verbal hostility toward Christ's word and his followers. If we fail to recognize our culture's urbane put-down of biblical truth (in the press, entertainment, academia, etc.[23]) as a revival of the old stratagem of persecution through words, Christians run the risk of being silenced by intimidation, embarrassment, and shame, paralyzed not by the threat of jail cell or sword, but merely by the possibility of appearing foolish. However, if we learn how our King expects us to respond to the wounds that words inflict, we will also be fortified by the Spirit to confront in confident hope whatever pain lies in the path of faithfulness.

RESPONDING TO SUFFERING

The responses to suffering that we see in the Christians portrayed in Acts are unnatural. Threats calculated to silence them only embolden them to spread the word further (Acts 4:18–20, 29–33; 5:17–21, 28). The slap of lashes that cause others to cry out and cringe in pain is followed by songs of praise from the lips of Jesus' servants (16:25). They plead to God for mercy on those about to crush out their lives (7:60). What explains these bizarre reactions?

Joy

We saw that in his sermon on the plain (Luke 6), Jesus linked integrity of conscience, suffering, and hope: those who suffer for the sake of the Son of Man can anticipate a great heavenly reward. The inseparability of these three things explains the surprising response to suffering that Jesus expects of his disciples: when men hate, exclude, and insult you, and reject your name as evil, because of the Son of Man, "rejoice in that day and leap for joy" (v. 23). Those who share in the hope of the kingdom respond with joy to the pains and insults that are necessary for the kingdom's present expansion and its full and final coming. This perspective, which grounds joy far more deeply than the transient circumstances on which so many rest their rootless happiness, molds the apostles' response to persecution in Acts.

The Honor of Suffering Dishonor

The apostles' response to persecution in Acts 5:41 is particularly striking: "They made their way from the presence of the Sanhedrin, rejoicing because they had been counted worthy of being treated shamefully for the sake of the Name." The leaders of Judaism had increased the intensity of their opposition from imprisonment and threats (Acts 3–4) to imprisonment, threats, and beating in response to the apostles' increasing influence (5:40). The apostles' response to escalating suffering was increasing joy, fulfilling Jesus' word (Luke 6:23). The reason for their joy was the *honor* of their *dishonor*. In the beating that they received, they "suffered dishonor," being treated as violators of the law by the judges of Israel.²⁴ Just as in Jesus' parable the messengers (prophets) sent to collect fruit from the vineyard (Israel) were beaten and "dishonored" by the tenants (kings and priests), so now Christ's apostles were receiving similar mistreatment.²⁵ Yet they regarded this dishonor as a privilege of which they had been "counted worthy" (καταξιοομαι). In its other two appearances in the New Testament, this verb speaks of people being counted worthy of the resurrection life of the age to come (Luke 20:35) and of the kingdom of God (2 Thess. 1:5)— honors indeed! Here, however, it was the suffering of dishonor that the apostles regarded as supreme honor, and their joy resulted from the recognition that God had counted them worthy of this privilege.²⁶

It was not, however, generic disgrace that was transformed into honor, or generic shame that was turned into glory. The apostles rejoiced in the honor of disgrace "for sake of the Name."²⁷ "The Name," as we have seen, is the name of Jesus Christ of Nazareth, which has the power to heal the lame (Acts 3:6, 16; 4:10) and is the only name in which salvation is found (4:13). It is the name that Saul would carry before Gentiles, kings, and Israelites, and for which he would suffer (9:15–16). The apostolic council would commend Judas and Silas to the Gentile churches as men "who have risked their lives for the name of our Lord Jesus Christ" (15:26). Paul would express his readiness to suffer not only bonds but death "for the name of the Lord Jesus" (21:13).²⁸ It is the name of Jesus, radiant with saving power to those who believe, that transforms the shame of suffering into glory.²⁹ Simon Peter, transformed from a shame-filled, Christ-denying coward into one of the joyful band of sufferers described in Acts 5:41, would later write: "Inasmuch as you share in the sufferings of Christ, rejoice, in order that in the revelation of his glory you may rejoice in exultation. If you are insulted in the name of Christ, you are blessed, for the Spirit of glory and of God rests on you. . . . If [someone suffers] as a Christian, he should not be ashamed, but glorify God in this name" (1 Peter 4:13–14, 16). Christians sensitized to the glory of the coming kingdom meet suffering "for the sake of the Name" with joy.

Boldness

Linked with this joy is boldness, an openness and freedom to speak the whole word of God without pulling back for fear of harm by human opponents.³⁰ Such uninhibited courage is not the fruit of the apostles' own fortitude. It is the gift of God, bestowed by his Spirit as the church presents the threats of her enemies before her Champion's throne and petitions for strength of heart to proclaim his message without reserve (Acts 4:29–31).

The boldness that sets Christ's servants free from fear of human enemies is rooted in a greater fear, as Jesus told his followers: "Do not fear those who kill the body and after this have nothing more to do. But I will show you whom you should fear: Fear him who, after the killing of the body, has authority to cast you into hell" (Luke 12:4–5). This holy fear of the supreme judge sets the threats of human authorities into proper perspective.

The judge we fear is not, however, an arbitrary tyrant whose coming occasions dread in those who serve him. Rather, the promise of his presence is their greatest source of security. When the slanderous antagonism of unbelieving Jews led to Paul's withdrawal from the Corinthian synagogue, "the Lord spoke to Paul in a vision: 'Do not fear, but speak and do not be silent. Because I am with you, and no one will seize you to harm you, because many people belong to me in this city' " (Acts 18:9–10). These words are a blend of the Lord's assurances to his servant in the prophecy of Isaiah and of his promise of protection to Jeremiah: "So do not fear, for I am with you; do not be at a loss, for I am your God, who strengthens you, and I will help you" (Isa. 41:10); "Do not fear their presence, for I am with you to rescue you" (Jer. 1:8).[31] The confidence of Christ's servants in the face of suffering is rooted in the assurance of his protective presence. Their boldness reflects the attitude of the suffering Servant: "Because the Lord has become my helper, therefore I will not be embarrassed. Rather, I have set [τίθημι] my face [πρόσωπον] like a firm rock [στερεὰν πέτραν], and I know that I will not be put to shame. He who vindicates me is near; who will condemn me?" (Isa. 50:7–8). In an earlier chapter, we noticed the allusion to this statement in Luke 9:51: Jesus "made firm [στηρίζω] his face [πρόσωπον] to go to Jerusalem," the place of his destined suffering. Similarly, Paul, the servant of the Lord, "determined" (τίθημι) in his spirit (or "in the Spirit") to travel to Jerusalem (Acts 19:21; see 20:22)—a resolve in which he persisted despite warnings of the sufferings awaiting him there (see below).[32] Calm confidence in the face of suffering springs from the assurance of our Defender's presence with us.

Obedience

One expression of the apostles' boldness was their determination to obey their Master despite opposition. When commanded to suppress the message entrusted to them by their Lord, they could only answer, "Whether it is right in God's sight to listen to you rather than God, you be the judges. For we are unable not to speak the things we have seen and heard" (Acts 4:19–20; see their stronger statement in 5:29). From the face of opposition they turned in prayer to the One who was their "Sovereign Lord"[33] (v. 24).

This confession of his absolute authority was no thoughtlessly used cliché, for the petition that they presented in this crisis was centered on the Master's purposes, not their own safety or comfort. They sought boldness to speak as he had commanded (v. 29).

This single-minded commitment to obedience, whatever the cost, was shown in the complexities of Paul's unswerving intention to travel to Jerusalem (19:21). On the one hand, the Spirit compelled Paul to undertake this pilgrimage (20:22), and we observe from Paul's epistles the importance that he attached to the offering he was bringing from Gentile Christians to the church in Jerusalem, to cement the unity of the church (Rom. 15:25–33; 2 Cor. 8–9). On the other hand, the same Spirit revealed to Paul and to Christian prophets along his way that sufferings awaited him in the city of David (Acts 20:23; 21:10–11; see Rom. 15:31). Why, then, did Paul not draw the conclusion that seemed so obvious to those who loved him, that he should avoid Jerusalem at all costs (Acts 21:12)? Obedient allegiance to Jesus made this trip to Jerusalem imperative, cost what it may: "City by city the Holy Spirit is testifying to me, saying that bonds and hardships are waiting for me. However, I attach no value to my life, so that I may finish the race and ministry that I received from the Lord Jesus, to testify to the gospel of God's grace" (20:23–24). "I am ready not only to be bound, but also to die in Jerusalem on behalf of the name of the Lord Jesus" (21:13). Accountability to their Master fortifies Christ's servants for faithful obedience that will not swerve in the face of suffering.

Compassion

The boldness that the Spirit gives is not a cocky, caustic arrogance toward opponents. In imitation of their Lord, Jesus' witnesses pray for the forgiveness of their persecutors (Acts 7:60).[34] They understand, without condoning, the ignorance that allowed Israel's leaders to blunder into their betrayal of the Messiah (3:17). Even when a leader abused his authority, Paul exhibited respect for the office, in deference to its divine source (23:1–5).[35]

Appeal for Justice

The apostles' gentleness did not preclude their making a forthright appeal for just treatment. Summoned before the Sanhedrin for healing in Jesus' name, Peter pointed out that he and John were accused of an "act of kindness" (ευεργεσια) (Acts 4:9). Paul and Silas refused to leave the Philippian jail until city officials came and publicly escorted them out, signifying the city's apology for having illegally flogged Roman citizens without due process (16:37–40). When a Roman commander desperately ordered

that the whip be used to wring from Paul the reason for the temple disturbance that Paul seemed to have provoked, the apostle frankly noted the
precarious legal ground on which the commander was standing: "Is it legal
for you to flog a man who is a Roman citizen and unconvicted?" (22:25).
Finally, rather than submit to a change of venue that would have resulted
in his assassination before trial, Paul played the trump card of his Roman
citizenship: he appealed to Caesar (25:1–12).

Although he was prepared to suffer imprisonment and even death, Paul
sought neither. Rather, with submissive firmness he claimed his civil rights,
not for his personal convenience or safety (as the dangers of the voyage to
Rome make clear), but for the honor of the name and word of Jesus in the
Roman world. Paul's steadfast insistence was that neither his conduct nor
his message constituted an attack upon Jewish law and the temple, the
Roman emperor, or civil order in general. This fact Theophilus needed to
see solidly established. Thus, Luke included in his portrayal of the Christian response to suffering these examples of Jesus' witnesses who challenged civil and religious authorities to deal justly.

The Dust of Judgment

On occasion, Christ's messengers responded to suffering in a way that
seemed futile, even silly; yet it constituted a chilling pronouncement of
judgment. They shook dust from their feet. This symbolic act was authorized by Jesus himself as a sign of God's abandonment of communities that
resisted the good news of the kingdom: "Shake the dust from your feet . . .
as a testimony against them [εις μαρτυριον επ᾽ αυτους]" (Luke 9:5). To
people who refuse to welcome them, the Messiah's messengers were to declare: "Even the dust of your city that sticks to our feet we wipe off against
you"; and that town's fate on the final day would make Sodom's fiery destruction pale (10:11). The long-suffering and nonviolent gentleness of
Jesus' servants should not be mistaken for a lack of divine authority. Their
message cannot be scorned with impunity. Rather, their dust-shaking cer-
emony previewed the day when God himself will make an utter separation
between those who have fled to him for refuge and those who have fled
from him in rebellion. In a terrifying prelude to the final division, Jesus instructed his emissaries to give certain cities what they wanted: to withdraw
the indicting and saving word of God from them. In Acts, the apostles mete
out this self-imposed sentence on groups of people who loved darkness
rather than light. In Antioch of Pisidia, when unbelieving Jews incited a
conspiracy of the local aristocracy to expel Paul and Barnabas from the area,
the apostles "shook the dust from their feet against them" and moved on

(Acts 13:50–51). In response to Jewish opposition in Corinth, Paul, "shaking out his garments, said to them, 'Your blood be on your own head! I am cleansed (of guilt). From now on I will go to the Gentiles' " (18:6).[36] The patience of God delays his judgment of those who resist his gospel. But a day of reckoning is coming, and to that fact Christ's messengers testified in this simple but terrifying gesture of abandonment by God.

GOD'S VICTORY OVER SUFFERING

The sufferings of God's servants cannot defeat God's redemptive purpose. God frustrates his enemies' attempts to suppress his message of salvation in Jesus, so they ask each another in confusion, "What shall we do with these men? The fact that a noteworthy sign has occurred through them is evident to all who live in Jerusalem, and we cannot deny it" (Acts 4:16). God laughs at his enemies by liberating his servants from imprisonment and sending them back into the temple courts to proclaim "all the words of this life" (5:17–20), or by sending his servant back to the praying church (12:6–19). Government officials dismiss the accusations brought by opponents, confirming the innocence of Christ's messengers (18:14–17; 19:37; 25:25; 26:31–32).

The Scattering of the Growing Word

The sufferings of God's servants even *advance* God's redemptive purpose. Stephen's speech in his own defense brought him not acquittal, but the crushing blows of boulders hurled by an angry mob. Nevertheless, his death detonated an explosion, a dispersion of life-giving witness to the ends of the earth. In the scattering caused by the impact of Stephen's martyrdom, Philip carried the word of God to Samaria (Acts 8:1) and to the coastal cities of ancient Philistia (v. 40), while others reached Cyprus and Antioch, breaking through an invisible but rigid socio-religious barrier to spread the word to Gentiles (11:19–21). Peter followed Philip's footsteps to the coast, and so found himself positioned by the Spirit to accompany messengers from Cornelius, to become God's witness to the Gentiles. Saul, a witness at Stephen's death who was fanned to flaming zeal by Stephen's message, restlessly resisted the word, trying to erase the memory of Jesus from the world. Nevertheless, it was in Saul that Stephen's suffering bore its sweetest fruit, for Jesus had chosen that violent persecutor to become his suffering witness to the nations (9:16). Jesus had said, "Truly I tell you, unless a kernel of wheat, falling into the ground, dies, it remains alone. But if it dies, it bears much fruit" (John 12:24). These words, preeminently true of their speaker, also came true through his servant-witnesses.

Christ's Power in Paul's Sufferings

The experience of Paul provides a prime example of God's power to disperse the seed of his word through the sorrows of his sowers. Commandeered to carry Jesus' name before Gentiles, kings, and Israelites (Acts 9:15), he had to understand that suffering for that name would be intrinsic to his mission (v. 16). Slanderous opposition by unbelieving Jews turned Paul out into the fruitful field of Gentile mission (13:44–49). Expelled from the environs of Pisidian Antioch, he carried the word to Iconium (vv. 50–51), and then, escaping a murderous plot at Iconium, he went on to Lystra and Derbe, still preaching the good news (14:5–7). False accusations placed Paul and Silas in a Philippian jail, there to sing God's praises among the prisoners and to proclaim to the jailor and his family the salvation that comes only by faith in Jesus (16:25–34).

Made the target of a lawless disturbance in the temple, Paul seized the opportunity to bear his witness concerning Jesus the Righteous One (22:1–21). Over forty Jewish persecutors swore an oath to kill Paul (23:12–15). Although their immediate objective was thwarted, determined opposition by Jewish leaders and the greed and political caution of Gentile governors prolonged Paul's imprisonment and compelled him to appeal to Caesar (25:1–12). Travel to Caesar's court in Rome entailed further dangers and sufferings, from storm and shipwreck (27:13–20), from self-serving sailors (vv. 27–32) and soldiers (v. 42), and from a serpent bite (28:3–6). Yet all these miseries advanced Paul's gospel mission.

The drama and danger of Paul's trials and travels must be seen in the light of the Lord's promise to Paul, "As you have been testifying about me in Jerusalem, so you must [δεῖ] also testify in Rome" (23:11). Paul had to testify in Rome, of course, because that was the sovereign plan of his Lord. Integral to that divine plan were the afflictions that befell the apostle along the way. God used his enemies' devious hostility to transport his servant to the center of worldly power, there to bear witness that Jesus alone is Lord.

When Paul reached Rome, no negative report about him had reached the Jewish leaders there, although they knew that the "sect" he represented was being spoken against everywhere (28:21–22).[37] Their response to Paul's message, like that of earlier audiences, was mixed: some were convinced, but others were not. As Paul had earlier written to the Corinthians, his message of Christ sounded like folly and weakness to some, while for others it proved to be God's wisdom and power, bringing rescue (1 Cor. 1:22–24; see 2 Cor. 2:15–16).

The paradox of the gospel's victory through its bearers' suffering is shown in the apostle's circumstances at the end of Acts. On the one hand, Paul was suffering in the restriction of imprisonment. Guarded constantly by a soldier (Acts 28:16), he was apparently prohibited from moving freely about Rome. This prevented him from seeking out the synagogue, the marketplace, or the halls frequented by philosophers, as he had done in the cities of the East. Instead, he had to await visitors to his prison house—for which he himself paid the rent (v. 30). What onerous captivity that was for one whose ambition was to preach the gospel where Christ was not known (Rom. 15:20)!

Yet, even within the confines of his custody, Paul enjoyed sufficient freedom to accomplish the witnessing mission for which his Lord had sent him to Rome. He could receive not only Jewish leaders but "all who came to see him" (Acts 28:30). When they came, he preached the kingdom of God and taught the things concerning the Lord Jesus Christ "with all boldness, without hindrance." "Without hindrance" (ἀκωλύτως) is in fact the final word of Acts, the word that Luke leaves ringing in our ears.[38] From a later imprisonment, Paul would write about his gospel "for which I am suffering even to the point of being chained like a criminal. But God's word is not chained" (2 Tim. 2:9 NIV). This is the point that Luke leaves with us: The bearers of God's word may be afflicted and restricted, but the message itself goes forward unchained, unrestrained, and without hindrance, even through their sufferings.[39]

SUFFERING AND HOPE TODAY

Can Jesus' call to suffering for righteousness' sake permeate our society's childish self-centeredness, its fixation on "security, comfort, and pleasure"? Does the church dare declare today what the apostles told new believers long ago: "We must go through many hardships to enter the kingdom of God"? Can this bitter pill be made marketable to choosy baby-boomer church (s)hoppers? The only church that has the credibility to summon people to the sufferings we have surveyed is the church that is centered on the transcendent hope proclaimed by the apostles, the hope of the kingdom of God. That kingdom has invaded history in the incarnation, the words and deeds, the death, resurrection, and heavenly enthronement of Jesus, the anointed Servant-King. It is advancing even now to the peoples at the ends of the earth, bringing salvation in the power of the Spirit, poured out by the Servant-King upon his servant-witnesses. It will bring this history of present sufferings and witness to a climax when the Servant-King returns in clouds of glory (Acts 1:11; see 3:19–21). Nothing less than the gospel of that kingdom and that King can shake self-absorbed pleasure-seekers from their shortsighted "felt needs."

For the church to proclaim this living hope that fortifies people to face suffering with courage and to take risks for the right, Christians must live their hope. When we enjoy religious freedom, material comfort, and financial security, these are kind reflections of our Father's generous providence. But they also pose real and present danger to our spiritual health. They sweetly seduce us into complacency, self-trust, or a nervous protectiveness of the feeble props of artificial security. They distract our heart's view from the hope of the New Jerusalem, resplendent with the blinding beauty of the Lamb; instead, they set our sights lower and closer: a yuppie paradise of tennis, golf, and surf, teaming with tanned, trim pleasure seekers.

Whether we think of Israelite prophets, apostolic witnesses, or modern martyrs, the suffering church has made an impact on the world because its hope has not been confined to the world. Christians can afford to lose all that the world can take from them, because they have an inheritance that can never perish, spoil, or fade, reserved in heaven for them (1 Peter 1:4). Whatever suffering may be required of Western Christians in the years ahead, nothing less than a vibrant, growing hope in the kingdom of God —in the coming of the King himself—can instill in us an integrity that is impervious to intimidation. Christians who can say with the imprisoned apostle that their eager expectation is that "Christ will be exalted in my body, whether by life or by death" (Phil. 1:20 NIV), are set free from fear, emancipated to proclaim Christ's salvation to the ends of the earth "without hindrance."

Notes

1 P. D. James, *The Children of Men* (New York: Alfred A. Knopf, 1993), 60, 89, 118.
2 Ibid., 89.
3 Ibid., 112.
4 Charles Colson with Ellen Santilli Vaughn, *The Body* (Dallas: Word, 1992).
5 Ibid., 43.
6 Ibid., 44, citing John Dart, "It's Not All in a Name for Some Churches," *Los Angeles Times*, December 22, 1990, S-1.
7 Richard N. Ostling, "The Generation That Forgot God: The Church Search," *Time*, April 5, 1993, 44–49 (quotation from p. 45).

⁸ Ibid., 49.

⁹ The "blessings" and "woes" structure of this portion of the so-called Sermon on the Plain (Luke 6) is reminiscent of the covenantal blessings and curses that sealed God's ancient bond with Israel. Those words were to be solemnly recited by the people after they entered the Land of Promise (Deut. 27–28). Because Jesus is Lord of the new Israel, his words define the faithfulness that leads to blessing—and the disloyalty that brings condemnation and woe.

¹⁰ Luke's vocabulary draws a parallel between the suffering of the prophets and that of Jesus' followers: Jesus charged the generation to whom he preached with "approving of" (συνευδοκεω) their fathers' murder of the prophets in times past (Luke 11:48). In fact, such persecutions had been predicted by the Wisdom of God: "I will send them apostles and prophets, some of whom they will kill and others they will persecute" (v. 49). Although this is not an Old Testament quotation, it summarizes Israel's history in concepts similar to Jer. 7:25–26; 25:4 (see 2 Chron. 36:15–21). In Luke (in contrast to Matt. 23), apostles (αποστολους) are linked with prophets. *Apostles* can mean "emissaries" in a generic sense, but here it seems to designate the representative witnesses appointed by Jesus. Like the Old Testament prophets, New Testament apostles would suffer persecution and martyrdom. Note Luke's only other uses of the verb "approve of" (συνευδοκεω), describing Saul's approval of the killing of Stephen (Acts 8:1; 22:20). A connection exists between the Israelites' opposition to the prophets, to Jesus the Righteous One, and to his witness Stephen.

¹¹ As Luke's gospel opens with a prediction of the verbal opposition (αντιλεγω) to be suffered by the Messiah, so Acts concludes with the comment by Jewish leaders "that people everywhere are talking against [αντιλεγω] this sect" (Acts 28:22). See also Acts 13:45; 28:19.

¹² Luke's characterization of the church in this summary section, "having favor [χαρις] with all the people," echoes summary descriptions of the church's Lord in Luke's gospel: "And Jesus grew in wisdom and stature, and in favor [χαρις] with God and men" (Luke 2:52 NIV). "All spoke well of him and were amazed at the words of grace [χαρις] that came from his lips" (4:22). Other positive responses to Jesus' ministry are recorded in 7:16, 29; 18:43; 19:48; 21:38.

¹³ The chief priests accuse Jesus of "subverting [διαστρεφω] our nation" (Luke 23:2), "stirring up [ανασειω] the people all over Judea" (23:5), and "inciting [αποστρεφω] the people to rebellion" (23:14). Pilate, on the other hand, finds no basis for these charges (23:4, 14–15). The verb in Acts 16:20 is εκταρασσω (BAG: "agitate, throw into confusion"); the verb in 17:6 is αναστατοω (BAG: "disturb, trouble, upset . . . raised a revolt" [see 21:38]); and in 24:5 Paul is accused of "stirring up riots [κινεω στασεις]." LN judge that διαστρεφω and αποστρεφω have the semantic field "lead astray" (88.264). They consider ανασειω and εκταρασσω to be virtually synonymous ("cause to riot," 39.44), and αναστατοω ("incite to revolt, rebel," 39.41) and κινεω στασις ("provoke insurrection," 39.34) to have distinct, but closely related, meanings.

¹⁴ On the other hand, from the perspective of the adherents to the Artemis cult, the apostles' assessment of Hellenistic polytheism would have constituted blasphemy against Artemis.

¹⁵ The only other instance of this verb in Luke-Acts ties the jealousy of the apostles' opponents to the pattern of Israel's ancient resistance to God's servants: "Because the patriarchs were jealous (ζηλοω) of Joseph, they sold him as a slave into Egypt" (Acts 7:9 NIV).

¹⁶ Note 1 Peter 4:14–16 NIV: "If you are insulted because of the name of Christ, you are

blessed, for the Spirit of glory and of God rests on you. If you suffer, it should not be as a murderer or thief or any other kind of criminal, or even as a meddler. However, if you suffer as a Christian, do not be ashamed, but praise God that you bear that name."

¹⁷ Jesus' parable of the tenants (Luke 20:9–19) dramatizes this indictment by the Chronicler.

¹⁸ Greek: καταγελαω, in the New Testament only here and in the parallel passages (Matt. 9:24; Mark 5:40). Note 2 Chronicles 30:10 LXX, in which King Hezekiah's messengers, sent to summon Israelites from the Northern Kingdom to observe the Passover in Jerusalem, are met with scorn (καταγελαω) and ridicule.

¹⁹ Luke 23:35 alludes to Ps. 22:6–7 (21:7–8 LXX), in which David laments being despised by the people (λαος), for "all who behold [θεωρεω] me mock [εκμυκτηριζω] me." So Luke, after describing the distribution of Jesus' garments in the words of Ps. 22:18 (v. 34), describes the people (λαος) beholding (θεωρεω) Jesus as the leaders mock (εκμυκτηριζω).

²⁰ Greek: διαχλευαζω. This word occurs only here in the New Testament. An uncompounded form is in Acts 17:32.

²¹ Greek: χλευαζω. This word occurs only here in the New Testament, but a compounded form is in Acts 2:13.

²² First Peter devotes particular attention to the verbal abuse that was heaped upon first-century Christians. Unbelieving Gentiles spoke maliciously (καταλαλεω) against Peter's Christian readers (1 Peter 2:12; 3:16), ridiculing their self-controlled behavior as "strange" (ξενιζω, 4:4) and insulting (ονειδιζω) them because of the name of Christ (4:14; see Luke 6:22). In the midst of such verbal assaults, believers can find strength to persist in purity and patience through the living hope of their abiding inheritance (1 Peter 1:3–9).

²³ Stephen Carter, *The Culture of Disbelief* (New York: HarperCollins, 1993).

²⁴ Deut. 25:2–3 set a limit of forty on the number of lashes with which an Israelite could be beaten. "If he is flogged more than that, your brother will be degraded [ασχημονεω = "put to shame"] in your eyes."

²⁵ Luke 20:11 and Acts 5:41 contain the only uses of ατιμαζω in Luke-Acts.

²⁶ The passive voice of the verb κατηξιωθησαν ("were counted worthy") is a so-called divine passive, implying that God himself was the one who bestowed this distinction on his servants.

²⁷ Greek: υπερ του ονοματος.

²⁸ In each of these the wording is υπερ του ονοματος.

²⁹ In 2 Thess. 1:5, Paul speaks of the Thessalonians' being "counted worthy" (καταξιοομαι) of God's kingdom and of their suffering for that kingdom.

³⁰ The verb "to speak boldly" (παρρησιαζομαι) appears seven times in Acts (9:27, "spoke boldly in the name of Jesus"; 9:28, "speaking boldly in the name of the Lord"; 13:46; 14:3, "speaking boldly in the Lord"; 18:26; 19:8; 26:26) and only twice elsewhere in the New Testament (Eph. 6:20; 1 Thess. 2:2). The noun "boldness" (παρρησια) appears five times in Acts (2:29; 4:13, 19, 31; and 28:31—the climactic, concluding sentence of the book!).

³¹ The Greek text of Acts 18:9–10 is μη φοβου . . . διοτι εγω ειμι μετα σου. The LXX text Isaiah 41:10 is μη φοβου, μετα σου γαρ ειμι. μη πλανω, εγω γαρ ειμι ο θεος σου (41:10). See also Isa. 43:5. In Jer. 1:8 the LXX reads, μη φοβηθης απο προσωπου αυτων, οτι μετα σου εγω ειμι του εξαιρεισθαι σε. See Jer. 1:19, where the conjunction "because" is διοτι, as in Acts 18:10. Also see Moses' assurance to Joshua: "Do not be terrified; do not be discouraged, for the LORD your God will be with you wherever you go" (Josh. 1:9 NIV).

³² On this and other parallels between Paul's sufferings and those of Jesus, see David P.

Moessner, " 'The Christ Must Suffer': New Light on the Jesus–Peter, Stephen, Paul Parallels in Luke-Acts," *NovT* 28 (1986): 220–56 (esp. pp. 249–56).

[33] Greek: δεσποτης, used elsewhere in the New Testament for the owners of slaves (1 Tim. 6:1–2; 2 Tim. 2:21; Titus 2:9; 1 Peter 2:18) and as a divine title (Luke 2:29; 2 Peter 2:1; Jude 4; Rev. 6:10).

[34] Luke 23:34 ("Father, forgive them, for they do not know what they are doing," NIV) is absent from an important early papyrus (p75) and other reliable manuscripts (e.g., B), but it is present in other early textual witnesses (ℵ, A, C) and the vast majority of later manuscripts.

[35] Some scholars, finding it incredible that Paul would not have recognized the high priest by his clothing or seating place before firing off his imprecation, suggest that Paul's apology was ironic and constituted in fact a further attack on Ananias the high priest, suggesting sarcastically that his conduct made his office unrecognizable (J. B. Polhill, *Acts* [NAC; Nashville: Broadman, 1992], 467; I. Howard Marshall, *The Acts of the Apostles* [Grand Rapids: Eerdmans, 1980], 263–64). Paul's address to the Sanhedrin as "brothers" and his citation of the Law (Ex. 22:28) suggest, on the other hand, that Paul's apology was genuine, however we explain his failure to recognize that Ananias was the high priest. Paul's attitude thus corresponded to the theology of human authority that he had penned to the Romans some weeks or months before (Rom. 13:1–7). See also 1 Peter 2:13–17.

[36] BAG suggests that shaking out one's clothes "is a gesture protesting innocence" (whereas shaking the dust off one's feet indicates "the breaking off of all association"). Paul's words accompanying the action, however, affirm not only his innocence (inasmuch as he has fulfilled his responsibility as God's watchman, Ezek. 33:2–9), but also his resistant hearers' liability to judgment and his withdrawal as bearer of God's word in order to take the message of life to the Gentiles. Paul's Old Testament pattern is provided by Nehemiah, who shook the dust out of his robes as a symbol of God's rejection and the expulsion of the unfaithful from his presence (Neh. 5:13). See H. Cadbury, "Dust and Garments," BC 5:269–77.

[37] That the Christian message would be "spoken against" (αντιλεγω) was predicted by Simeon when he held the infant Messiah in his arms. See Luke 2:34.

[38] The adverb ακωλυτως appears only here in the New Testament. On the other hand, the cognate verb κωλυω, "hinder," appears a number of times. Noteworthy uses in Luke-Acts include: no one should hinder children from coming to Jesus (Luke 18:16); nor should an Ethiopian (Acts 8:36) or Roman centurion (10:47) be hindered from being baptized— because, after all, no one can hinder God as he extends his grace to outsiders (11:17).

[39] Paul's joyful observation to the Philippian church illustrates and confirms Luke's climactic statement: "What has happened to me has really served to advance the gospel. As a result, it has become clear throughout the whole palace guard and to everyone else that I am in chains for Christ" (Phil. 1:12–13 NIV). Note also the greeting he extends to them even from the saints belonging to Caesar's household (4:22).

INDEX OF SCRIPTURE

SERIES OF INTEREST

Explorations in Biblical Theology: This new series seeks to integrate Bible-based Reformed theology with the application of Scripture. *Election & Free Will: God's Gracious Choice and Our Responsibility* is the first book in the series.

The Gospel According to the Old Testament: A series of studies on the lives of Old Testament characters, written for laypeople and pastors, and designed to encourage Christ-centered reading, teaching, and preaching of the Old Testament. Titles include *Immanuel in Our Place: Seeing Christ in Israel's Worship* and *From Famine to Fullness: The Gospel According to Ruth.*

Reformed Expository Commentary: Aimed at both pastors and lay teachers, this series provides careful exposition of biblical text from a Reformed perspective while focusing on Christ through the lens of redemptive history. Volumes include *Daniel, Galatians,* and *Hebrews.*

A Theology of Lordship: These three books by John Frame explore theological, ethical, and spiritual truths: *The Doctrine of the Knowledge of God, The Doctrine of God,* and *The Doctrine of the Christian Life. The Doctrine of God* received the 2003 ECPA Gold Medallion Award in the Theology and Doctrine Category.

For more information on these series and
other titles, please visit our website:

WWW.PRPBOOKS.COM